The Handbook of
Good English

The Handbook of Good English

by Edward D. Johnson

(First published as *The Washington Square Press Handbook of Good English*.)

Facts On File Publications
460 Park Avenue South
New York, N.Y. 10016

The Handbook of Good English

First published as *The Washington Square Press Handbook of Good English* by Pocket Books, a Simon & Schuster division of Gulf & Western Corporation, 1230 Avenue of the Americas, New York, N.Y. 10020

Library of Congress Cataloging in Publication Data
Johnson, Edward D.
  Handbook of good English.
  Includes index.
  1. English language — Grammar — 1950-   . I. Title.
PE1112.J54   1983   428.2   82-21101
ISBN 0-87196-141-5

Printed in the United States of America

CONTENTS

INTRODUCTION

This book is strict rather than permissive, because it assumes that those who consult it want to be protected from criticism. Its four chapters are a series of rules, each rule followed by examples, explanations, and exceptions. The rules are for the most part the familiar ones taught in primary and secondary schools, but I have tried to extend them far enough to be useful to sophisticated adult users of the language, those whose thought is complex and whose verbal dilemmas are correspondingly complex.

The Glossary/Index at the back of the book both serves as an index to the rules and provides information and advice on specific matters of English usage; it also defines the grammatical terms used throughout the book. When the Glossary/Index does not answer a question directly but refers the reader to a rule, I advise reading the entire rule, even though some of them are rather long; an understanding of the general principles underlying each rule is important.

Good English changes over the course of time, and at any given time there is some disagreement about what it is. All of us have occasional problems with it, and those whose problems are frequent are understandably impatient with its rules and strictures and even contemptuous of them. Good English is, after all, a kind of institutionalized snobbery—those whose English is good look down on those whose English isn't good; those whose English isn't good are either in constant fear of giving themselves away or find some more or less self-respecting way of defying those whose English is good. Grammar and usage are therefore touchy subjects. We expect occasional correction from a parent or a teacher, but any friend who corrects us had better be a good friend indeed.

My advice is to take good English seriously—it is, after all, a standard of communication, and standards are necessary—but not to worship it. We take the rules and bounds of a game such as baseball or tennis seriously, because otherwise the game can't be played, but we don't worship such rules and bounds. Communication is much like a game, and those who know its rules—those who have a command of good English—play it better than those who don't; they can both please themselves and please others with their play. I hope those who use this book will find that it helps them take pleasure in their language.

1

GRAMMAR

We learn the basic grammar of our native language, along with its basic vocabulary, at a very early age and without conscious effort. Then we discover that there is such a thing as *correct* grammar, which has to be learned consciously. We are exposed to special terms—*conjunction*, *gerund*, *predicate*—that many of us never quite grasp and that almost all of us let fade from our minds when we leave school behind.

This book is concerned with correct grammar. It uses some special terms, because there is no practical way to discuss correct grammar without using them. However, when I introduce a term that I think some readers may have difficulty with, I define it or give a simple defining example of it, and all grammatical terms used in the book are included as entries in the Glossary/Index.

Throughout this chapter and this book, when I claim that something is ungrammatical or is bad or faulty grammar, I am misusing the term *grammar* as it is defined by scholars of language, who use it to mean not a set of rules that govern the use of language but a set of rules that reflect how a language is actually used. To a scholar of language, *bad grammar* can only mean a use of language that demonstrates a lack of fluency. A prescription such as "Never use *he* as the object of a preposition" is useless to the scholar, because in fact *he* is often used as the object of a preposition by fluent speakers of English.

I have chosen to use the term in the somewhat vague but nevertheless well-understood common sense: Good grammar employs word relationships and form changes that are accepted as correct by grammarians and the well-educated, and bad grammar employs word relationships and form changes that are condemned by them. When grammarians and the well-educated differ among themselves, I discuss the differences.

The rules and explanations in this chapter are intended to help writers and speakers avoid common errors—that is, avoid bad grammar. They include some advice, such as on parallel construction, concerned with effective use of language rather than strictly with matters of grammar—that is, concerned with good language, not just good English grammar. Often it is the choice we make among grammatical structures rather than merely the rightness or wrongness of those structures that determines the overall quality of our expression.

Conversely, some matters that could be considered part of grammar are not covered here but in other chapters—especially Chapter 2, on punctuation, which is much affected by grammar—and in the Glossary/Index. The Glossary/Index should be helpful to those who need answers to specific questions; sometimes it answers a question directly, and sometimes it refers to the appropriate rule in this chapter or one of the others.

It is often difficult for someone who does not know the name of the error he may be committing to find the discussion of that error in a reference book. I have done my best to reduce this difficulty by careful listings in the Glossary/Index, but the reader may sometimes have to do some skimming among the rules. To help the skimming eye, I have subdivided many of the longer rules and have begun paragraphs with key types of sentences.

THE SENTENCE

Most of us don't have to be told what a sentence is—which is a good thing, for it is possible to poke holes in any simple definition. We can say that a sentence is a word group that expresses a complete thought, but *I said yes* is a complete sentence yet hardly a complete thought; like many sentences it depends on its context to complete its meaning. We can say that a sentence is a word group that includes a subject and a verb, but *Yes* can be a complete sentence even though it has neither subject or verb, and *When I came to dinner* can't be a sentence—at least out of context—even though it has both subject and verb. Either the complete-thought definition or the subject-and-verb definition could be expanded enough to make it valid for just about all sentences, but we'd no longer have a simple definition.

Since the subject of this chapter is grammar, we might try the following definition: A sentence is a group of words that is not grammatically dependent on anything outside itself. This definition excludes too much—an independent clause is only part of a sentence, but it is not grammatically dependent on anything outside itself (see Rule 2-1 in the next chapter for a discussion of types of sentences). However, it does emphasize one important aspect of the sentence: the grammatical dependency we expect the words within it to have on one another.

Grammatical dependency is what determines whether a group of words is a sentence, whether the group contains enough words or too many, and whether the relationships of the words are easy or difficult for a listener or reader to understand. The following five rules are concerned with the basic structure of good sentences—sentences that are both good grammar and good uses of good grammar.

1-1   Write in whole sentences, not in fragments.

The fragment is easy to see in *I discovered the overalls. When I was ladling out the chowder.* The second "sentence" is merely a dependent clause of the first sentence and shouldn't be separated from it by a period; in this example even a separating comma would be wrong (the *when* clause is a defining construction; see Rule 2-1).

Here is a more complicated example: *The President, whose term in office had barely begun when the opposition in Congress, which included members of his own party, capitulated to public opinion, changing the nature of his party leadership.* Was it the President or the opposition that capitulated? The context might make it clear, but the sentence is still a bad one. If it was the opposition that capitulated, the whole sentence is a fragment; *The President* is obviously supposed to be the subject of the sentence but has no verb. If it was the President that capitulated, then *the opposition*, just as obviously supposed to be the subject of a dependent clause, has no verb, so the clause is a fragment.

Such fragments are surprisingly common, particularly in journalism. A hurried writer, or his hurried editor, may feel something is amiss but not see the error—after all, it's hard to see what isn't there, and it's what isn't there that makes a sentence or clause a fragment. Whenever something seems wrong with a sentence but it's not clear what, check for fragments.

Permissible fragments

Except in formal writing, fragments are acceptable to produce special effects: *I said a year ago this company was headed for trouble. Which is where we've arrived, as these figures will show.* The device should be used sparingly.

And, *but*, *or*, *for*, *so*, *yet*, and other so-called coordinating conjunctions are often used to begin sentences, despite an older rule, still sometimes heard, that sentences should never begin with conjunctions. It is true that a sentence that begins with a conjunction—something joining its thought to that of the preceding sentence—can hardly be anything but a fragment of thought, yet such sentences are now accepted except in very formal writing; I use them frequently in this book. To avoid them we must either (1) actually connect the sentence to the preceding sentence, which may be undesirable; (2) replace the conjunction with a conjunctive adverb or adverbial phrase (such as *In addition* for *And*; *However* for *But*; *Alternatively* for *Or*), which usually also requires adding a comma after the adverb and may give excessive emphasis to the connection to the preceding sentence; (3) just drop the conjunction, which may remove a helpful transitional connection; or (4) completely recast the sentence. It's better to allow an occasional sentence to begin with a conjunction.

Elliptical sentences

Many sentences are elliptical—that is, they leave out one or more words that the listener or reader can be expected to supply. The missing word or phrase is called an ellipsis. An elliptical sentence is not a fragment; fragments are bad grammar, but elliptical sentences are usually quite respectable.

"When did you discover the overalls?" "When I was ladling out the chowder." In this exchange, the answer is severely elliptical, leaving out the entire main clause *I discovered the overalls*—but any listener or reader could supply the missing words, and we could not call the answer bad grammar.

A more typical example of ellipsis is *John loves money more than Mary*, in which *more than Mary* is an elliptical dependent clause. The sentence is good grammar, but we do have the problem of ambiguity; we don't know whether the filled-out elliptical clause is *more than Mary loves money* or *more than he loves Mary*, though the context would probably make it clear. See also Rule 1-3.

1-2   Don't omit grammatically necessary words.

Even when a listener or reader would have no real trouble supplying an omitted word, the omission may be an error if the word is essential to the grammar of the sentence.

Omission of parts of phrase pairs

The stock has always performed as well or better than expected attempts to be a compact sentence and does leave out some dispensable words, but the second *as* in the construction *as well as* should not be omitted; it should be *as well as or better than expected.* The error is common whenever sentences include phrase pairs such as *as well as . . . or better than* and *as much as . . . if not more than*. When it's the second phrase in the pair that is incomplete, the omission is often not so apparent—*It has gone up as much as IBM if not more*; *It has gone up more than IBM, not only just as much*. This omission is tempting, because fixing it requires not just supplying the omitted *as* or *than* but repeating at least one word from earlier in the sentence—*more than IBM*; *as much as IBM*—and the sentence begins to sound clumsy. Most grammarians don't consider this omission an error but merely ellipsis (Rule 1-1). But it is acceptable only if it is the second phrase in the pair that is incomplete; all grammarians consider it an error when the first phrase is incomplete.

Omission of verb forms

He either will or has already left and *He either will leave or has already* are wrong; it should be *He either will leave or has already left*. Similarly, *The country has already and will continue going to the dogs* is wrong; it should be *has already gone*. In the first example, the auxiliary verbs *will* and *has* require specific forms of the base verb, *leave* and *left*; in the second example, *has* requires *gone* and *will continue* requires *going*. When a verb is used with an auxiliary and is repeated, it can't be omitted unless its form is the same in both constructions, as in *He either is leaving now or will be soon*, in which *leaving* is the correct form in both constructions.

When no auxiliary verb is involved but a verb changes form because of a change in person, the verb can be omitted in the second construction: *I sin more than she*; *I supply his financial support, his mother his emotional support*. When an auxiliary verb is involved and changes form because of a change in person, the whole compound verb can be omitted as long as the form of the actual verb is the same: *I am going to jail, you to your just reward*; the omitted auxiliary verb is *are*, but the omitted actual verb is *going*, the same form as in the first clause, so the omission is all right.

You better do it right now actually leaves out the main verb completely. In speech, *You had better* is quite properly contracted to *You'd better*, then improperly blurred to *You better*; people come to consider it some sort of idiom and permissible even in writing. It's incorrect in either speech or writing, though like any other error it can legitimately appear in dialogue, especially in fiction.

Omission of words in subordinate constructions: false comparison

Like the robbers, the cops' view of law enforcement is complex omits too much and makes a false comparison between *the robbers* and *the cops' view of law enforcement*. The phrase *view of law enforcement* does not have to be repeated in the subordinate construction, but *robbers* must at least be made possessive to show that the phrase goes with it too: *Like the robbers', the cops' view of law enforcement is complex*. Somewhat similarly, *Profits were not so high as the preceding year* makes a false comparison between *Profits* and *the preceding year; they were in* is supposed to be understood between *as* and *the*, but some readers may have difficulty supplying so much—a pronoun, a verb, and a preposition. At least the preposition *in* should be supplied—*Profits were not so high as in the preceding year*—to make it immediately clear that *Profits* and *year* are not being directly compared.

Such excessive omissions are usually the result of hasty writing and can be caught by routine checking for grammar; see Rule 4-13.

Omission of prepositions

We disagreed only with regard to what the disaster was due is an incorrect omission of *to*, which is required after *due* as well as after *regard*: *We disagreed only with regard to what the disaster was due to*. The repeated *to* may at a glance seem like a redundancy, but it is not; it is necessary in both places.

I did it the same way omits the preposition *in*; the complete sentence would be *I did it in the same way*. Such omissions are standard with adverbial phrases such as *in the same way*, and usually we have no doubt when such a preposition can be omitted and when it can't be.

1-3   Don't omit words necessary to prevent ambiguity or momentary misreading.

John loves money more than Mary is ambiguous because the *than* clause is elliptical. In most contexts, the meaning would be clear and the sentence therefore acceptable, but in some contexts it might be unclear, in which case the *than* clause must be at least partially filled out: *than Mary does* or *than he does Mary*.

He was expelled for failing physics and gambling is ambiguous because of an omitted preposition; it should be *He was expelled for failing physics and for gambling*. It takes special alertness to catch omissions that are grammatically correct but permit misreading.

The word *that* is often omitted in such constructions as *I believe I'll go home* and *He said I could stay*. These omissions are fine, but sometimes when *that* is left out it is not clear where it belongs. *The expectation is falsely high earnings will be reported* could mean either *The expectation is that falsely high earnings will be reported* or *The expectation is falsely high that earnings will be reported*. Sentences with *that* omitted should be inspected with extra care.

Omission of relative pronouns

He is the man whom I supported but who turned out to be a crook is both clear and balanced. Both the relative clauses, *whom I supported* and *who turned out to be a crook*, define *man*; the man is singled out both from all other men I may have supported and from all other men who may have turned out to be crooks. *He is the man I supported but turned out to be a crook*—with both relative pronouns omitted, as is grammatically permissible—may mean the same thing or it may not. Perhaps it means *He is the man whom I supported, but he turned out to be a crook*, with *turned out to be a crook* not meant as a relative clause helping to define *man* but as the second half of a compound predicate, picking up the subject *He* from the beginning of the sentence. We can omit the first relative pronoun in this example without ambiguity—*He is the man I supported but who turned out to be a crook*—but there is some loss of balance; the sentence has the flavor of faulty parallelism (Rule 1-5) even though it is not truly faulty.

That's the book I want is certainly more natural than *That's the book that I want,* and *He is the man I supported* is more natural than *He is the man whom I supported.* Usually the omission of a relative pronoun in a defining clause is an improvement. Nevertheless, when we omit a pronoun we should make certain that no ambiguity results.

1-4   Omit redundant and unnecessary words and phrases.

The traffic was as usual as ever is a typical careless redundancy; *as usual* and *as ever* mean virtually the same thing. This kind of redundancy repeats the same idea in different words. Often the repetition of the idea is not so obvious: *The stolen money was discovered to be missing the next morning* is redundant for *The money was discovered to be missing the next morning* or simply *The theft was discovered the next morning.*

Please refer back to the previous section is typical of a much more common type of redundancy, in which the redundant element is an unneeded modifier. *Refer* does not need the modifier *back,* since the *re* in *refer* has the same meaning as *back.* There are dozens of familiar expressions that are redundant: *consensus of opinion* means *consensus*; *free gift* means *gift*; *variety of different choices* means *variety of choices*; *large in size* means *large*; *plans for the future* means *plans.* Occasionally such a redundancy may be justifiable as intensifying the meaning: *I may possibly be able to go* is redundant because the verb *may* incorporates the idea of possibility, but it does seem more tentative than *I may be able to go.* Much more often there is no justification. I have learned from past experience—I mean, *I have learned from experience,* or perhaps even just *I have learned*—that it is not easy to eliminate redundancies; they are insidious. We should do our best to weed them out.

Wordiness and flourishes

Because of the fact that I had occasion to be in possession of the money, they were of the opinion that I was guilty is wordy for *Because I had the money they thought I was guilty*. Such wordiness occasionally has a function, emphasizing some element or giving it a slight twist, but usually it suggests confusion, pomposity, or both. It is not an error of grammar but an error of composition (see Rule 4-12).

I venture to say you wouldn't find me so contemptible if I'd split the money with you begins with a somewhat quaint flourish. There's nothing the matter with that. An occasional flourish is not only permissible but desirable; flourishes add nuance and expression to otherwise bald statements. Of course, the speaker or writer who uses *I venture to say* to begin every other sentence—there seems to be at least one such person at every conference table—is adding off-flavor nuances; he is nervous, or pompous, or uncertain of what he is saying, or just clumsy with language.

1-5   If there are elements in a sentence that are parallel in meaning and in grammatical function, make them parallel in grammatical form.

This is a basic rule of clear expression. Violation of the rule is a feature of what one might call deliberately bad writing—the writer consciously varies the grammatical form of parallel elements because he thinks the variation will make his sentences more interesting and impressive. Such variation may violate rules of grammar and will almost certainly make sentences needlessly confusing and clumsy.

Items in a series not parallel

He liked sailing, swimming, and to fish is a crude example; most of us don't have to be told that the third item should be *fishing*, which makes it a series of three gerunds rather than two gerunds and an infinitive. The grammar is correct but the series is clumsy.

How about *He liked sailing, beachcombing forays, and swimming*—is the series properly parallel? No, it's not, though it looks parallel at a glance and the offense to ear or eye is subtler than in the first example. We still have the gerunds *sailing* and *swimming*, but *beachcombing* is not an independent gerund—it merely modifies the noun *forays*. Thus the series is made up of two gerunds and a modified noun and is not parallel. If we take out *forays*, then *beachcombing* is an independent gerund and the series is parallel.

Note that *He liked sailing, swimming, and other seaside activities* is not a case of faulty parallelism; the third item in the series is not parallel in meaning and significance to the other two, but characterizes them and sums them up.

He liked to sail, swim, and to walk on the beach has a series of three infinitives, but they aren't properly parallel; *to* should either be eliminated before *walk* or be supplied before *swim*. In putting *to* before the last infinitive but not the middle one, the writer may be hoping to discourage if not eliminate a possible but unlikely misreading; *on the beach* could grammatically go with all three infinitives, as in *He liked to sunbathe, drink, and sleep on the beach all day*, though it would take a perverse reader to notice the grammatical possibility in the original example. If there is a real possibility of misreading such a series, a better solution than making the series nonparallel is recasting or rephrasing.

He liked to sail, swim, and had a passion for beachcombing is in worse trouble; the last item is not a true part of the series at all but is the second part of a compound predicate. For some reason the error is very common. *He liked to sail and swim and had a passion for beachcombing* is correct: two predicates to go with *He*, and two parallel objects to go with *liked*. If we want to avoid the run-together look of *sail and swim and had*, we can put a comma after *swim* (a comma is usually unnecessary and undesirable between compound predicates, but is permissible to avoid confusion; see Rule 2-3), or we can put in the comma and also repeat *he* before the second predicate, making it an independent clause: *He liked to sail and swim, and he had a passion for beachcombing*.

Either . . . or, not only . . . but also: correlative elements not parallel

Correlative elements in a sentence are ones indicated by pairs of conjunctions such as *either . . . or, whether . . . or,* and *not only . . . but also.*

He has either gone swimming or someone has taken him sailing is faulty parallelism—and bad grammar—because the second element is not a second predicate sharing the subject *He* with the first predicate, but an independent clause with its own subject, *someone.* The sentence can be made grammatical simply by changing the position of *either*: *Either he has gone swimming or someone has taken him sailing.* This is correct, because the correlative elements are now both independent clauses. Another solution would be *He has either gone swimming or been taken sailing.* Neither solution produces complete parallelism—in the first, the subject is different in the two clauses, and in the second, the first predicate is active, the second passive. However, both are correct, and we can't perfect the parallelism without losing some of the meaning: *He has either gone swimming or gone sailing* loses the implication that he can go swimming on his own but wouldn't be expected to go sailing without someone else. Correlative elements have to be parallel enough to be grammatical, and they should be parallel enough to be easily understood, but they don't have to be so parallel that we can't say what we mean.

Note that the simple sentence *He has either gone swimming or gone sailing* can be made nonparallel all too easily by misplacing *either. He has either gone swimming or sailing* omits a necessary repetition of *gone. He either has gone swimming or gone sailing,* with *either* in a different position, omits a necessary repetition of *has. He has either gone swimming or has gone sailing,* with *either* moved again, incorrectly repeats the *has.* All these examples fail to make the correlative items grammatically parallel.

He is going sailing whether you want to go or not may seem like an error of parallelism, after all the discussion above. It is quite correct—the second element is merely elliptical, with *not* taking the place of the entire clause *you don't want to go.*

More than, as much as: comparative elements not parallel

Comparative elements in a sentence are ones joined by phrases such as *more than* and *as much as*. Leaving out a necessary *than* or *as* is an error covered in Rule 1-2. Failing to use the right case for a pronoun, as in *He sails more than me*, could be considered an error in parallelism but is discussed in Rule 1-6 as an error in case.

He didn't like swimming as much as to sail is clearly nonparallel and ugly, though it is not incorrect grammar. The lack of parallelism can be much less apparent in more complicated sentences: *He learned to swim that summer, but more than swimming with his friends on the broad public beach he liked to sail far offshore with his uncle.* In such a sentence the lack of parallelism between *swimming* and *to sail* could be defended as a conscious or unconscious device to give special emphasis to the second item in the comparison. Parallelism is not the only important element of good writing.

Not . . . but: antithetical constructions not parallel

Antithetical constructions are signaled by *not . . . but* and sometimes by *but not* or simply *not*. *He liked not sailing and swimming but to walk on the beach* is faulty parallelism; so is *He liked to walk on the beach but not sailing and swimming.* The grammar is correct but awkward.

True grammatical errors can occur in antithetical constructions in the same way they do in correlative constructions: *He has not gone swimming but sailing* omits a necessary repetition of *gone*, and so on.

Mistaken parallels with certain verbs

He is crazy already and fast driving his wife crazy may look like a proper parallel construction, but it is flawed. The verb *is* is first used as a linking verb—*He is crazy*—and then as an auxiliary verb—*He is . . . fast driving.* It should be *and is fast driving.*

The faulty parallelism occurs with verbs, like *is* in the

example, that can play two or more distinct roles—*I have gone*, *I have a gun*; *I boil with anger*, *I boil an egg*. There are many such verbs. *Keeping himself fit, his family from disintegrating, and to his resolution to remain sober became his goals* uses *keeping* in three different senses. The sentence might be defended as producing a rather quirky special effect, and the multiple-meaning word is a standard device of poetry. Still, the effect would probably be better in the example if *keeping* were repeated in each phrase, making a straightforward series of parallel noun phrases all formed with gerunds—but see also the discussion of elegant variation in Rule 4-11; there may be little point in using the same verb in each phrase.

He bolted the door and his dinner and *He took his hat and his leave* use the multiple meanings of their verbs for a deliberate humorous effect, which would be lost if the verbs were repeated. If the sentences amuse, the device—which is called syllepsis or zeugma—is justified. But often syllepsis is not deliberate but accidental, making a sentence not humorous but just vaguely disturbing. We may have to study such a sentence quite carefully to discover that we have made a single verb have two meanings.

SUBJECTIVE, OBJECTIVE, AND POSSESSIVE: THE CASE OF NOUNS AND PRONOUNS

The case of a noun or pronoun is determined by the function of the word within the sentence it is part of—whether it is the subject of a verb, the object of a verb or preposition, or the possessive modifier of another word. English nouns have only two forms for the three cases, since the subjective form and the objective form are the same; the possessive is formed by adding an apostrophe plus *s* or sometimes just the apostrophe (see Rule 2-29). Some pronouns, such as *one* and *anybody*, also have only two forms, but some others have not just three but four. *I*, *me*, and *my* are subjective, objective, and possessive, and there is also a so-called independent possessive, *mine*, which instead of merely modifying another word acts like a noun and can even itself be made possessive: *Let's take your car; mine's tires are flat.*

Except for the independent possessive, possessives are

actually modifiers, and they are discussed later in this book (Rule 1-19), although Rule 1-7 concerns the use of the possessive case for the subject of a gerund. The three other rules in this section concern only the pronouns that have different forms for the subjective and objective cases.

1-6   Put the subject of a sentence or clause in the subjective case.

Since nouns have the same form in the subjective and objective cases, violations of this rule occur only with a few pronouns—the personal pronouns *I*, *me*; *he*, *him* and *she*, *her*; *we*, *us*; and *they*, *them*; and the relative or interrogative pronoun *who*, *whom* and its indefinite form *whoever*, *whomever*. But because these pronouns are common, errors are common.

Pronouns as part of compound subjects

Johnny and me want to go swimming is amazingly difficult to stamp out of an eight-year-old's speech. This may be one of the times that natural grammar—the grammar we absorb as we learn to speak and long before we go to school—is at real odds with standard English; the child perhaps considers *Johnny and me*, or even *me and Johnny*, to be a single idea that should keep the same form whether subject or object. Eventually, parents and teachers convince Johnny's friend that the pronoun in a compound subject has to have the same case that it would if it were standing alone—*I want to go swimming*—and we begin to hear *John and I want to go to Europe this summer*.

Pronouns as part of their own phrases or clauses

I avoid him who has the plague is correct; *him* is the object of *avoid*, and *who* is the subject of *has*, the verb in its own clause. Those who make it *I avoid he who has the plague* may just be afraid of the objective case, having in childhood been corrected so often about *Johnny and me want to go swimming*, but more sophisticated people make the error too, because it does seem to have some logic going for it.

The entire word group *him who has the plague* acts as a unit—in the example, the direct object of *avoid*—and the *who* in the subordinate clause seems to attract the *him* of the main clause to its own case. Don't let it.

I invited people whom I thought would get along together is just as wrong as *I thought them would get along together.* The pronoun *whom* is the subject of *would*, not the object of *thought*, and it should therefore be *who*. Often a relative clause such as *who would get along together* is interrupted by another clause such as *I thought. I thought* does indeed have an object in the example, but it is not the pronoun *who*, it is the entire surrounding clause *who would get along together*—and the case of the pronoun is determined by the part it plays in its own clause, not by the part the clause plays in the sentence. Similarly, *Whom did you say was being invited?* is wrong; *did you say* is just an intrusion in the clause *Who was being invited.* Sophisticated people make this error too, particularly in passive constructions.

Note that *I saw a man whom I thought better dressed than I* can be correct, if it is considered elliptical for *whom I thought to be better dressed*, with *whom* in the objective case as the subject of the infinitive *to be* (see **infinitive** in the Glossary/Index).

Pronouns in elliptical clauses

He sails better than her seems wrong to most of us, and probably to all of us if the elliptical clause is filled in: *He sails better than her sails.* Some modern dictionaries accept *than* as a preposition, which makes *He sails better than her* correct, but I advise against using it this way. When in doubt, just imagine the elliptical clause with the ellipsis filled in. See also **than** in the Glossary/Index.

Pronouns in apposition

John, he of the big mouth, won't be invited and *Let's not invite John, him of the big mouth* are both correct. In the first sentence, *he of the big mouth* is in apposition to *John*, the subject of the sentence, and the pronoun is in the subjective case. In the second sentence, *him of the big mouth* is again in apposition to *John*, but *John* is the object of the sentence, and the pronoun is in the objective case. The case of a pronoun in apposition is determined by the function of the word that it is in apposition to. (See also Rule 1-19 for special problems with possessives.)

T. S. Eliot's line *Let us go then, you and I* is technically an error; *you and I* is in apposition to *us*, and it should be *you and me*. However, I do not intend a sneer at Eliot. When a pronoun in apposition does not immediately follow the word it is in apposition to, its case may shift if it "sounds better" that way, even if there is no grammatical defense for the shift.

It's me or *It's I*? Pronouns as subjective complements

A subjective complement is something that follows a linking verb such as *is*; it's the *that* in *This is that*, and it's the *gray* in *All cats look gray*. A complement isn't the object of a verb but something linked to the subject by a verb. The rule for complements is very simple: They should be in the same case as the subject they are linked to, which is, of course, the subjective case.

So, should it be *It's me* or *It's I*? *That's him* or *That's he*? How about *I looked for bottlenecks at the plant and discovered that the worst one was I*—does that sound like standard English?

We should feel free to break the rule when the subjective pronoun seems stiff or unnatural. Nevertheless, sometimes it's better to follow the rule and use the subjective in formal writing, and even when trying to speak with special dignity: *It is I, your employer, whom you are cheating by your tardiness.*

1-7   Put the subject of a gerund in the possessive case, if possible.

I dislike that man's wearing a mask and *I dislike that man wearing a mask* are different statements. In the first, the wearing of the mask is disliked; in the second, the man is disliked. In the first statement, *wearing* is a gerund—that is, a special form of a verb that functions as a noun. In the second statement, *wearing* is a participle—that is, a special form of a verb that functions as an adjective.

She approves of the teacher handing out extra homework as punishment would probably not be misunderstood; almost certainly the approval is of the handing out of the homework, not of the teacher observed to be handing it out. But at least in theory it is just as wrong as *She approves of the teacher discipline*, in which the gerund phrase has been replaced by a noun. In both cases it should be *teacher's*. The subject of a gerund is really something that "owns" the action of the gerund—and owning is expressed by the possessive case.

There are times when it makes no difference, or almost none, to the sense of a sentence whether an *ing* verbal is understood as a participle or as a gerund, and then we can take our choice; usually the objective sounds smoother. For example, *I saw the plane landing* and *I saw the plane's landing* mean very nearly the same thing, and unless there is a reason for emphasizing the landing rather than just describing what was seen, the possessive + gerund has no advantage over the objective + participle. But often there is a difference in meaning, and then the distinction is worthwhile.

Many writers and editors, and indeed many of the grammarians whose books they use for reference, consider it not an error but merely standard idiomatic English to use the objective case for the subject of a gerund. To me, this seems a fuzzing of a grammatical signal that can be useful; I advise following the rule.

When the possessive is impossible

When the subject of a gerund is not a simple noun or pronoun but a group of words, it may be impossible or at least bizarre to use the possessive: *Many of us don't approve of a man whom we voted against's being elected*. We have to recast such sentences—and they frequently are clumsy anyway—or else accept the construction as a necessary violation of the rule. Quite frequently, the violation is necessary, or at least preferable to an awkward alternative. Nevertheless, when the violation seems necessary, we should inspect the sentence carefully for a general sloppiness;

gerunds and participles are versatile word forms and sometimes give us more rope than we can handle.

Many constructions are acceptable as virtual idioms: *There is no sense in both of us going.* Still, the fastidious will make it *There is no sense in our both going.*

1-8 Put the object or indirect object of a sentence, clause, or verbal in the objective case.

Like Rule 1-6, this rule is violated only with the few pronouns that have different forms for the subjective and objective cases.

Pronouns as part of compound objects

Our parents sent John and I to Europe and *Our parents gave John and I a trip to Europe* are embarrassing errors, much worse than the childish *Johnny and me want to go swimming*; they not only are incorrect but suggest a self-conscious effort to be correct, a fault sometimes called hyperurbanism. Once *Johnny and me want to go swimming* is eradicated, some of us go too far and give up the objective case completely. If in doubt, just imagine the pronoun standing alone instead of being part of a compound: *sent I to Europe* and *gave I a trip* can't be right.

Pronouns as part of their own phrases or clauses

I avoid he who has the plague is incorrect, because *he* is the object of *avoid*—the verb in its own clause—and should be *him*. See Rule 1-6 for more discussion of this point.

Pronouns as objects of verbals

The objects of verbals—that is, of gerunds, infinitives, and participles—are always in the objective case. The subjects of verbals are not necessarily in the subjective case: Rule 1-7 prescribes the possessive for the subjects of gerunds; the subject of an infinitive is always in the objective case, as in *I want him to build my house*; and the subject of a participle may be either subjective or objective, depending on the subject's role in the sentence. But the objects of gerunds, infinitives, and participles are always in the objective case: *I hate saluting him*; *I hate to salute him*; *The man saluting him must be his son.*

A problem: who and whom, whoever and whomever

Who is the subjective case and *whom* is the objective case, and we can, if we like, apply the rules strictly: *Whom are you going to invite to your party? You just guess whom I'm going to invite.* But for a century and a half, language arbiters from Noah Webster on have been pointing out that educated speakers and writers are apt to use *who* for the objective, especially when it occurs earlier in the sentence than the verb or preposition it is the object of and when it is not immediately preceded by a preposition. *To who will you send invitations?* and *I'm going to invite whoever I want to* still sound ungrammatical to most of us, but *Who did you send invitations to?* and *Whoever I invited, it's no business of yours* are more likely to get by, and their correct equivalents can seem labored and prissy. For some reason, *whom* and *whomever* have always had a la-di-da flavor.

In formal writing it is best to be strict and use *whom* in every objective situation. In less formal writing and in speech, it is wiser to use *who* whenever it seems more natural. This way we are at least less likely to make the foolish error of using *whom* when it should be *who* and ending up both la-di-da and incorrect.

1-9   Put the object of a preposition in the objective case.

I don't understand what's going on between he and Joan and *She wrote the most lovely apology to John and I* are embarrassing, foolish errors. The broken rule is almost the same as Rule 1-8; in fact, in the second example, *John and I* could be made the indirect object of the verb by changing the word order, and thus this example breaks Rule 1-8 too. I have made a separate rule for objects of prepositions because I have noticed that people who would never say *Joan gave John and I a lift* or *Joan drove John and I home* may make the same error when the pronoun is the object of a preposition rather than the object of an immediately preceding verb. Don't ever make the error.

Note that a pronoun may directly follow a preposition but not be the object of the preposition. *Between his house and mine stood a fence* is an obvious example. We should expect the objective case after a preposition, but not let our expectation lead us to break Rule 1-7: *I object to his going so soon,* not *I object to him going so soon*; *his* is not the object of *to* but the subject and modifier of the gerund *going* and thus should be possessive.

Everyone but I left and *Everyone left but I* are common errors, perhaps because in many other constructions *but*, a versatile word, is not a preposition but a different part of speech. In the examples, *but* is a preposition, with the same meaning as the preposition *except*, so it should be *Everyone but me left*. Note that *Everyone left but I* cannot be passed off as elliptical for *Everyone left, but I didn't*, which creates a logical impossibility; one of the clauses has to be inaccurate. If in doubt, see what other word or phrase can replace *but*; if the replacement is a preposition or prepositional phrase, *but* must be a preposition too.

Don't act like I'm going to bite you is a very common error. Since *like* is a preposition, the example does violate Rule 1-9, but the error is usually committed not because of ignorance of the rule but because of a misunderstanding of the word *like*, which should not be used to mean *as* or *as if*; see *like* in the Glossary/Index.

AGREEMENT

Long before the schoolteachers get hold of us, we learn that in an English sentence certain words must agree in form with certain other words—that *He don't* and *John and Mary is in love* are bad grammar. A verb's form may be affected by whether its subject is in the first person (*I*), the second person (*you*), or the third person (*he*) and by whether the subject is singular or plural, and we pick up this part of grammar as we learn to talk.

Applying the principles of agreement is not really very difficult, since English, unlike many other languages, does not have separate inflections, or form changes, for every situation. Nevertheless, complexities do occur, and disagreement in number (Rules 1-11 and 1-12) is common even in simple situations. Also, the very simplicity of English inflection can be a problem, since a word may be in grammatical agreement with too many other words in the sentence, causing ambiguity (Rule 1-13).

1-10   Make a subject and its verb agree in person.

You are crazy and *I am not crazy* are straightforward examples of subject and verb agreement in person. But should it be *Either you or I is crazy*, or *am crazy*, or *are crazy*? The rule is to let the person of the verb be determined by the subject nearer to it: *Either you or I am crazy*, and similarly, *Neither you nor I am crazy*. However, these constructions are forced compromises and are apt to sound clumsy. We may be better off sidestepping the problem, which is usually easy enough: *Either you're crazy or I am*, or *One of us has to be crazy*. Note that *Neither of us is crazy* is correct; it is elliptical for *Neither one of us is crazy*, with *one* the real subject and *us* merely the object of the preposition *of*.

A different rule applies when one subject is positive, the other negative: *You, not I, are crazy*. The verb takes its person from the positive subject, whether or not it is closer.

The quandaries above may come up occasionally, but actually, mistakes of person are uncommon among those who write and speak standard English. (They are a feature of nonstandard English dialects—*She go home*—and in such dialects can't really be called mistakes; a dialect has its own grammar.) There are very few verb forms to choose among. The verb *be* has three forms denoting person in the present (*I am, you are, he is*) and two forms in the past (*I was, you were*). Almost all other verbs have only two forms in the present (*I write, he writes*) and only one in the past. A few verbs never change at all to show person (*can, should, must*).

1-11   Make a subject and its verb agree in number.

The boy swims, *the boys swim*; *John is going*, *John and Mary are going*. We learn the simple grammatical principle of agreement in number as we learn to talk, and we have very few verb forms to choose among. Thus it would seem unlikely that errors of agreement in number between subject and verb would occur. But they do occur, sometimes because of momentary confusion and more often because it can be difficult to determine whether a subject is singular or plural.

Simple confusion

My suitcase was stolen is unlikely to cause any problem, but if a subject is separated from its verb by several other words, we may lose track of its number: *The suitcase with all my business records, which I need for this week's IRS audit, were stolen*. It takes only a moment's inspection to see that *The suitcase . . . were stolen* is incorrect, but in speech and in hasty writing we may not take even that moment; after all, it's the plural *records* rather than the singular *suitcase* we are worried about.

Subjects joined by *and*

My suitcase and briefcase were stolen. Simple enough—though at the moment the theft was discovered we'd be likely to hear *Hey, where's my suitcase and briefcase?* The reversed position of subject and verb and the contraction of the verb—and, of course, the speaker's alarm—make the error easier to commit.

Meat and potatoes, *profit and loss*, and many other compounds with *and* have a singular rather than a plural import and hence correctly take a singular verb. *Profit and loss are shown in this column*, while not wrong, is apt to seem a rigidly unnatural application of the basic rule. *Profits and losses are shown in this column* is natural enough, because the elements of the compound are themselves plural, but this principle doesn't always hold either; we'd correctly say *Pork chops and potatoes is his favorite dish*, because the "idea" of the subject is still singular.

Similarly, when phrases joined by *and* are used as the subject of a sentence, the verb is singular or plural depending on whether the "idea" of the compound subject is singular or plural: In *Reaching for my suitcase and finding it gone was heartbreaking*, the idea of the subject is singular, but in *Being too trusting and carrying too much cash always get you in trouble*, the idea is plural.

When singular subjects joined by *and* are merely a wordy or joking way of referring to a single thing, the verb is singular: *My son and heir was supposed to be keeping an eye on the luggage*.

Finally, an important and frequently violated rule: When two singular subjects are joined by *and* but preceded by *each* or *every*, the verb must be singular: *Each suitcase and briefcase has to be checked*; *Every tourist and business traveler has had similar experiences*; *Every girl and boy is to bring his or her own lunch* (see also Rule 1-12). This is true even if the *each* or *every* is repeated for the second element: *Each suitcase and each briefcase has to be checked*.

Subjects joined by or and nor

The bellboy or the taxi driver was probably involved. The subjects are not exactly sharing the verb, but using it in turn, so the verb is singular, agreeing with each subject individually. When one of the subjects is singular and the other is plural, the number of the verb is determined by the number of the closer subject: *The bellboys or the taxi driver was probably involved*; *The taxi driver or the bellboys were probably involved*. *Nor* follows the same rule: *Neither the bellboys nor the taxi driver was involved*.

Like the rule for determining the person of the verb in such cases (see Rule 1-10), this rule permits sentences that are correct but may be clumsy. Such sentences can be rewritten to avoid the problem, but the pairing of singular and plural subjects comes up a lot more often than the pairing of subjects of different persons. Furthermore, sometimes rewriting will just make a sentence clumsier or change its meaning. *The taxi driver or the bellboys probably had some-*

thing to do with it, with *had* in agreement with both subjects, might do for the example.

The verb in a relative clause can be plural even when the relative pronoun refers to two or more singular subjects joined by *or*: *The bellboy or the taxi driver, who were both right here, was probably involved.* However, this construction is awkward and is apt to lead to the simple confusion discussed above, with the sentence incorrectly ending *were probably involved.*

Positive and negative subjects

I think the bellboys, not the taxi driver, were involved; *I think the taxi driver, not the bellboys, was involved.* The positive subject determines the number of the verb whether or not it is closer to the verb. This construction usually does not sound too clumsy, but if it does, the negative subject can be repositioned: *I think the bellboys were involved, not the taxi driver.*

Subjects that look singular but are plural— or may be

Collective nouns, such as *family*, *group*, and *committee*, can take either singular or plural verbs, depending on whether they are being thought of as singular or plural. *The committee is qualified to decide* makes a statement about the committee as a unit; *The committee are not all qualified to decide* makes a statement about the individual members. (The British almost always use the plural—*The committee are qualified*, and even *The government are in confusion.*) A frequent mistake with collective nouns is forgetting whether we're considering them singular or plural and trying to have it both ways: *The committee is qualified to decide, but are not all as well informed as they might be.* The number of a collective noun should be consistent not just within a sentence but throughout a statement or any written work, though violations of this principle are sometimes justified and unobjectionable, as when the same term is used differently in different parts of a book.

Some nouns look singular in English but are plural in the language they were adopted from, such as *agenda* and *data*, which are both Latin plurals. Whether or not such a word takes a singular verb is a question of usage rather than rules. *Agenda* has long been accepted as a singular, with the plural *agendas*. *Data* has not yet crossed the line but may be on its way. *The data is incomplete* is considered an ignorant error by many people, but some handbooks, such as the stylebook of the *Los Angeles Times*, already prescribe the singular for *data*, and others allow the singular when the meaning is essentially singular—that is, a collection of information thought of as a unit rather than as many separate items. It is wise to be conservative and use *data* as a plural, simply to avoid the appearance of error. When in doubt about the status of a given word, consult a dictionary—a good and recent one that, unlike the most recent editions of Merriam-Webster dictionaries, distinguishes between good and poor usage.

Subjects that look plural but are singular—or may be

Physics is almost always a singular, but *The physics of the device are sophisticated* is correct. *Statistics* is singular if it means the field of study, plural if it means a collection of specific information. There are many similar words. Unlike the collective nouns, they can switch back and forth from their singular to their plural meanings quite freely, even in the same sentence: *Physics was his field, but the physics of this device were beyond him.*

Five boys is certainly a plural—what could be more plural than a plural noun modified by a number larger than one?—and yet *Five boys is not enough even for a scrub game* is correct. In that example, the plural *are* could be used too, but sometimes it cannot be. *Five dollars are too much* is wrong, or at best unidiomatic; a sum of money is thought of as singular. Usually we know without thinking about it whether a noun modified by a number is really plural, as in *Five boys were enrolled for soccer*, or just a unit that is plural in form. We can switch back and forth freely: *Seven bright pennies were exposed on the grubby palm, but seven pennies was not enough for a candy bar.*

Subjects and complements of different number

In *The secret is more controls*, the singular subject *secret* is linked to the plural complement *more controls* by the singular verb *is*. The subject, not the complement, determines the number of the verb. *More controls are the secret* reverses subject and complement, and the verb is plural.

In a long sentence, the verb may end up much closer to the complement than to the subject and mistakenly fall into the complement's number: *The secret of holding down taxes, maintaining services, and eliminating unexpected shortages are more controls*. It should be *is more controls*, to agree with the subject, *secret*.

Parenthetical subject between true subject and verb

John, and his parents, was at the zoo yesterday is correct. The pair of commas around *and his parents* takes the words right out of the grammar of the sentence, just as parentheses or dashes would: *John (and his parents) was*; *John—and his parents—was*. A parenthetical subject has no effect on the number of the verb.

The Roman Empire, and subsequent empires, were eventually destroyed is an error of grammar if the writer means something like *The Roman Empire, like subsequent empires, was eventually destroyed*. It is an error of punctuation if the writer means *The Roman Empire and subsequent empires were eventually destroyed*; a series of three or more items should be separated by commas (see Rule 2-6), but not a series of two items, and a comma at the end of the series wrongly separates subject and verb (Rule 2-4). Writers who make the error—whether it is their punctuation or their grammar that is at fault—are apt to have a generally vague style and be vague thinkers, and their meaning may not be entirely clear even in context.

John as well as his parents was entranced by the monkeys is correct. The construction *as well as his parents* is parenthetical, even though it is not set off by commas (see Rule 2-1). It could be so set off, giving the sentence a slightly different effect.

1-12   Make a pronoun and its antecedent agree in number, person, and gender.

The antecedent of a pronoun is the noun or noun phrase that it is intended to represent. In *I asked Bill, but he can't go*, the antecedent of the pronoun *he* is *Bill*.

Pronouns do not always have antecedents, and some logically can't have antecedents. In the question *Who can go?* the interrogative pronoun *who* has no antecedent—how could it? In the statement *Anyone can go*, the indefinite pronoun *Anyone* has no antecedent. Frequently when there is an antecedent, it is in an earlier sentence: *I asked Bill. He can't go*.

When there is an antecedent, the pronoun must agree with it in number, person, and gender.

Disagreement in number

Everybody will be responsible for their own welfare is a common error. *Everybody* is singular; *their* is plural. It should be *his own welfare* or *his or her own welfare*. Similarly, it should be *Every boy and girl is to bring his or her own lunch,* not *their own lunch*. (*Every boy and girl* is a singular subject; see Rule 1-11.) The error is becoming more and more common, because the use of masculine pronouns to cover mixed sexes has been attacked in recent years, and making the pronoun plural seems to be a way to avoid the cumbersome compounds *he or she*, *him or her*, and so on. The compounds are indeed annoying when repeated again and again—and perhaps for enhanced fairness there should be an alternation of *he and she*, *she and he*; why should the masculine pronoun always come first? We may have to recast: *All girls and boys are to bring their own lunches*, or *Every child is to bring a lunch*.

Anyone, *everyone*, and *someone* also require singular pronouns: *Anyone who forgets to bring their lunch will go hungry* is the same kind of error as discussed above.

Disagreement in person

Anyone who forgets his manners is going to be sorry you were born is wrong because the antecedent of the second-person pronoun *you*, like the antecedent of *his*, is the third-person indefinite pronoun *Anyone*. It should be *he was born*. However, it is sometimes permissible to let the person shift. *I hope none of you forget your manners* is, strictly speaking, incorrect, since the antecedent of *your* is *none*, a third-person pronoun, but *none of you* strongly suggests the second person. A rigid grammarian might make it *forgets his manners*, but *forget your manners* is as acceptable and more natural.

Failures of agreement are most likely to occur when a pronoun's antecedent is in an earlier sentence: *No one is to forget his manners. If you do, you'll be sorry.* The shifting person between sentences is not an error of grammar, since grammar functions only within a sentence, but it is a poor choice of words.

The *he or she* problem mentioned in the preceding section has made disagreement in person more frequent, and avoiding it can be irritating: *No one is to forget his or her manners. If she or he does, he or she will be sorry.* By thinking ahead, we can sometimes sidestep the problem, perhaps with a loss of force: *Don't forget your manners. If you do, you'll be sorry.*

Careless writing and speech often drifts from person to person: *He told me to look out for live wires, and if you touch them you'll be sorry. But I thought that as long as you're careful no one could get hurt.* There are grammatical problems here, but the basic problem is a vagueness not just of language but of identity; the writer or speaker doesn't quite know who he is (or she is) or *you* is.

Disagreement in gender

The dog didn't come when I called him, and the next morning it was still missing is wrong because of the shift in gender from *him* to *it*. We can use a masculine or feminine pronoun for an animal—and usually should if the animal is identified as a stallion or a mare, a mother or a father, a

Knight Errant III or a Princess Suzie—but we shouldn't then switch to a neuter pronoun.

However, there is nothing wrong with writing *The chickadee, in spite of its commonness, is an interesting bird* and a sentence or so later *The chickadee lays her eggs one at a time* and still another sentence or so later *The bird has a particular call to show that in the competition for mates he is a winner*. As long as the reader will not be confused, the gender can be governed by the context and can shift whenever common sense dictates.

Disagreement in case

There is usually nothing wrong with this disagreement—a pronoun doesn't agree with its antecedent in case, except by coincidence. (A pronoun does, however, agree in case with a word it is in apposition to; see Rule 1-6.) In the sentence *The dog didn't come, though I called him and rattled his dish, and the next morning he was still missing*, the pronoun is first objective as the object of *called*, then possessive as a modifier of *dish*, and then subjective as the subject of *was still missing*.

The car is really my wife's, who dented the fender is, however, an error. A noun or pronoun in the possessive case is usually functioning as an adjective, and an adjective cannot be the antecedent of a pronoun (see Rule 1-19). There are some situations in which a possessive noun or pronoun is not just an adjective and can be the antecedent of a pronoun: *Let's take my car, not my wife's, which has a dented fender* is correct, because *wife's* is not an ordinary adjectival possessive here but a so-called independent possessive, a possessive that functions more like a noun than like an adjective. Most of the personal pronouns have special forms for the independent possessive: *mine, yours, hers, ours, theirs*.

Special problems with *each*

Each of us brought our own lunch is wrong because *Each of us* really means *Each one of us*. The true subject is the understood singular third-person pronoun *one*, and thus *our* is wrong in both person and number. It should be *Each of us brought his own lunch*, or for mixed sexes, *his or her own lunch.* It could be rephrased to *We each brought our own lunch,* because here *each* merely modifies the subject, *We.* (The singular *lunch* is permissible by a principle sometimes called distributive possession; each member of the possessing group possesses one of the possessed items.)

1-13 Don't let a pronoun have more than one likely antecedent.

Joan and Sarah are both married to lawyers, but I don't think her husband is a partner in his firm could have several meanings. The first pronoun, *her,* could refer to either Joan or Sarah. The second pronoun, *his,* could refer to *husband,* but could refer to the other husband. In context there may be no ambiguity, and if the words are spoken the inflections of speech may reduce ambiguity. Still, we often have to correct and amplify ourselves in conversation: *—I mean, I don't think Sarah's husband works with Joan's; he must be a partner somewhere, the way they spend.*

True ambiguity

The resources of the Ruhr were very great, but the capacity of the war industries to take advantage of them was much reduced when they became a prime target of Allied air raids is a well-composed sentence, except that we can't tell whether it was the resources of the Ruhr or the war industries that became a prime target. The context might make it clear or might not; during World War II the mining and heavy industry of the Ruhr were a prime target, but so were specialized armament and equipment industries both in the Ruhr and elsewhere in Germany. Perhaps the best clue is the word *capacity*—the writer probably wouldn't have used that word if he had meant that the war industries were affected indirectly rather than directly by the air raids. A reader shouldn't have to work that hard and still end up with a probable meaning rather than a certain one.

John trusted Bob, but wasn't sure that he had checked every facet of his situation before making his decision to leave it up to him is stunningly ambiguous out of context. In context, it could well be clear to most readers, but some would certainly slip off the track and find it impossible to get back on. The names should replace the pronouns in enough places to make the meaning unambiguous.

Momentary ambiguity

Don't trim the enlargement's border if you're going to put it in a frame is momentarily ambiguous; for an instant the reader may think it's the border, not the enlargement, that is going in the frame. *Don't trim the border of the enlargement if you're going to put it in a frame* is still ambiguous. *If you're going to put the enlargement in a frame, don't trim its border* is clear. Surprisingly, putting the pronoun before the antecedent, which is not a grammatical error but does often make confusion more likely, turns out to be another solution here: *If you're going to put it in a frame, don't trim the enlargement but leave its border*.

There are many, many other types of sentences that permit pronouns to be ambiguous or confusing, but the solution is always the same: careful checking to make sure that no misreading is possible. It may well be that there is a possible misreading but it is too unlikely to worry about. This decision is quite sensible, especially when changing the sentence would make it less effective in other ways, but it should be a conscious decision.

VERB TENSES: PAST, PRESENT, AND FUTURE

The basic tenses are past, present, and future, but English has a lot more than three tenses—by some counts, more than thirty. We have not just *I cooked*, *I cook*, and *I will cook*, but the present perfect *I have cooked*, the past perfect *I had cooked*, and the future perfect *I will have cooked*. These tenses—now there are six—also have progressive forms: *I was cooking*, *I am cooking*, *I will be cooking*, *I have been cooking*, *I had been cooking*, and *I shall* (or *will*) *have been cooking*. Some tenses have a special emphatic form: *I do cook*, *I did cook*. Various verb forms that can be considered separate tenses make complicated uses of auxiliary verbs: *I was going to cook*, *I would be cooking*, *I would have been going to cook*, and so on.

Foreigners have trouble with English tenses, especially with the progressive tenses, but most of us do not, having learned their proper use as young children. We know that *I cried when she appeared* and *I was crying when she appeared* do not mean the same thing. We also understand the function of auxiliary verbs—*be, have, will, shall, do*, and other common verbs—in forming tenses.

We do sometimes have problems with tenses when there is more than one verb in a sentence, or when the sentence includes a participle, infinitive, or gerund.

1-14   Keep the tense of a verb in proper relation to the tenses of other verbs in the sentence or passage.

This is a difficult rule. In some sentences the tense of a given verb is strictly determined by the logical relationship between the time of the verb's action and the time of some other verb's action. In other sentences the tense of the verb is affected by the tense of other verbs but not completely determined by them; we may have a choice of tenses, and the tense we choose may affect the meaning or may not. Although the basic purpose of tenses is to indicate the time of a verb's action, they often ignore calendar and clock.

Fortunately, applying the rule does not seem to be as difficult as explaining it. Most of us are quite safe just using the tense that "sounds right," and it is only when we think about it too much that we are in danger of using the wrong tense.

Relative time

We say *He assumes she is single* and *He assumed she was single*; the secondary verb follows the main verb into the past tense. However, we might also say *He assumed she is single*. The main verb does not necessarily force its tense on the secondary verb. Often a subordinate verb that expresses something that is always true, not just true at the time of the main verb's action, is in the present tense—*Galileo believed that the earth moves around the sun*—but *moved* would not be wrong either, and some would consider it preferable, since the present tense *moves* makes the verb seem more important than the past tense *believed*.

When a secondary verb does follow the tense of the main verb, it may go only part of the distance. We say *He had assumed she was single,* not *He had assumed she had been single*; we could even say *He had assumed she is single*. It may not follow the tense of the main verb at all; if we put *He assumes she is single* in the future tense, it becomes *He will assume she is single*, not *He will assume she will be single*. And when the actions of a main verb and a secondary verb clearly take place at different times, the verbs can often be either in the same tense or in the logically appropriate other tense: *He always goes out after he comes home* or *has come home*; *He went out after he came home* or *had come home*. Usually the same tense sounds more natural. However, when the main verb is in the future tense, the secondary verb usually must be either present or past, not future: *He will go out after he comes home* or *has come home*.

Just because we have a choice of tenses in many situations does not mean one is as good as the other. When a secondary verb expresses continuing action, rather than action that took place only at the time of a main verb that is in the past tense, the present tense is often preferable. *I heard the prices were going up* implies that prices have gone up; *I heard that prices are going up* implies that there may still be time for a quick trip to the store.

The disappearing past perfect

The basic function of the past perfect tense is to indicate action that takes place previous to the time of another verb in the sentence or passage that is in the past tense: *He assumed she had married*; *She discovered he had gone out*. However, more and more often, writers who are generally careful do not bother with the past perfect in dependent clauses when the time relationship is fairly clear anyway: *She missed John, who left the party early*; *John fell in the ditch which they dug for the well line*. I think it is better to use the past perfect—*had left* and *had dug* in the examples— as a matter of habit, because not using it does often permit more ambiguity than the writer realizes and does seem incorrect to many readers. Nevertheless, when a dependent clause includes a word such as *after* or has some other clear signal of the relationship of the dependent clause's time to the main clause's time, the past perfect may be not only unnecessary but somewhat illogical: *Minutes after he had left the party and had fallen in the ditch, she arrived* would be better off without the past perfect.

Ambiguity with the past and past perfect

She discovered that he had left the party and gone home does not mean the same thing as *She discovered that he had left the party and went home*. Because *go* is an irregular verb, with different forms in the past tense (*I went*) and the past perfect tense (*I had gone*), the first sentence must mean *he had . . . gone home* and the second sentence must mean *She . . . went home*.

If we make it *She discovered that he had left the party and walked home*, we no longer have the grammatical signal provided by *went* or *gone*. The sentence is grammatically correct but can be taken to mean either that she walked home or that he did. If he walked home, we can make the sentence unambiguous by repeating the auxiliary verb: *and had walked home*. If she walked home, we have to change the structure of the sentence by supplying a pronoun for *walked*: *She discovered that he had left the party, and she walked home*. This makes it a compound sentence—that is, one with two or more independent clauses—rather than a sentence with a single subject and compound predicate.

Past and past perfect in narrative

Smith said he had begun the day as usual—he arrived at the bank on time and went to the vault. The verbs are not in proper tense relation; since Smith's arrival and his going to the vault took place in the time previous to the time established by *He said*, it should be *had arrived* and *had gone*.

However, suppose Smith's narrative goes on for a long paragraph or even for pages. Are we required to let *Smith said* force every verb in the narrative into the clumsy and wordy past perfect tense? No. In such a circumstance it is not only permissible but desirable to let the tense sneak back to the simpler past tense, and the sooner the better. If we pick the right time to let the tense sneak back—not in the middle of a narrative but at its beginning, and usually not in the middle of a sentence—the reader or listener will probably not notice and will be spared a long succession of past perfect verbs.

When Smith's narrative ends and the time established by *He said* must be reestablished, the transition must be made carefully so that the reader can follow it without effort: *The police did not question Smith further but told him not to leave town* could begin the paragraph following the end of Smith's narrative.

Subjunctive verb forms

If they swim well their father smiles contains two indicative verbs, both in the present tense—*swim* and *smiles*. If they don't swim well and we want to state what the effect on their father would be if they did, we use the subjunctive: *If they swam well their father would smile*. The verb forms *swam* and *would smile* may look like past tenses, but there is no "pastness" to their meaning; they are subjunctive forms. The sentence is intended as a speculation about the present, not a statement about the past. (In another context it might be a straightforward indicative statement about the past: *The children were sometimes good swimmers. If they swam well their father would smile*.)

Just as a secondary verb does not always follow a main verb into the main verb's tense, a secondary verb does not always follow the main verb into the main verb's subjunctive mood. In fact, the secondary verb may have more influence on the main verb than the other way around.

If you can pay me now, I will be grateful is an indicative sentence. *If you could pay me now, I would be grateful* is a subjunctive sentence, with both verbs in the subjunctive mood. However, both *If you could pay me now, I will be grateful* and *If you can pay me now, I would be grateful*— that is, a mixture of indicative and subjunctive moods—are now considered permissible in English. We could consider these sentences failures of parallelism, but lack of parallelism alone is not an error of grammar; the nonparallel elements can be correct grammatical structures, just badly chosen combinations of them. Lack of parallelism may be desirable if it expresses subtleties of meaning or emphasis— that is, if meaning and emphasis are not exactly parallel anyway.

In other sentences, both verbs do have to be in the same mood: *We would jail him if he were clearly guilty* can't be changed to either *We will jail him if he were clearly guilty* or *We would jail him if he is clearly guilty*. See also Rule 1-17.

A common error with subjunctive forms in past-tense sentences is carrying them too far: *If you'd have paid me, I'd have been grateful*. The contraction *you'd* must mean either *you had* or *you would*, neither of which is correct in the sentence; it has to be *If you'd paid me* or *If you had paid me*. Expanding the contraction should make the error apparent: *If you would have paid me, I would have been grateful* is obviously wrong.

1-15   Use the present participle and present infinitive to indicate time that is the same as the time of the main verb, whatever the tense of the main verb is; use the past participle and the past infinitive to indicate time previous to the time of the main verb.

Being a thief, he knew how to open the safe; Being a thief, he knows how to open the safe; Being a thief, he will know how to open the safe. In all these sentences, the man is a thief at the same time that he knows how to open the safe. Suppose we make it *Having been a thief, he knew how to open the safe* and so on. In all the resulting sentences, the man was a thief at a time previous to the time when he knows how to open the safe; we can't tell for sure whether or not he remains a thief, but the use of the past participle leaves it as a strong possibility that he's gone straight.

The infinitive works the same way: *He was proved to be a thief, He is proved to be a thief, He will be proved to be a thief; He was proved to have been a thief, He is proved to have been a thief, He will be proved to have been a thief.*

Sometimes in a sentence with several verbs in the past tense the infinitive will mistakenly get drawn along into the past: *The evidence was conclusive to the judge, and even though there had been no eyewitnesses to the crime he found Smith to have been the thief.* Even if Smith went straight between the time of the crime and the time of the trial, the judge *found Smith to be the thief.* But sometimes the past infinitive is precisely correct: *The judge ruled that the prosecution could not show Smith to have been a thief except by Smith's own testimony*—that is, the prosecution was not allowed to reveal Smith's previous record.

The present infinitive very frequently has a future implication: *I am to go tomorrow.* In this construction it functions like the present progressive tense, which can also express future time: *I am going tomorrow.*

Tenses of gerunds

Cooking the meal pleases her and *Cooking the meal pleased her* are the same statement, first in the present tense and then in the past. *Having cooked the meal pleases her* and *Having cooked the meal pleased her* are a quite different statement, first in the present and then in the past. The tense of a gerund is locked up tightly in the meaning of the gerund itself—the gerund's tense does not affect and is not affected by the tense of verbs in the sentence. *Cooking* and *Having cooked*, as gerunds, are like two nouns with different meanings; one means the process or activity of cooking, the other means the fact of having cooked.

1-16   Don't use the present participle to indicate action just previous to the action of the main verb.

Crossing the room, he sat down is incorrect unless he actually did sit down while in the act of crossing the room, in which case the event might be described less flatly. *Having crossed the room, he sat down,* with the participle in the past tense, makes the sentence correct, but may give the act of crossing an inappropriate significance.

The simplest way to indicate consecutive actions is to use consecutive verbs: *He crossed the room and sat down.* Someone who has just written several sentences of similar construction may want to provide some variation and so fall into the *Crossing the room* error. In fact, the error is routine for many careful and respected writers; they may be good writers but they abuse the special modifying effect of the participle.

The time of the participle is bound to the time of the main verb (Rule 1-15), and bound very tightly. There is some flexibility when the participle describes action of a different type from the action of the main verb—but not much. *Noticing that his knees were shaking, he sat down* is all right, because the noticing and the sitting are different types of action, one internal and the other external, and the noticing can go on throughout the act of sitting and even beyond. *Knowing that the market would drop, he sold out* is all right, because the knowing can go on before, during, and after the selling. *Hearing that the market would drop, he sold out* begins to be not all right, and *Hearing that the market would drop, he called his broker* is well along the path to not all right, with its definite suggestion of simultaneous listening and talking. *Hearing that the market would drop, he learned that selling out quickly might save him* is definitely not all right; the hearing and learning couldn't be simultaneous.

VERB MOODS: INDICATIVE, IMPERATIVE, AND SUBJUNCTIVE

The indicative mood is the familiar, standard mood of verbs: *He touches the lamp*; *He eats his breakfast.* The imperative mood, though not as common, is just as familiar, perhaps because we hear it so often in infancy: *Don't touch that lamp! Eat your cereal!*

The subjunctive mood may seem comparatively difficult and rare, though it is actually common. It does not express what something is or what something does, as the indicative does, or a direct command, as the imperative does. It expresses what something might be or do, should be or do, or must be or do. In a way it is the most distinctively human of moods, because it expresses the idea of possible being or action rather than actual being or action. Animals can exist only in the real world, but much of our mental life is spent in the worlds of if, might, ought, and must.

Most of the time the subjunctive form of a verb is identical to a past-tense indicative form, which makes it possible for grammarians to claim that the subjunctive is passing out of the language—they can say that a given construction uses the past tense of the verb and avoid saying that the form is subjunctive. But in a common construction such as *I should go*, it doesn't make sense to consider *should* the past tense of *shall*. There is no "pastness" to the meaning; *should* in this sentence is a subjunctive. The subjunctive is still very much a part of English, and we use it effortlessly all the time.

It is true that certain distinctive subjunctive forms seem to be passing out of English. These forms are the subject of the one rule in this section. Some tense problems with the subjunctive are discussed in the earlier section on tenses (see Rule 1-14).

1-17   Use the subjunctive forms *I were* and *he, she,* or *it were* in clauses that are contrary to fact, but be wary of using them in other situations.

I wish I were rich is a typical example of the condition contrary to fact. The clause *I were rich*, which looks very strange standing alone, is a subjunctive form used for statements that are known to be untrue, or are at least assumed to be highly unlikely by the speaker or writer, and that are presented just as hypotheses or desires. Often the condition contrary to fact is in an *if* clause: *He wouldn't wear those clothes if he were rich*.

A common error is to use the subjunctive form in any *if* clause that is in the past tense: *I wondered if she were single*; *If he were rich you couldn't tell it by his clothes*. It should be *was* in both sentences; the *if* clauses are merely in the past tense, they are not subjunctive. We aren't apt to make this error in the present tense—we use the correct indicative form: *I wonder if she is single*; *You can't tell from his clothes if he is rich*. See also **subjunctive** in the Glossary/Index.

Special subjunctive forms were used in more grammatical situations a generation ago than they are now, and they are more common in Britain than they are in the United States. An Englishman may well use *I were* in an *if* clause that is not contrary to fact, and he is being correct if perhaps slightly old-fashioned; when an American does the same, he is probably trying to be tony and revealing an uncertain grasp of American grammar. An Englishman might also say *I wonder if she be single*, another subjunctive form, which survives in constructions that are standard here too, such as *He insisted that he be paid* and *I insist that he be polite*. *I wonder if she be single* sounds quite affected in this country.

I wish I was rich is no longer considered incorrect in the United States; even in the contrary-to-fact construction, the distinctive subjunctive form *were* is no longer prescribed by many grammarians and is no longer the preference of many educated writers and speakers. Note that in *I wish I was rich*, *was* is still subjunctive, even though the distinctive *were* form isn't used. The indicative would be *I wish I am rich*, which is clearly wrong. In the past tense, *I wished I was rich* may seem to be using *was* as an indicative past, as in *I discovered I was rich*, but it is really still a subjunctive.

I wish I were rich and *I wished I were rich* are better usage at present. Perhaps in another few generations both they and *I wish I was rich* will seem affected, as *I wonder if she be single* does now, and we will all be saying *I wish I am rich*.

The subjunctive for the future conditional

President Reagan, whose English is good, said in August 1981, *If there were some kind of international crisis, we would correct that with new legislation*—using the distinctive *were* form of the subjunctive for a conditional sentence about the future, which cannot logically be a condition contrary to fact. This use of the subjunctive is one of those that grammarians have been waving farewell to for years, but it has remained alive and seems to be becoming more common, perhaps because the contrary-to-fact implication makes the unthinkable expressible: *If there were to be an all-out nuclear attack, we would reevaluate our SALT stance.*

The more straightforward subjunctive without the distinctive *were* form seems less conjectural: *If there should be an all-out nuclear attack . . .* Even the *should* form is not advised by most established grammarians, many of whom established themselves before the atom did; they favor the scary indicative: *If there is an all-out nuclear attack, we will reevaluate our SALT stance.*

I think the use of the distinctive *were* forms for the future conditional is defensible; it permits a special degree of doubt to be expressed about the future condition. It has always been common among the well-educated. It is perhaps a bit fussy, and regular guys may choose to stick to the indicative, but it does not invite derision the way *It is I* and *Whom do you want to invite?* may. Those who have been told that the distinctive forms should be used only in conditions contrary to fact may find fault with their use for the future conditional, but those who are either broader-minded or unaware of such arbitrary points of grammar will not object.

VERB VOICES: ACTIVE AND PASSIVE

The active voice is simple and direct: *She kissed John.* The passive voice reverses the position of the agent of the verb and makes the object of the verb its subject: *John was kissed by her.* The passive voice takes more words than the active voice, and it can be cumbersome and distracting. However, it has its legitimate uses.

1-18   Don't be afraid of the passive voice.

First we were shown the wall paintings in the main part of the house, and then we were taken by the guide, who was a very friendly man, over to a refreshment area to wait while the grown-ups went to see some other paintings in a room where we children weren't permitted. Poor little guy—he used the passive for all the *we* clauses, reserving the active for the clauses in which adults were the subject, and some schoolteacher is going to tell him to avoid the weak passive voice and make him rewrite it: *First we saw . . . then we went to a refreshment area with the guide . . . a room where we children couldn't go.* The comparatively swashbuckling account that results from the rewriting is not as good, as a child's expression, as the original tale of being taken—not of going—to Pompeii.

Children perceive themselves as objects of action more than as subjects of it, and they use the passive voice even though it takes more words and requires more complicated constructions. It is a feature of their expression. It does sound weak, compared to adult expression, and therefore teachers try to get them away from it. This is not stupid or wrong of the teachers, though a teacher may be insensitive about the problem. Children do have to become adults, do have to learn to think of themselves as the subjects of action rather than the objects of it.

This book is for adults—and we can forget that "Avoid the passive" rule. The passive voice is respectable, is capable of expressing shades of meaning that the active voice cannot express, and is sometimes more compact and direct than the active voice.

The troublesaving passive

Smith was arrested, indicted, and found guilty, but the money was never recovered has four passive constructions. It is simpler and more direct than *The police arrested Smith, the grand jury indicted him, and the trial jury found him guilty, but the bank never recovered the money,* which has four active constructions. The use of the active voice requires naming the agent of the verb, because in the active voice the agent and the subject are the same, and a verb must have a subject. The passive voice permits not naming the agent of the verb, because the object of the active verb has become the subject of the passive verb. If the agent is too obvious, too unimportant, or too vague to mention, the passive is usually better.

The passive to emphasize the agent

The money was stolen by a man, judging from those footprints emphasizes the agent because it puts it at the end of the clause, which is a prominent position that the reader expects to have some stress. *A man stole the money, judging from those footprints* could be inflected just as clearly in speech by extra emphasis on *man,* but in writing the passive voice supplies the emphasis.

The pussyfooting passive

The money was stolen while Smith was in the vault states the crime and describes the circumstances but avoids making a direct accusation. This tact, frequently desirable in life, would be more difficult to achieve were it not for the passive voice.

The pussyfooting passive is admittedly much abused. *These arrears cannot be overlooked, and if payment is not made promptly, our legal staff will be notified and more rigorous action will be taken* is an offensive, falsely polite way of saying *Our firm cannot overlook these arrears, and if you do not pay us immediately we will take rigorous legal action.* The much shorter *Pay up* is both meant and understood, of course; statements such as this do require a little extra verbiage. They don't require the pussyfooting passive; the active is both clearer and less offensive.

The pussyfooting passive is essential in journalism—often the writer does not know who did something or is not free to say who did it, but he wants to say it was done.

MODIFIERS

Adjectives and adverbs are the parts of speech that the term *modifier* brings to mind—adverbs modify verbs, adjectives, and other adverbs, and adjectives modify nouns and sometimes pronouns. However, the term also includes phrases and dependent clauses that define or elaborate on other words or other phrases and clauses.

Modifiers are misused in various ways. They can be forced into double duty as both modifier and noun, they can be badly positioned in a sentence so that it is not clear what they modify, they can occur in sentences in which they have nothing to modify, and they can just be the wrong type of modifier—an adjective where an adverb is called for, or vice versa.

1-19   Consider a possessive form to be
         a modifier; don't use it as an
         antecedent for a relative pronoun,
         and don't let a noun not in the
         possessive be in apposition to it.

The hat is John's, who forgot it uses the possessive form
John's as the antecedent for the relative pronoun *who*, which
is incorrect. *The hat belongs to John, who forgot it* is correct; *who* now has a real noun, not a modifier, as its antecedent. *The hat is John's; he forgot it* is another solution,
permissible because the personal pronoun *he* is not as tightly
bound to the antecedent as a relative pronoun; as long as the
meaning of *he* is clear (see Rule 1-13) it can have a possessive form as its antecedent.

The hat is John's, the young man who is so forgetful* uses
the phrase *the young man who is so forgetful* in apposition to
the possessive *John's*, which is also incorrect. We could use
man's in the appositive phrase, to agree in case with *John's*,
but then *who* would have the possessive antecedent *man's*,
another error. In other examples, making the appositive
noun a possessive might work: *Is that John's—my husband's—hat?* In the original example, *The hat belongs to
John, the young man who is so forgetful* is the quickest
repair.

My husband John's hat is nevertheless acceptable—the
phrase *my husband*, though not restrictive, since a woman
has only one husband, is tightly combined with *John* into a
single phrase, which is then made possessive. This is often
possible when the second term is more specific than the first
term: *his friend John's hat*, but not *John his friend's hat*.
Some grammarians do permit *John, his friend's, hat*, but if
we take out the parenthetical *his friend's*, which we should
be able to do without affecting the grammar of what remains,
we have *John hat*. (See also the discussion of parenthetical
and defining appositives in Rule 2-1.)

Exception: the independent possessive

*If you need a hat take John's, which has been here all
week* uses the possessive *John's* as antecedent for the rela-

tive pronoun *which*, but it is nevertheless correct. The antecedent of *which* is not John himself but the thing he owns, his hat. We might consider the example an elliptical sentence—*John's* is short for *John's hat*—but actually *John's* is functioning as a so-called independent possessive, a possessive form that can function as a noun and both serve as antecedent for a relative pronoun and have another noun in apposition to it.

The distinction is clearly seen when we use personal pronouns, some of which have distinctive forms for the independent possessive: *I needed a hat and took yours, which you had left behind*; *If you need a hat take mine, the gray one*. The forms *yours* and *mine* are possessives but really act as nouns, unlike the forms *your* and *my*, which act only as modifiers.

1-20   Position modifiers in a sentence so that they modify the right word and only that word.

Since word order is the most significant indication of the meaning of an English sentence—*John loves Mary* and *Mary loves John* are an obvious example of the effect word order can have on meaning—a misplaced modifier can make a sentence unclear or at least momentarily confusing.

Adjectives and adjective chains

Adjectives almost always either directly precede the word they modify, as in *gray cats*, or directly follow it and a linking verb, as in *Cats are gray*. Errors with position of an adjective and the word it modifies are uncommon.

However, when two or more adjectives modify the same word, there is often some question what order to put them in. Sometimes all the adjectives stand in the same direct relation to the word they modify, and the order does not greatly matter: *a gray, cold, fretful sea* has a string of three descriptive adjectives that could be put in any order. Usually adjectives that all directly modify the same word are separated by commas. We can test whether or not the adjectives all directly modify the same word by seeing if *and* can be put between the adjectives—*a gray and cold and fretful sea*—without changing the meaning.

More often, there is some progression in the order of adjectives from the most specific to the least specific, as in *my three beautiful Belgian rabbits*. Each adjective modifies the whole word group that follows, and tampering with the order of the adjectives sounds wrong or changes the meaning. The possessive adjective *my* is a definitive adjective—other definitive adjectives are the articles *the* and *a* and the demonstrative adjectives *this*, *that*, *these*, and *those*—and definitive adjectives come first, modifying the whole following word group. Then come numerical adjectives—*three* in the example—modifying what remains of the word group. Then there are adjectives implying judgment or opinion of some kind, such as *beautiful*. Then there are purely descriptive adjectives, such as *Belgian*. When there are two or more descriptive adjectives in the series, they are usually in the order of adjectives expressing size, adjectives expressing shape, and adjectives expressing other qualities: *large round furry Belgian rabbits*.

All this is breaking it down rather fine; actually the line between judgmental and descriptive adjectives can be hard to draw and the best order for a string of descriptive adjectives hard to judge, so a good deal must be left to the ear. However, the fact that such a series of adjectives does progress can be tested by trying to insert *and* as we did with adjectives that do not progress: *my and three and beautiful and Belgian rabbits* is obviously not English. Yet we can double the adjectives in each category and join the pairs with *and*, and the result is English, even though clumsy: *your and my third and fourth beautiful and courageous Belgian and French rabbits*.

Note that when the string of adjectives forms a progression, commas are usually not desirable to separate the adjectives. Since each adjective modifies the whole word group that follows, a comma would separate the modifier from the modified phrase, which is a misuse of the comma (see Rule 2-5).

Adverbs

Adverbs are prone to wander. In *The young man swims badly* the adverb *badly* immediately follows the verb, and in *The young man almost failed to finish* the adverb *almost* immediately precedes the verb. This closeness is common, but it is also common to find the adverb well separated from the verb: *I can't believe how badly that young man swims.*

In sentences in which the position of an adverb is critical, we are unlikely to make mistakes. *Harshly, he asked how they could be punished* and *He asked harshly how they could be punished* and *He asked how harshly they could be punished* and *He asked how they could be harshly punished* and *He asked how they could be punished harshly* all express different ideas; there is some overlapping of possible intended meanings in the five examples, but almost everyone would unerringly pick the best word order for his meaning. The first two examples have almost the same meaning, but the *Harshly, he asked* example uses *Harshly* to modify the entire sentence, not just *asked*, and thus suggests that the entire situation, both the manner of asking and the question, was harsh; the *He asked harshly* example concentrates the effect of the adverb on the verb *asked*, and thus suggests only the manner of asking the question was harsh.

However, because they can wander and because they can modify adjectives, other adverbs, and whole sentences as well as verbs, there may be several words in a given sentence that an adverb can modify, and this makes confusion and ambiguity possible even in sentences that are grammatically correct.

We can't follow completely false logic is ambiguous. It should be either *We can't completely follow false logic* or *We can't follow logic that is completely false*; for the second meaning we have to make the sentence more complicated and use a relative clause, because there is nowhere in the original sentence that we can put *completely* that will make it clearly the modifier of *false*. This kind of misplaced modifier is sometimes called a squinting modifier—it seems to look in two directions at once. Squinting modifiers can be hard to find when we are looking over what we've written, because we ourselves, of course, know what we mean, and the grammar is not actually incorrect, just ambiguous.

I'm almost having the best time of my life is not ambiguous—except by a very perverse misreading—but it is careless and graceless; it should be *I'm having almost the best time of my life*. The adverb usually should not be separated from the word it does modify by any other word that it is grammatically possible for it to modify, though adverbs are too wily to permit this principle to be stated as a definite rule.

I'm only going to tell you once has a misplaced modifier—it should be *I'm going to tell you only once*—but it is not ambiguous, and it is not graceless either; it is almost an idiom. The "correct" version may sound a little stiff compared to the more natural alternative; sometimes taste must determine when the precise positioning of a modifier is desirable and when it is too fussy. I recommend allowing *only*—an especially vagrant word even among the adverbs—to wander with some freedom in speech, but positioning it precisely in anything but the most casual writing; the habit can have a surprisingly pervasive good effect on our expression, because it is by just such attention to detail that prose becomes truly good instead of merely workmanlike and adequate.

Split infinitives

It was impossible to completely follow his logic is far better than *It was impossible to follow completely his logic*, which is unnatural, or *It was impossible completely to follow his logic*, which is both unnatural and ambiguous. As is frequently the case, we do have an alternative to splitting the infinitive: *It was impossible to follow his logic completely*.

The rule against the split infinitive is an arbitrary one, a hangover from the nineteenth century, when grammarians attempted to make English grammar conform to Latin grammar. The Latin infinitive cannot be split—but only because it is all one word, not because there is any rule against it. Fewer and fewer writers, and few grammarians, subscribe to the rule against the split infinitive. And yet there are arguments for following it. Arbitrary it is, but arbitrariness alone is no reason to violate a rule; many rules of grammar and particularly of usage are arbitrary. To me—perhaps because I am old enough to have been made to follow the rule as a student—split infinitives still retain some fragrance of ignorance and sloppiness. I have no way of knowing how small the minority I am part of has become, but I suspect that it is still a sizable if silent one.

Nevertheless, splitting the infinitive is better than putting the infinitive's modifier in an unnatural or ambiguous place. If we choose to avoid split infinitives—perhaps because we consider such avoidance a kind of gesture of respect for the language and the readers we are addressing—we should also take the trouble to recast sentences to avoid putting the modifier in an unnatural place. Occasionally a writer seems to go out of his way to put the modifier in an unnatural place, perhaps as a kind of showing off—the writer wants his readers to notice that he knows enough not to split infinitives.

Participles and participial phrases

He was the only man in the group dancing is ambiguous; it could mean either *He was the only man dancing in the group* or *He was the only man in the dancing group*. Participles are used as adjectives, but they wander more like adverbs.

He was the only man in the group wearing makeup has the same ambiguity; either he was the only person wearing makeup or none of the others in the group wearing makeup were men. The word *group* is right next to the participial phrase *wearing makeup*, but that does not prevent ambiguity; *wearing makeup* is drawn at least as strongly to *man*, which is the complement of the subject of the sentence, *He*. Similarly, *I met her going to the store* is ambiguous; the participial phrase *going to the store* must modify either *I* or *her*, but we can't tell which. If it modifies *I*, we can make the sentence unambiguous by repositioning the participial phrase—*Going to the store, I met her*—but that is hardly natural; often it is better to recast and avoid the participial phrase: *I met her on my way to the store* or *on her way to the store*.

Thus participles and participial phrases must be watched carefully; like adverbs, they can cause confusion and ambiguity.

Dependent clauses

He was flown to Miami for combat training, where he was commissioned is not ambiguous and not truly an error, but it does separate the *where* clause from the word it modifies, *Miami*. When a dependent clause modifies a specific word or phrase in a sentence, it is best to put the clause directly after the modified word or phrase: *He was flown for combat training to Miami, where he was commissioned.* If this makes the sentence seem awkward, it should be recast to avoid the dependent clause: *He was flown to Miami for combat training and was commissioned there.*

1-21   Don't let modifiers dangle with nothing to modify.

Inspecting the books, the error was immediately apparent is an example of the famous dangling participle. The sentence does not have too many words that *Inspecting* could grammatically modify—the concern of Rule 1-20—but only one, *error*. However, that one is not possible, because an error can't inspect. The word the participle should modify must be some word signifying whoever inspected the books, and it is not in the sentence at all. The error is almost always just that simple, and is easily avoided: Just remember that a participle, like any adjectival word, must have something to modify.

Inspecting the books, the error was immediately apparent to us may seem better, because it does supply *us* for the participle to modify, but it too is wrong. When a participle or participial phrase begins a sentence, it must modify the subject of the rest of the sentence (or the subject of the following clause, if the sentence has more than one clause). Thus this example is still a dangling participle; *us* is not the subject and *Inspecting* can't modify it. *The error was immediately apparent to us, inspecting the books, but not to them, inspecting their monthly royalty* is correct, because the participial phrases do not begin the sentence and immediately follow the words they modify.

Shown the books, the accountant's hands began to shake

has a dangling participle. The participial phrase *Shown the books* is intended to modify *accountant,* but *accountant* is in the possessive case—*accountant's*—and thus is not a noun but an adjective, and a participle cannot modify an adjective (See Rule 1-19). The only word available for the participle to modify is the noun *hands*, which is obviously not the intended meaning. This error is quite common, especially with possessive pronouns, as in *Mulling over the options, his perplexity only increased.*

Considering the state of the books, the error was found surprisingly quickly technically contains a dangling participle; *Considering* has nothing in the sentence to modify. However, there are many similar common expressions in English that are accepted as correct and that it would be troublesome and pointless not to accept. Actually they do have something to modify—the whole rest of the sentence. They are essentially sentence modifiers, as *however, therefore*, and similar adverbs usually are. *Regarding, looking, judging, allowing, excepting*, and similar participles that express some kind of generalized mental activity permit such sentence-modifying phrases. Dictionaries are apt to identify the most common of these participles, such as *considering* and *regarding*, as prepositions and conjunctions, which in a rather weasely way gets them off the hook; it lets us call *considering the state of the books* a prepositional phrase rather than a dangling participial phrase.

The books having been inspected, the error was apparent is correct; it is not a dangling participle. *The books having been inspected* is a so-called absolute construction. The phrase itself includes the word the participial form *having been inspected* modifies: *books*. Absolute phrases do not have to modify any specific word in the rest of the sentence. They modify the whole rest of the sentence, just as an introductory dependent clause does: *When the books had been inspected, the error was apparent.*

Many dangling constructions aren't as famous as the dangling participle but are just as common.

Other danglers

By being prepared and giving a brief show of your best work, your family and friends will think you are quite a photographer is not a case of the dangling participle; *being prepared* and *giving* are not participles but gerunds. It's still a dangler, because the gerunds that introduce the sentence are in adverbial phrases, and these adverbial phrases should relate to the subject and verb of the main clause—that is, they should modify either the verb or the whole sentence. To correct the sentence the main clause must be rewritten: *you will make your family and friends think you are quite a photographer*. Now the adverbial phrases relate correctly to *you will make* and modify the whole sentence.

In *They made him, a proved incompetent, head of the department*, the phrase *a proved incompetent* is in apposition to *him*, and the sentence is correct. However, *A proved incompetent, they made him head of the department* is wrong; the appositional phrase dangles. When an appositional phrase begins a sentence, it must be in apposition to the subject of the sentence, which in the example is *they*, not *him*.

It pays to be suspicious almost anytime a sentence begins with a subordinate element, whether the element· is a modifier, a prepositional phrase, or some other construction. *At the age of five, his father died* is a classic example; the sentence doesn't contain any word that *At the age of five* can relate to, since *his* is merely adjectival (see Rule 1-19) and the father couldn't be a father if he died at five. (*When he was five, his father died* does not dangle, though it does invite perverse misreading.) Another similar example is *In no real need of money, nevertheless greed proved his undoing*. Sometimes the problem is only that the subordinate element comes first, and the sentence can be made grammatically correct simply by shifting order: *Fat and wheezy, the run was too much for John* can be made *The run was too much for fat and wheezy John* or even *for John, fat and wheezy*. Shifting order may at least make the basic problem of a bad sentence more evident.

1-22   Don't misuse adverbs as adjectives, and don't misuse adjectives as adverbs.

Adjectives that should be adverbs

He drives really good is wrong because *good* modifies the verb *drives* and thus should be the adverb *well*. *He drives real well* is wrong because *real* modifies the adverb *well* and thus should be the adverb *really*. *He drives real good* is a double error. Using an adjective as an adverb is debased, substandard English, and few of us are likely to make such errors except when being deliberately slangy.

I drive slow in town is not an error. Some common adverbs have two forms; both *slow* and *slowly* can be adverbs, though the only adjectival form is *slow*. Don't automatically correct an "adjectival" form that seems idiomatic as an adverb; check the dictionary—it may be a legitimate adverb too.

Adverbs that should be adjectives

I feel badly about it is the most common type of error; the example itself is so common that some authorities accept it as standard English. The verb *feel* is a linking verb in this construction, not an ordinary verb as it can be in other constructions, such as *The doctor feels carefully along the patient's spine*. A linking verb links its subject to the following word or phrase. *I* is a pronoun and cannot be modified by or linked to an adverb. It can be modified by or linked to an adjective. Thus it should be *I feel bad*.

An occasional expression such as *I feel badly* may infiltrate the speech and writing of those who are conscious of grammar and know something about it, but not enough; they think the verb *feel* has to be followed by the adverb *badly*, so they carefully tack on the *ly*. It's an embarrassing error, because it suggests a self-conscious attempt to be correct. To avoid embarrassment we have to pay special attention to expressions involving linking verbs. The most common linking verb is, of course, *be*; other common verbs that can be linking verbs are *seem, appear, look, become, grow, taste*, *feel*, *smell*, *sound*, *remain*, and *stay*. Most of them are not always linking verbs. The verb *smell* is not a linking verb in *He vigorously smells the wine* or in *He smells less acutely than the winemaster*, but it is a linking verb in *He smells strong after his sessions in the wine cellar*.

You have to hold the camera vertical for close-up portraits is correct. It's the camera, not the holding of it, that has to be vertical; *hold the camera vertically* would be the same sort of error as *feel badly*, though it does not involve a linking verb. It involves an object complement—a noun or adjective that follows the actual object of the verb to complete the meaning. *Let us see it clear and plain* is a similar use of object complements.

Precision can be important. In opening his poem on his father's dying with the line *Do not go gentle into that good night*, Dylan Thomas, not just a master but a grandmaster and ringmaster of language, was being precisely correct; he wanted his father to be ungentle about the prospect of dying, but he did not want his father to die ungently—that is, he did not want the death to be ungentle and painful, which *Do not go gently* would mean.

2

PUNCTUATION

Punctuation can be thought of as a means of indicating the pauses and changes of tone that are used in speech to help communicate the meaning of sentences. The marks of punctuation evolved partly as indicators of pause and tone—a comma usually indicates a pause, a question mark usually indicates a rising tone, and so on—and they retain this significance. Consequently, in this chapter I often point out that a comma, question mark, or some other mark of punctuation can be "heard" at a given point in a sentence.

However, we cannot rely completely on our sense of proper spoken delivery when we are punctuating written sentences. For one thing, muttering sentences to ourselves as we're writing is inefficient, like lip reading, and also uncertain, because a sentence muttered over a few times somehow loses its meaning and we soon can't decide how we would speak it. More important, punctuation goes well beyond its function as an indicator of pause and tone, even though it retains that function. In the early seventeenth century, Ben Jonson developed a theory of syntactical punctuation—that is, punctuation based on the relationships between words in a sentence rather than only on pause and tone in spoken sentences—and ever since, punctuation has had something of a life of its own, independent of spoken English though usually not in serious disagreement with it.

Punctuation cannot reproduce the variety of pause and tone available in speech. On the other hand, speech cannot indicate with equal clarity everything that the marks of punctuation can indicate in written English. Some complicated sentences can be clear and balanced in writing, but cannot be spoken, or even read aloud, without extreme awkwardness and ambiguity. A single written sentence can introduce a subject, discuss it, indicate the relative importance of the items of the discussion, and sum it up, leaving the reader with a complete idea—complete in the way a musical composition or a painting is complete, and admirable in the same way. Spoken language, rich and beautiful as it can be in other respects, must often be less compact and complex, because it does not have the precise syntactical signals that marks of punctuation give to written language.

Like the preceding chapter, on grammar, this chapter focuses on common errors and problems. It is divided into obvious major sections. The first section concerns sentence structure; the rest of the sections concern the individual marks of punctuation. I have not provided a section on the period, because it has only one major use—to end a declarative sentence. However, the problems that come up when the period is used with other marks of punctuation are discussed in the rules for those marks of punctuation, and the various conventional uses of the period, such as to indicate an abbreviation, are discussed in Chapter 3.

Punctuation practices change more quickly than grammatical rules, and there is more disagreement about them from authority to authority, from stylebook to stylebook. Therefore I have had to list many exceptions and qualifications and to defend some rules that are my own preferences.

SENTENCE STRUCTURE

Punctuation within a sentence is largely determined by the structure of the sentence. Structure includes grammar, but it is not just another word for grammar; several of the terms used in this chapter to describe structure are not necessary at all in the preceding chapter, which is specifically on grammar. The first rule in this chapter and the lone one in this section includes a review of some of the necessary terms.

2-1   Consider the structure of a sentence when punctuating it.

Sentence structure is a basic part of language, and ordinarily we don't have to think about it very much. However, when we are not sure how to punctuate a sentence, we do have to think about its structure, and usually in terms of three basic questions:

1. Is it a simple sentence, a compound sentence, or a complex sentence?
2. If the sentence includes a dependent clause or phrase, is the dependent clause or phrase parenthetical or defining?
3. Does the sentence begin with the main clause, or with an introductory word, phrase, or dependent clause?

Each of the terms used in these questions is discussed below.

Simple sentences

John writes is the simplest sort of simple sentence, containing just a subject, *John*, and a verb, *writes*. *John writes me letters* is still a simple sentence, though now the verb has the direct object *letters* and the indirect object *me*. *John and Mary write* is also a simple sentence, though it has the compound subject *John and Mary*. And *John writes and telephones* is a simple sentence, though it has the compound verb *writes and telephones*.

A sentence can get quite long and complicated and still remain a simple sentence. *Until recently, John and Mary, my grandchildren, wrote me letters twice a month and telephoned every Sunday afternoon* is a simple sentence, even though it includes an introductory phrase, a compound subject with an appositive, a compound verb, a direct and an indirect object for one of the verbs, and an adverbial phrase for each of the verbs. It is simple because in spite of its complexity, it still merely connects one subject or set of subjects to one action or set of actions. The following discussion of other types of sentences should make the nature of the simple type somewhat clearer.

Compound sentences

John writes, and Mary telephones is a compound sentence. It consists of two clauses, either of which could stand alone: *John writes. Mary telephones.* They are independent clauses—that is, not only does each have its own subject and predicate (the minimum any clause must have), but neither one is dependent on the other. A compound sentence is merely a group of two or more simple sentences (or complex sentences, discussed below) that have been made one sentence by punctuating them appropriately and often by using a conjunction such as *and*.

Complex sentences

John, who is my grandson, doesn't write anymore contains the dependent clause *who is my grandson. Mary still gets the urge to telephone just before the rates go up on Sunday* contains the dependent clause *just before the rates go up on Sunday.* Both are complex sentences—that is, sentences with one or more dependent clauses. The clause *who is my grandson* is obviously not an independent clause (unless one makes it a question); it is an adjectival clause modifying *John.* The clause *just before the rates go up on Sunday* is not independent either; it is an adverbial clause modifying *gets the urge to telephone.* Each dependent clause merely modifies something in the main clause.

Compound/complex sentences

They wanted to go on writing and telephoning, but after they moved into my house I told them to stop has an independent clause up to the comma and another independent clause after the comma, so it is a compound sentence. The second independent clause includes not just the main clause *I told them to stop* but the modifying dependent clause *after they moved into my house*, so the sentence is also a complex sentence. Thus we have a compound/complex sentence.

Punctuating simple, compound, and complex sentences

As can be seen in the examples above, a simple sentence may have quite a lot of punctuation, a compound or complex sentence very little. Many of the remaining rules in this chapter deal with the specific problems that come up in specific types of sentences: Rule 2-2 is about compound sentences, Rule 2-3 is about simple sentences with compound predicates (that is, compound verbs), and so on. The discussion just below of parenthetical constructions and defining constructions will help in punctuating complex sentences.

Parenthetical constructions

His son, who is a good swimmer, made the rescue contains the parenthetical dependent clause *who is a good swimmer*. The pair of commas around the clause—one before and one after—are exactly like a pair of parentheses: *His son (who is a good swimmer) made the rescue*. Omitting one comma or the other would be just as bad an error as omitting one of the parentheses.

Parenthetical constructions are often called nonrestrictive, because they do not restrict the meaning of the word or words they relate to but instead expand on that meaning; they could be removed from the sentence without changing the basic meaning.

The rescue was made by his son, who is a good swimmer contains the same parenthetical clause as the first example. We don't use the second comma, because we have reached the end of the sentence and use a period instead, but if we substitute parentheses for the commas, it's easy to see that the clause is still parenthetical: *The rescue was made by his son (who is a good swimmer)*. It is unusual for a parenthetical clause to begin a sentence, but when it does, the first comma is, of course, omitted: *Although he swims well, he has no lifesaving training.* The second comma—in the example, the one after *well*—is optional but usually desirable, as explained in the discussion of introductory constructions below.

Parenthetical—or nonrestrictive—elements don't have to be clauses; they can also be phrases or even single words, as explained more fully below in the discussion of appositives. *His son, John, made the rescue* has the parenthetical element *John. John, swimming strongly, reached the child in time* has the parenthetical element *swimming strongly.* Again, the two parenthetical commas are reduced to one if the parenthetical element occurs at the beginning or end of the sentence: *We saw your son, John*; *We saw John, swimming strongly.*

Defining constructions

His son who is a good swimmer made the rescue is quite a different sentence. The subject is no longer just *His son*, but a specific son who is a good swimmer, as distinguished from other sons who aren't. There are no commas, because *who is a good swimmer* is now a necessary, integral part of the sentence. Similarly, *His son John made the rescue* singles that son out from others with different names—but see also the discussion of appositives below.

Defining constructions are often called restrictive, because they restrict the meaning of the word or phrase they relate to. Like nonrestrictive elements, restrictive elements can be single words or phrases as well as clauses. They should not be separated from the words they relate to with commas, because they are an essential part of the meaning.

It is apparent that only the person who is writing about the water rescue can know whether he means *who is a good swimmer* to be restrictive or nonrestrictive, defining or parenthetical. If he punctuates properly, he makes his meaning unmistakable; if he doesn't, it is uncertain what he means. In speech, we can hear slight pauses for the parenthetical construction and a run-together failure to pause for the defining construction. In writing, the presence or absence of commas (or other marks of punctuation, such as dashes or parentheses) makes the distinction.

His son John who is a good swimmer made the rescue is good news but bad punctuation. It is punctuated as if both *John* and *who is a good swimmer* are defining elements, but that can't be the case, because surely only one son is named John. The clause *who is a good swimmer* must be considered a parenthetical element and set off with commas. *John* can be considered either parenthetical or defining, depending on whether there is only one son or more than one; if it is parenthetical, commas should ordinarily be used around it, but see the discussion of appositives just below.

Parenthetical and defining appositives

An appositive is a noun, or a group of words acting as a noun, that immediately follows another noun to explain it or further define it. *My friend Mary is getting married* uses *Mary* as a defining appositive, narrowing down *friend* to a specific friend, and no commas are used. *Mary, my friend from school, is getting married* uses *my friend from school* as a parenthetical appositive, and parenthetical commas are used. Note that a defining appositive restricts the meaning and makes the word it is in apposition to more specific, whereas a parenthetical appositive, though it may clarify and elucidate meaning (many people are named Mary), does not really restrict it (*Mary* is already a specific person, unlike *friend*).

When a noun and another noun in apposition to it are equally specific, the noun in apposition is considered parenthetical: *My husband, John, is at work*; *John, my husband, is at work*. Both *John* and *my husband* are completely specific.

My sister Mary is getting married is punctuated (or rather not punctuated) to indicate that there is more than one sister—that is, *Mary* is defining, and necessary to indicate which sister is meant. *My sister, Mary, is getting married* is punctuated to indicate that there is only one sister, and *Mary* is parenthetical rather than defining. However, the parenthetical commas can often be omitted in phrases such as *my husband John* and *my sister Mary*, even though there could be only one husband and there might be only one sister. *My husband John* can be considered a unit, somewhat like *my Uncle Bob*, rather than an ordinary case of noun and appositive; it often would be spoken without pauses. *My sister Mary* can also be considered a unit when the existence of other sisters is unknown or irrelevant; and conversely, *my sister, Mary,* with *Mary* treated as parenthetical, may be quite all right even if there are a dozen other sisters as long as Mary is the only possible one meant in the context. Some writers and editors always try to make the punctuation conform to the actual genealogical facts, but this can be a violation of common sense. Usually commas can be inserted or omitted in such phrases by ear rather than by genealogical reasoning.

Defining appositives are very often incorrectly set off by commas. *In his essay, "Self-Reliance," Emerson celebrated individualism* is typical; since Emerson wrote more than one essay, *"Self-Reliance"* is defining, not parenthetical, and there should be no commas setting it off (though the second comma is desirable, as explained below).

Introductory constructions

An introductory construction is anything that precedes the main clause of a sentence. It may be a single word, such as *However*; it may be a phrase, such as *In view of the circumstances*; it may be a dependent clause, such as *When I'm ready*. Usually an introductory construction is followed by a comma, which serves as a signal that the main clause is about to begin.

I'll call you when I'm ready contains the defining dependent clause *when I'm ready*. *When I'm ready, I'll call you* puts the dependent clause first, as an introductory construction; *When I'm ready* is still a defining clause, restricting the meaning of *I'll call you*, but because it is introductory it is set off with a comma. Thus after an introductory construction, the comma is not the signal of a parenthetical element but simply a clarifying pause.

A comma is not always required following an introductory construction—*When I'm ready I'll call you* is fine, since the introductory clause is short and very closely related to the main clause—but it is usually permissible, often desirable, and sometimes necessary. We can usually "hear" whether the comma is desirable or necessary. *When we're eating local politicians are excluded as a topic of conversation* requires a pause after *eating* in speech and a comma after *eating* in writing, to keep *local politicians* from being momentarily misunderstood to be the direct object of *eating*. We can also "hear" when the comma is not permissible: *In the dining room, were twelve quarrelsome people* should not have the comma after *room* (see also Rule 2-5, especially the discussion of inverted sentences).

Therefore, *however*, *in addition*, and many similar words and phrases are usually followed by a comma when they are used to introduce a sentence: *Therefore, let's talk about something else*. There is some flexibility when such words are used in a compound sentence to introduce a second clause: *Tempers were beginning to rise, and therefore we changed the subject*. A comma after *therefore* would not be incorrect, but would give the sentence a loose look, with no distinction made between the major pause after *rise* and the minor or missing pause after *therefore*. *Tempers were beginning to rise; and therefore, we changed the subject* uses a semicolon for the major pause and a comma for the minor one, which is correct but gives the sentence more punctuation than it really needs. (Grammar books of a century ago would require a comma between *and* and *therefore* as well— an example of the changes that "correct punctuation" has endured; we use lighter punctuation today.)

COMMA

The comma is by far the most frequent mark of punctuation within the sentence, and it is the most frequently misused. In principle, it is very simple: It is always a means of separating one word, phrase, or clause from another. However, it is not the only mark of punctuation that has this function. Semicolons, colons, parentheses, and dashes are separators too. Errors with commas frequently occur because the writer is unsure whether the comma or one of the other separators is required.

2-2   Separate independent clauses joined by *and, or, but, for,* and similar coordinating conjunctions with a comma or a semicolon.

We're going to discuss it, and then we'll decide what to do is a compound sentence—that is, it has two independent clauses. *We're going to discuss it* can stand alone as a complete sentence, and so can *Then we'll decide what to do.* When joined by *and*, the clauses are separated by a comma. A semicolon could be used instead, and if the *and* is omitted, a semicolon should be used (see Rule 2-12). When the *and* is supplied, a semicolon is usually an unnecessarily strong mark of punctuation and the comma is better.

Often when the second independent clause begins with an introductory construction (Rule 2-1), the comma is misplaced: *We're going to discuss it and, when we've worked it out, we'll let you know* should have a comma after *discuss it* and no comma after *and*. The comma after *out* is optional in this example. See Rule 2-8 for similar problems with introductory constructions.

Exceptions

Let's sit down and I'll tell you a story is a compound sentence and could have a comma after *down*, but the comma is optional. This is often the case when the clauses of a compound sentence are short and closely related.

I'll tell him that we're going to have lunch and then we'll discuss it also omits the comma between the clauses—but notice that they are no longer independent clauses but together make up the object of *I'll tell him*; they are noun clauses, a special type of dependent clause. Omitting the comma makes the sentence clearer in this example; if there were a comma after *lunch*, the reader couldn't be sure whether or not *then we'll discuss it* is one of the things *I'll tell him*—it might be an independent clause.

It's an unusual problem and no one knows much about it, but we're going to discuss it and then we'll decide is a double compound sentence—two independent clauses joined by *and* are connected to two other independent clauses joined by *and*. We could put commas after *problem* and *discuss it*, but if we do, we had better change the existing comma after *about it* to a semicolon to avoid a loose string of three commas: *It's an unusual problem, and no one knows much about it; but we're going to discuss it, and then we'll decide*. This would have been considered the best way to punctuate the sentence a generation ago, but the trend today is to use light punctuation. With only one internal mark of punctuation, the comma after *about it*, the sentence is smoother and just as easy to understand.

When the board met yesterday, the topic came up and I discussed it with John has an introductory *when* clause followed by two independent clauses that are not separated by commas. The meaning is clearly that the discussion with John took place during the board meeting—that is, the introductory *when* clause modifies both the following clauses, not just the first one. If we make it *When the board met yesterday, the topic came up, and I discussed it with John*, the meaning is no longer so clear; the discussion with John may have taken place after the board meeting. If it took place after the meeting, the sentence could be made unambiguous by adding a modifier—*and later I discussed it*—but if it took place at the meeting, the missing comma between the independent clauses makes it clear enough. As a general principle, it is sensible to omit a comma between independent clauses that are both modified by the same dependent clause or introductory phrase. *In the morning, I'll come over, and we'll have lunch together* is not such a case—the second independent clause is not modified by *In the morning*. But *In the morning, I'll come over and we'll have breakfast together* is such a case, and though the comma omission is not required for clarity in this example, it is desirable to indicate the shared relationship with the introductory phrase. If in a given example of a shared introductory phrase the sentence begins to seem unwieldy and to require a comma just for ease of reading, it is likely that the sentence has outgrown its structure and should be divided or recast.

2-3   Do not separate compound predicates with a comma except for good reason.

We'll check the books, and let you know contains a compound predicate: *We'll check . . . and let you know.* The comma after *books* is unnecessary, though we cannot rule it out as definitely wrong. In some sentences, such an unnecessary comma can cause confusion: *I told him that we'd checked the books, and found the error in his own records* is not clear, because the meaning could be either *I told him that we'd . . . found the error in his own records* or *I . . . found the error* after telling him *we'd checked the books.* Omitting the comma does not completely eliminate the ambiguity, but it helps.

When commas are unnecessary, they should be omitted, just as unnecessary words should be omitted (see Rule 1-4).

Exceptions

We'll check the books, and let you know next week justifiably uses the comma to make it clear that *next week* modifies only *let you know*, not *check the books.* Often a comma is helpful to counter the tendency of adjectives, adverbs, and other modifiers to link themselves to the wrong word or phrase.

He left the room, and a moment later reappeared with a tray of drinks justifiably uses the comma to indicate a lapse in time. *He left the room, and reappeared with a tray of drinks* is even more justifiable, since the explicit time-lapse signal *a moment later* has been dropped. If the sentences were spoken, we would probably hear a pause after *room* in the first sentence and would almost certainly hear a pause in the second.

He is doing well, and will rise to the top if he keeps it up justifiably uses the comma to separate predicates that are quite different in significance—one is a statement about the present and the other is a prediction about the future. When the verbs in a compound predicate are in different tenses, as they are in the example, a comma is often justifiable. Somewhat similarly, *He was not doing well, and was eaten by a bear* has a justifiable comma; the verb in the first predicate is active, the verb in the second predicate passive.

He was poor, and was deficient in looks as well is justifiable because the second predicate, *was deficient in looks as well*, is being presented as a parenthetical construction (see Rule 2-1). The comma after *poor* could be eliminated, but the sentence would then have a slightly different effect; the second predicate would no longer seem a humorous afterthought.

He paints landscapes, and flirts with other arts uses the comma justifiably to make it less likely that *flirts* will be taken as a noun—that is, he paints flirtatious women.

He left the room, mixed a tray of drinks, and returned has commas simply because there is a series of three predicates, not just two; see Rule 2-6.

Often a sentence with a compound predicate can be made to conform strictly to the rules by inserting a pronoun and making it a compound sentence: *He paints landscapes, and he flirts with other arts* is a good sentence, perhaps better than the original example. However, *He left the room, and he reappeared with a tray of drinks* is tedious; that sentence is better left with its compound predicate separated by a comma. There are many other occasions when it is justifiable to separate compound predicates with a comma.

2-4   Do not separate subject and verb, verb and object, or preposition and object with a comma.

The cavalry, artillery, and light infantry, were drawn up in order incorrectly has a comma after *infantry*, as if the writer began inserting commas between the elements of the compound subject and forgot to stop.

The sun shining through the unshuttered window, woke him early incorrectly has a comma after *window*—or else, if the writer is considering *shining through the unshuttered window* to be a parenthetical phrase rather than a defining phrase (see Rule 2-1), there should be a comma after *sun* as well as a comma after *window*. For some reason this error is very common, though even the quickest check of what we've written should make it apparent. (Note that a parenthetical construction and its enclosing commas can come between a subject and its verb: *The sun, shining through the unshuttered window, woke him early.* This doesn't really separate subject and verb, since the parenthetical construction is outside the grammar of the basic sentence.)

The figures do not prove but clearly suggest, that trouble is ahead incorrectly has a comma after *suggest*, separating it from the *that* clause that is its object. The error is common before *that*. Note that in the example, adding a comma after *prove* would make *but clearly suggest* a parenthetical construction, and the comma after *suggest* would then be not only correct but required. Sometimes an object is accidentally severed from its verb because the writer has omitted one of the parenthetical commas.

He praised and gave recommendations to, Smith, Brown, and Jones incorrectly has the comma after *to*, separating the preposition from its objects. This could also be an error with parenthetical commas—a comma after *praised* would make the comma after *to* correct—but I believe it is more often the result of a mistaken feeling that a list such as *Smith, Brown, and Jones* needs some sort of punctuation to introduce it. No punctuation is needed when the list fits into the grammar of the sentence (see Rule 2-16).

Exceptions

Whatever is, is right is indeed right, because the comma helpfully separates *is* from *is*. With the comma omitted, the sentence is not wrong but is more difficult to read. (*Whatever exists, is right* is not quite right; the comma isn't needed.) The comma is frequently desirable to separate repetitions of a word: *Whoever feels, feels sorrow now*; *Those who vote only infrequently, infrequently are satisfied with their representation.* Such repetition of words is usually a rhetorical device to give special force to speech, and as we might expect, the rule-flouting comma is very clearly heard if the examples are read aloud.

We who breathe, love requires the comma, because *love* could be misread as a noun rather than a verb—that is, as the direct object of *breathe*. Again, the comma would be clearly heard in speech, separating the two stressed verbs.

The fact is, you're wrong is right, though again the comma could be omitted. The comma could be interpreted as substituting for the elliptical word *that*: *The fact is that you're wrong*. It could also be interpreted as a way of countering the strong tendency of *is*, and any form of the verb *to be*, to link itself with whatever immediately follows, as it does in *The expectation is falsely high earnings will be reported*, which most readers would have to read twice to get the meaning, and they couldn't be absolutely sure of it then. Either a comma or *that* inserted after *is* would make it clear—or a *that* inserted after *high* if that is the intended meaning.

There are other exceptions, but they tend to fall into the two categories already covered: the rhetorical, such as *Whatever is, is right*, and the casually elliptical, such as *The fact is, you're wrong*. If what we're writing is neither rhetorical nor casual, exceptions to the rule are apt to be unnecessary.

2-5   Do not put a comma between an adjective or adverb and a following word or phrase that it modifies. When an adjective or adverb follows the modified word, usually set off the adjective, but not the adverb, with a pair of commas.

A sunny, day is too obvious an error for almost anyone to make, but *Day broke on a gray, cold, fretful, sea* is an example of a surprisingly common pattern. It may be an absent-minded error; the writer may simply forget when to stop putting in commas to separate the series of adjectives (see also Rule 1-20) or may have it in mind to add a fourth adjective and be unable to think of one. In the same way, *We were not only becalmed but foully, despicably, damnably, becalmed* incorrectly has a comma between the last adverb and the modified verb.

When the modifier follows the modified word

The sea, fretful, lashed the ship is the typical pattern for adjectives that follow the word they modify. The comma after *sea* is not really separating adjective from noun, it is one of a pair of commas that make the adjective parenthetical. The adjective is added almost as if it were an afterthought; it really is parenthetical. When the modifier is not a simple adjective but a participle or an adjectival phrase or clause, it is set off by commas if it is parenthetical but not if it is defining (see Rule 2-1): *The boy, swimming rapidly, reached the child in time*; *The boy swimming rapidly is his son.*

The sea lashed fretfully at the ship is the typical pattern for adverbs that follow the word they modify. A single comma after *lashed* would be incorrect, and parenthetical commas around *fretfully* would be pointless. However, parenthetical commas can be used in many adverbial constructions: *The wind blew, fitfully but energetically enough for some progress, until late afternoon.* Similarly, *The afternoon lull was expected and therefore accepted, gratefully by the crew and resentfully by their captain*; this is really a parenthetical construction too.

Inversions

Sunny and warm, September is the best month has a comma between adjective and noun but is nevertheless correct. It is an inversion of *September, sunny and warm, is the best month*, in which *sunny and warm* is parenthetical, and when the sentence is inverted the comma after *warm* is retained to show that *sunny and warm* is still parenthetical—descriptive rather than defining.

Days sunny and warm gave way to days dank and cold omits parenthetical commas for the following adjectives, but is correct because of the strongly defining function the adjectives have; the adjectives are not meant to be parenthetical, and commas would destroy the sentence.

Sentence modifiers

Imperceptibly, the becalmed ship lost ground to the current separates adverb from verb with the subject of the sentence—*the becalmed ship*—as well as with a comma. The comma is optional; its absence or presence affects the tone of the sentence but not its basic meaning. Adverbs can wander from the words they modify (see Rule 1-20), and when they do wander we have considerable freedom with commas. In the example, the comma encourages *imperceptibly* to be understood as a modifier for the entire sentence, not just the verb, as in the comparatively flat *The becalmed ship imperceptibly lost ground to the current*, in which the adverb is closely linked to the verb by its position.

However, therefore, and similar words often begin sentences. They are considered adverbs, but they usually modify everything that follows—they are sentence modifiers, not just word or phrase modifiers, and they serve somewhat like conjunctions, relating what follows to what precedes. Usually a comma after such introductory adverbs is desirable, and often it is necessary to prevent misreading: *However the captain screamed orders and organized the men into whaleboat parties* reads at first like a sentence fragment (Rule 1-1), with *However* meaning *in whatever fashion* rather than *but*.

Complications in inverted sentences

Toward the hazy cape, rowed the weary whalers is faulty because of the comma after *cape*, not because of the unnatural but permissible word order. *Toward the hazy cape* is a participial phrase with a clearly adverbial function—modifying *rowed*—and should not be separated from *rowed* by a comma. It is generally true that when the subject of the main clause follows the verb—that is, when the usual word order has been inverted—an introductory phrase should not be cut off by a comma.

Toward the hazy cape, the weary whalers rowed, with subject and verb in the usual order but modifying phrase and verb still in inverted order, is also faulty, though less obviously so; in fact, older grammar books advise setting off such adverbial phrases with a comma.

Toward the hazy cape, the weary whalers spied a far-off sail filled with heaven-sent air can have the comma, though it could be omitted too. However, note that *Toward the hazy cape* has become somewhat hazy itself; it's not clear what it modifies. It probably indicates the direction in which the rowers spy the sail, but if so, it does not directly modify *spied* but an understood participle: *Looking toward the hazy cape . . .* Or it could be taken as an adjectival phrase, rather than an adverbial one, modifying *sail*: *The weary whalers spied a far-off sail toward the hazy cape.* Or it may be meant as an adjectival phrase modifying *whalers* to describe their location when they spy the sail: *Nearing the hazy cape, the weary whalers spied a far-off sail*, and, considering the necessary rearward-facing posture of the rowers, the sail is not in the direction of the cape but somewhere in the opposite quadrant. The comma is permissible only because the function of the participial phrase *Toward the hazy cape* is no longer clear; there are several ways of reading it, and thus there is no longer a specific word to be incorrectly separated from it by a comma, which is rather a lame justification for a comma.

Adverbs and adverbial phrases can be puzzling, especially in inverted sentences, but Rule 2-5 still applies. If such sentences become confused and ambiguous, it is not the fault of the rule, and inserting commas in violation of the rule will not repair them. They must be recast, usually by reversing the inversion and linking the modifying phrase clearly to the word it modifies.

2-6   Use a comma before *and*, *or*, or *nor* preceding the last of a series of three or more words or phrases.

The safe contained coins, jewelry, and documents has a series of three nouns. *He emptied the safe slowly, carefully, and completely* has a series of three adverbs. *He came in, sat down, and began to tell his story* has a series of three predicates. *His manner was not shifty, shy, or sheepish, but his flying, fluttering, and flouncing hands suggested some deep anguish* has a series of three adjectives and a series of three participles. In all such cases, I advise using a comma before the *and* that connects the last item in the series to the preceding items.

This rule is old-fashioned. Most newspapers and magazines do not use the comma before *and*—called the final serial comma—and some book publishers recommend not using it. Don't use it if you don't want to. However, Rule 2-6 is splendidly simple, and I think it is defensible on two grounds.

First, the comma is clearly heard in a spoken series. We say *coins and jewelry* with no pause, but we say *coins, jewelry, and documents* with a pause after *coins* and an equal pause after *jewelry*. Omitting the comma ignores one of the functions of the comma—to indicate a pause in speech.

Second, even those who prefer not to use the final serial comma should use it sometimes.

I opened, he raised, and you folded is a series of three clauses—and even if it were only two clauses, as in *I opened with the last of my red chips, and he began to bring out his blue ones*, the comma before *and* would be defensible and desirable to separate the independent clauses (Rule 2-2). Thus those who omit the final serial comma may have to make an exception for a series of clauses.

I remember the gleam of the rain-washed pavement, the distant clatter of streetcars, the food smells wafting from the restaurant downstairs and the simple dress she wore is one of those jocose sentences invented by writers like me to bully readers and attempt to amuse them. But such sentences do occur. Thus those who omit the final serial comma must take special care to make an exception when the final item in the series can be misread as part of the preceding item. The ambiguity can happen in many ways, and is very apt to happen when the items in the series are not just single words but phrases or words modified by phrases, participles, and dependent clauses.

Why bother? Play it safe and use the final serial comma.

When *and, or,* or *nor* occurs more than once in the series

The safe contained coins and jewelry and documents is the conventional way to punctuate a series with *and* repeated after each but the final item—that is, to not punctuate it; no

74

commas are needed. Similarly, *His manner was not shifty or shy or sheepish* and *His manner was neither shifty nor shy nor sheepish.* Commas can be used, however, to produce a deliberate cadence: *His manner was not shifty, or shy, or sheepish.* Usually if the commas are used they should be used consistently after every item, including the last—*His manner was not shifty, or shy, or sheepish, but seemed strained*—because they make each item after the first a parenthetical addition, and by Rule 2-1 the commas should be in pairs.

Various complexities are permitted the sure-handed. *His manner was not shifty, or shy or sheepish, or even much of a manner at all; yet his hands, flying, fluttering and flouncing, and flirting with each other, suggested some more than ordinary concern* uses the commas and absence of commas with deliberate intent to connect some items in the two series more closely than others.

When *and, or,* or *nor* does not occur at all

The safe contained coins, jewelry, documents must have the comma between the last two items, since the conjunction is missing. Problems come up when the sentence goes on after such a series: *Coins, jewelry, documents, covered the floor* or *Coins, jewelry, documents covered the floor*? When we leave out the conjunction, should the last item in the series be followed by a comma as well as preceded by one?

The missing conjunction is essentially a rhetorical device. Sometimes it indicates that the series is to be imagined as continuing: *The coins, the jewelry, the documents, lay scattered in wild profusion* uses the comma after *documents* defensibly to indicate that other items as well as the named ones may have been scattered. At other times the missing conjunction indicates that the series is logically complete and can't be continued. *Men, women, children, lay asprawl on the sand* has an unhelpful comma after *children*; *Men, women, children* sums up all of humanity, and the series has no logical continuation.

Usually in such constructions we can "hear" the comma if it is desirable. If we cannot hear it, or cannot hear its absence, it may be better to put the conjunction in and make the series straightforward.

2-7 Don't automatically use commas to set off a negative element from a following positive element in *not . . . but* constructions.

He opened the book, not to read it, but to seem occupied is, in my opinion, overpunctuated. The comma after *book* would rarely be heard in speech; the comma after *it* might not be heard either.

Most grammar books do prescribe commas around a negative element such as *not to read it*. I don't know why they do. The *not to read it* is not a parenthetical element (see Rule 2-1); if it were, then *He opened the book but to seem occupied*, with *not to read it* omitted, would be a good sentence, and it isn't. The commas have no necessary function at all, either as signals of spoken delivery or as indications of grammatical structure. *I brought you here not to praise you*, with no positive element but only a negative element, could have no comma after *here*; why, then, are commas desirable if we make it *I brought you here, not to praise you, but to flay you*?

There is a strong tendency to punctuate such sentences as they would be spoken: *He opened the book not to read it, but to seem occupied*. I hope this tendency prevails, but meanwhile I must point out that it breaks the accepted rule.

However, it is permissible to omit both commas: *He opened the book not to read it but to seem occupied* is acceptable according to at least some major modern handbooks of usage, such as *Words into Type*, and it follows the current trend toward light punctuation. The omission is virtually required by idiom when the negative element is very short: *They advised making not war but love*; *He gave not time but only money to the cause*; *I think not she but he is to blame*. I recommend omitting both commas whenever the sentence reads better without them—and I would not condemn anyone who omitted just the first comma, though I cannot in good conscience advise that.

When a negative element follows a positive element

He opened the book to seem occupied, not to read it is the conventional and unobjectionable way to separate a positive element from a following negative element. The comma is clearly heard if the sentence is spoken. In certain constructions, however, the comma can justifiably be omitted: *He came to conquer not to serve, and he will leave in shame not in honor.* Commas could be used in this example, but the omission gives the sentence a rhetorical effect—it reflects a special way the sentence might be spoken.

He opened the book to seem occupied, not to read it, and to conceal the spot on his tie requires two commas to set off the negative element between two positive elements. The negative element can be considered a parenthetical construction, since if it is removed the sentence remains a good one.

Confusion with *not only . . . but*

He opened the book, not only to read it, but to seem occupied is a misapplication of the rule about setting off negative elements. The sentence has no negative element; *not only to read it* is not negative in the way that *not to read it* is. There should be no commas.

Not only did he hope to seem occupied, but he wanted to read the book is a different situation; the comma is correctly used to separate two independent clauses, though it would not be incorrect to omit it in this example (Rule 2-2).

2-8   **Don't ordinarily put a comma after *and, but, or,* and similar conjunctions, or after *that, if, when,* and similar words when they are subordinating conjunctions, if what follows is an introductory phrase or clause.**

The wind had risen, and, throughout the night, the rain beat against the windows and *The storm was over, but, in its aftermath, the heavy rain continued* are overpunctuated. The *and* in the first sentence and the *but* in the second are coordinating conjunctions, connecting independent clauses. There is no reason to have commas after them; a conjunction should not have its joining function contradicted by a comma. The commas after *night* in the first sentence and *aftermath* in the second are optional to set off the introductory phrases (see Rule 2-1), but are really unnecessary, since the phrases are short and directly modify the verbs in the clauses they introduce—they are merely out of their usual order (see the discussion of inversions in Rule 2-5). Moreover, it is the presence of those commas that makes the definitely undesirable commas after *and* and *but* seem to belong—the phrases *throughout the night* and *in its aftermath* are made to look like parenthetical constructions. But they are not parenthetical and should not be set off with commas.

When *that*, *if*, *when*, and similar words introduce subordinate clauses, they are acting as subordinating conjunctions. *That* is also considered a conjunction when it introduces a noun clause that acts as the object of *said* or a similar verb, as in *He said that he would go*. The same principles of punctuation apply with these conjunctions as with *and* and *but*, and thus *He said that, if it rained, he would stay home* is excessively punctuated. The clause *if it rained* is set off as if it were parenthetical, but it is not—it is a defining clause, as is clear if the order of the clauses is changed: *He said that he would stay home if it rained*. In the original sentence, the comma after *that* should definitely be omitted; the comma after *rained* is optional but would be better omitted, since the introductory clause is very short and since the omission makes it clearer that the entire word group *if it rained he would stay home* is the object of *He said*.

If, in the first part of the year, the market rallies, we'll be rich is also excessively punctuated. Omitting the first two commas improves the sentence. It could be further improved by a more natural word order: *If the market rallies in the first part of the year, we'll be rich*.

Similarly, *I love the time when, under the twisted apple boughs, windfalls dot the stubbled grass* has unneeded and illogical commas, but in this case taking out the commas or changing the word order may not be an improvement—the writer may want the commas to indicate pauses in his somewhat self-conscious sentence, and he may prefer the word order he has to *I love the time when windfalls dot the stubbled grass under the apple boughs*, which makes *under the apple boughs* modify *grass* rather than *dot*. A writer who inserts the commas not automatically but after thoughtful consideration of the alternatives is not breaking Rule 2-8—he is merely using his own judgment, which may be good or bad.

He said that, although he couldn't stay long, he would come is different from the examples above because the dependent clause *although he couldn't stay long* is not defining but parenthetical (as is any clause beginning with *although*, since the word can't really restrict the meaning of anything but can only elaborate on the meaning). Nevertheless, there is no real justification for the comma after *that*. The entire word group *that although he couldn't stay long, he would come* is the object of *He said*. The fact that *although he couldn't stay long* is parenthetical to the clause *he would come* (which is not an independent clause but a noun clause, acting as the object of *He said*) does not justify putting a comma between *that* and *although*, as may be more obvious if we substitute parentheses for the commas: *He said that (although he couldn't stay long) he would come*. This makes the *although* clause parenthetical to what *He said* rather than to the fact that *he would come*—and that is not the intention of the sentence.

We had thought that, considering your position, we might buy you out is a similar case, with an unnecessary comma between *that* and the parenthetical participial phrase *considering your position* (which looks like a dangling participle but is nevertheless acceptable—see Rule 1-21).

I must admit that I very frequently see these unnecessary and illogical commas in carefully edited books and magazines. They are a hangover from past centuries, when commas were used much more heavily; they violate the overriding general principle of modern punctuation—to use punctuation lightly and omit it when it is unnecessary. There are times when an introductory construction that follows a conjunction is so much an interruption in the sentence that a comma is required or at least desirable both before and after the interruption. *He was relieved when, the weather having turned bad, he didn't have to go* is correctly punctuated; the absolute phrase *the weather having turned bad* requires the commas. *The storm was over, but, apparently because of the heavy rain, the river was in flood* has a desirable comma after *but* to help set off the strongly parenthetical *apparently because of the heavy rain*. But these times are rare.

Note that *It had better rain, or, he thought, he would have to go* and *Smith, Jones, and, somewhat later, Brown arrived* are not violations of Rule 2-8, which concerns conjunctions followed by introductory constructions; they are standard uses of parenthetical commas (see Rule 2-1).

2-9 Don't use a comma to indicate an understood word unless the sentence requires it for clarity.

His office gave him little satisfaction, and his wife, none requires the comma after *wife* so that the reader can be certain that something has been omitted there—a repetition of *gave him*. Without the comma, the sentence could easily be taken to mean *His office gave him little satisfaction and gave his wife none*. (The comma after *satisfaction* in the original sentence does not prevent this misreading, because it may be there just to give the second predicate a parenthetical effect; see Rule 2-3.) Note that the comma after *wife*, though correct, is really rather a nuisance; *His office gave him little satisfaction, and his wife gave him none* gives more satisfaction as a sentence.

He quit his job, and his wife her excessive social involvements does not require a comma after *wife*, because the only possible meaning is *his wife quit her excessive social involvements*. We can take out the comma and still be sure both where a word is missing and what the word is. Since the comma has no function, it should be taken out.

He had always had a secret yearning for a more contemplative life, she for a life of toil and accomplishment requires no comma after *she*, even though the omission—*had always had a secret yearning*—is quite long.

He now has ample time to dream, she the self-respect of the breadwinner, they the loving marriage both had longed for, and I the suspicion that their solution would not work for us requires no commas to indicate the omissions, even though the omitted word changes form: *she has*; *they have*; *I have*. (See also Rule 1-2.)

The use of a comma to indicate an understood word or group of words is apt to make a sentence seem old-fashioned and fussy. If a sentence does seem to require such a comma for clarity, perhaps the sentence can be improved by supplying the omitted word or words or by otherwise changing the sentence to make the comma unnecessary.

2-10   Use commas to set off names and similar words in direct address.

I am writing, Mr. Smith, to confirm our agreement and *Tell me, my friend, whether this is a sensible course* are typical examples of forms of address that interrupt the course of a sentence. If the commas are omitted in the first example, *Mr. Smith* becomes the indirect object of *writing* and the meaning of the sentence changes completely. If the commas are omitted in the second example, there is no change in meaning. However, the commas are required in the second case too; they cannot be eliminated just because they are not essential to prevent misreading. The interjection of a form of address is actually a parenthetical construction (see under Rule 2-1), so commas should be used.

If the name or other form of address occurs at the beginning or end of the sentence, it is, of course, set off with only one comma: *Mr. Smith, I am confirming our agreement*; *I wonder if this is wise, my friend*.

Exception

But officer, I wasn't speeding and *Oh my friend, what a fool I've been* omit the first of the parenthetical commas. The omission helps indicate the way the sentences would be spoken. Similarly, *Yes sir* and *No sir*—sometimes *Yes sir* is spelled *Yessir*, and considerably less often *No sir* is spelled *Nosir*—indicate a failure to pause in speech before the form of address. It is quite proper to omit the first comma when quoting speech and perhaps in some cases when trying to give written words some of the immediacy of speech, but in writing that is meant to be read rather than imagined as spoken, Rule 2-10 should be followed and both commas used.

2-11 Use a comma, or some other mark of punctuation, before or after direct quotations to set off *he said* and similar attributions.

"I'm looking for a job," John said (or *said John*) and *John said, "I'm looking for a job"* show the standard form for attribution. The comma is required by convention rather than by grammar or logic. We might consider it an exception to the rule against separation of verb and object (Rule 2-4), since the quotation is essentially the object of *said*. However, it is a special kind of object, and the comma is clearly heard if the examples are spoken.

The most common verb in attributions is *said*, but there are many others—*he wrote*, *he shouted*, *he asked*, *he whimpered*—and they all follow Rule 2-11. Sometimes the verb is poorly chosen: *"Don't come any nearer," he hissed* is poor because there are no sibilant sounds in *Don't come any nearer* to hiss. Sometimes the verb has nothing to do with spoken or written expression at all but indicates manner or some accompanying action: *"Please come closer," he smiled*; *"I've never seen you before," he frowned*. This is a kind of shorthand for *he said with a smile* or *he said, frowning*; it is a convenient shorthand and has been in use for generations, but it is not logical and it annoys many readers. The easiest repair is to replace the comma with a period and make the attribution an independent sentence: *"I've never seen you before." He frowned*.

When *that* appears between *said* and the quotation

He said that, "regardless of the cost" he would pay is a serious error of punctuation. There should be no comma after *that* when it is used in this way as a subordinating conjunction (see Rule 2-8). This is true whether or not the quotation is just a fragment, as in the example, or a complete statement: *He said, "Britain will pay for this"* but *He said that "Britain will pay for this."* (Usually it is pointless and contrary to convention to introduce a directly quoted complete statement with *that*, but when it is done, there should be no comma.) The construction *he said* is a straightforward attribution that requires the conventional comma, but *he said that* is not a straightforward attribution and should not have the comma.

Other marks of punctuation

John said: "I'm looking for a job" replaces the comma with a colon. This is correct, and some writers always use the colon rather than the comma when the attribution precedes the quotation. However, the colon is a strong mark of punctuation, and it holds the reader up more than the comma does. It may be desirable to hold the reader up—perhaps to emphasize the importance of what follows or to introduce a quotation that is quite long—but otherwise the comma is smoother.

"I'm looking for a job!" John said, "I'm going to look—" John began, and *"Should I look for a job?" John asked* do not have commas because other marks of punctuation have displaced them—an exclamation point in the first example, a dash in the second example, and a question mark in the third example. It would be logical to use a comma as well as the other mark of punctuation—*"I'm looking for a job!," John said*—but this is contrary to the conventions of English punctuation; the comma is not used with the exclamation point, dash, or question mark but is displaced by the stronger mark. One does see such punctuation; it is wrong.

The position of quotation marks is also governed by convention rather than logic; see Rule 2-24.

When the attribution interrupts the quotation

"I," John said, "am looking for a job" shows the standard form when the attribution comes in the middle of a quoted sentence: comma before and comma after, making the attribution parenthetical. (If the interruption of the quotation is not an attribution, dashes should be used, not commas: *"I"*—

John paused and seemed to glow with self-esteem—"am looking for a job.")

"I'm looking for a job," John said, "will you let me marry your daughter?" is, however, incorrect, because the attribution comes between sentences, not in the middle of one. If we take out the attribution we have *"I'm looking for a job, will you let me marry your daughter?"*—two independent clauses joined by a comma, which is an error (see Rule 2-12). There could be a semicolon instead of a comma after *said*, but this is rarely seen; the simplest and clearest punctuation is a period after *said*, with *will* then capitalized as the beginning of a new sentence.

"I'm looking for a job," John said, and then, "Will you let me marry your daughter?" is correct, with the comma and *and then* connecting the independent quotations.

Exception: quotations as noun phrases

Sometimes a quotation is used as a noun within the grammar of a sentence: *His battle cry is "More benefits and fewer taxes"; His reply was "No comment."* This can be the case even with verbs such as *say* that normally are used in attribution: *We should never say "I agree" when we really do not; He was a poor pickpocket, for he had a habit of saying "Thank you" as he replaced each ravaged wallet*. In each of these examples the quotation is not an ordinary one but a group of words acting grammatically like a noun—the quotations in the first pair of examples are acting as subject complements, and those in the second pair are acting as direct objects, which are grammatical functions of nouns. When a quotation is so used—as a noun phrase—it should not have a comma before it, nor should there be one after it: *"No comment" was his reply*.

The crowd cried "Long live the king!" and "Down with the republic!" is typical of quotations that are in a gray area between true quotations and noun phrases. We could reason in either direction. It is often convenient to reason in the direction of considering them noun phrases—after all, they are samples of utterances of specific people in the crowd, not actual utterances in unison, or so one might argue—because otherwise we may have to insert commas that clutter the sentence and probably couldn't be heard if the words were spoken.

SEMICOLON

The semicolon has two main uses: to separate independent parts of a sentence, and to separate elements of a series when some of the elements already contain commas. It can be thought of as a very strong comma, though it has some special powers too—it can connect as well as separate.

Some writers use semicolons when commas would be sufficient, and the result is apt to be an unnecessarily choppy style that slows the reader down. Others don't use semicolons enough, and their sentences are apt to seem run-on and toneless. Still others don't use the semicolon at all, and unless they confine themselves to short and simple sentences, they commit real errors of punctuation by using commas when semicolons are required.

2-12   Use a semicolon to separate independent clauses that are not connected by *and*, *but*, or some other conjunction.

It's an unusual problem, no one knows much about it is an example of the so-called comma fault—using a comma to connect two independent clauses. The comma cannot be a connector; it is a separator. The semicolon, however, can function both as a connector and as a separator, and at the same time: *It's an unusual problem; no one knows much about it.* If we use the comma, then we have to supply a connector—that is, a conjunction such as *and*: *It's an unusual problem, and no one knows much about it* (see also Rule 2-2).

We're going to discuss it, then we'll decide what to do may seem less obviously a comma fault, because *then* seems to be performing the role of a conjunction. But *then* here is an adverb, modifying *decide*; it is not a conjunction (see Rule 2-13). The comma should be a semicolon, or else it should be followed by *and*.

Exception: the comma to emphasize

The problem was simple, the solution was difficult uses a comma instead of a semicolon to emphasize the contrast—in this case an antithetical contrast—between the two independent clauses. The comma is especially desirable if the second clause is made elliptical: *The problem was simple, the solution difficult*. If we make it *The problem was simple; the solution was difficult*, we lose some of the energy and pithiness of the original contrast.

We could quibble with this example and claim that it is not really an exception to Rule 2-12 but an elliptical sentence, with *but* understood after the comma: *but the solution was difficult*. An understood word—that is, a missing word—is often more conspicuous in its absence than it would be if it were present, because the reader has to supply it for himself.

In any case, the comma is occasionally desirable when the rule calls for a semicolon. *She was twenty, he was twenty-one* uses the comma not to emphasize contrast but to emphasize the slightness of contrast. *The problem was simple, the solution was simple* uses the comma to emphasize the absence of contrast. In all the examples of exceptions given here, the comma is not only justifiable but preferable.

If the independent clauses are considerably longer than they are in the examples above or if for any other reason the comma does not seem a sufficient signal to the reader that another independent clause is coming, it is better to follow Rule 2-12 and use the semicolon.

Exception: the comma to indicate a continuing series or to heighten parallels in a series

Smith couldn't vote because he was out of town, Jones couldn't vote because he was sick, Brown couldn't vote because he didn't know it was election day. Only 50 percent of the electorate turned out. This is an acceptable use of commas. A seemingly desirable *and* is omitted after *sick* chiefly to indicate that the series could go on (see Rule 2-6). Semicolons might not be quite as good, since the implication of an unfinished series wouldn't be as strong. At the same time, the commas make the parallel structure of each clause more evident. In a sense, a semicolon tells a reader to forget the grammar (if not the content) of what precedes, because a new independent clause is about to start. The comma makes it more likely that the reader will not forget the preceding grammar and will better appreciate the parallelism.

2-13   Use a semicolon to separate independent clauses that are connected by *however, thus, therefore, nevertheless*, and similar emphatic conjunctions.

The problem is difficult, however, we will solve it and *The problem is difficult, therefore we couldn't solve it* are far too loosely punctuated. In both examples the comma after *difficult* should be a semicolon.

Emphatic conjunctions such as *however* and *therefore* are not really conjunctions at all—they are adverbs. When they introduce clauses, they are classed as conjunctions or so-called conjunctive adverbs, but they don't lose their adverbial function and they don't gain all the powers of a true conjunction—that is, a coordinating conjunction such as *and* that connects elements of equal grammatical value. Therefore, failure to use the semicolon can be considered a violation of Rule 2-12, because the clauses are not connected with a true conjunction.

Note that most conjunctive adverbs—*however* is usually an exception—can be preceded by a true conjunction, making the comma correct: *The problem is difficult, and therefore we couldn't solve it.* (The semicolon could be used too, if a stronger pause is wanted.) We can't double up true conjunctions, such as *and* and *but*, but we can pair a true conjunction and a conjunctive adverb—which suggests that there is a considerable difference between the two types of conjunction.

2-14   Use a semicolon to separate items in a series when some of the items already contain commas.

The committee included Smith, Jones, and Brown is a straightforward series of three people. If we make it *The committee included Smith, the treasurer; Jones, the production supervisor; and Brown, the security officer*, we need semicolons to separate the items. Otherwise the series could be understood to be a series of four or five people (not six, since *and Brown, the security officer* has to signify a single person).

I spoke to the chairman, I notified the treasurer, and I wrote an account of the action into the company record is a straightforward series of three independent clauses. If we add a dependent clause to one of the independent clauses, we may still be able to get away with not using semicolons: *I spoke to the chairman, I notified the treasurer, who hadn't been at the meeting, and I wrote an account of the action into the company record*. But if we keep adding complications to the sentence, we soon need semicolons to help the reader distinguish major breaks from minor ones: *I spoke to the chairman, who told me he, like other members of the board, disapproved; I notified the treasurer, who hadn't been at the meeting; and I wrote an account of the action into the company record*. If only commas were used, the sentence would still mean the same thing, but it would be difficult to read.

COLON

The primary use of the colon is to introduce whatever follows: a list, a statement, an example, or anything else that the earlier part of the sentence has led the reader to expect. The use of the colon in the preceding sentence is typical.

The British use the colon more often than Americans do, and somewhat differently: they use it instead of a semicolon to separate clauses when the first clause leads to the second clause. The preceding sentence is an example of this use. Some American writers do this too, but few of them do it well; they have learned something about the British use of the colon by reading British prose, but they were never taught to use it properly and are vague about its function. I deal with the British practice as an exception to Rule 2-15.

The dash can often replace the colon (see Rule 2-17).

2-15 Capitalize the first word after a colon if what follows is a grammatically complete sentence; otherwise do not capitalize the word unless it is always capitalized.

Three men were there: Smith, Jones, and Brown has a capitalized word after the colon because the word is someone's name. *Three men were there: the chairman, the treasurer, and the security officer* has a lowercased word after the colon because what follows is not a complete sentence. *There were only two choices: We could fire the comptroller or go out of business* has a capitalized word after the colon because what follows is a complete sentence.

This very simple rule is the standard American practice.

Exceptions

Oil, gas, and coal: these are the resources to watch does not have a capitalized word following the colon, because the colon is like a dash in this sentence. If we consider the clause after the colon to be a separate sentence—that is, if we capitalize its first word—the opening phrase *Oil, gas, and coal* is orphaned. See also Rule 2-17.

Not one of the men showed up: they all claimed to be sick does not have a capitalized word after the colon, even though a grammatically complete sentence precedes the colon and another one follows it. However, note that the colon is not merely performing its basic function of introducing what follows. It is signaling a special logical connection between the first clause and the second clause. The second clause expands on the first clause. *Not one of the men showed up: two of them claimed they'd never even been notified* is a slightly different example; the second clause doesn't expand on the whole meaning of the first clause but gives some additional detail.

The standard modern American practice would be to use a semicolon or a dash rather than a colon in the examples in the preceding paragraph, or else to use a period and make two short sentences. The semicolon will do the job, but since the semicolon commonly separates clauses that not only have no grammatical interdependence but have no close logical connection, we lose the signal of a logical connection that the colon provides. The dash is somewhat better, since it does suggest a logical connection between the clauses. The main objection to the dash is that it is so versatile, able to play the roles of several other marks of punctuation. The colon is more precise.

Most American writers do use the dash to indicate a logical connection between clauses, but some use the colon. British writers are much more likely to use the colon than the dash. The British use of the colon is sometimes very effective. It permits long, complicated sentences that are nevertheless clear and easy to read, because of the extra precise signal provided by the colon. It does permit some ambiguities too. *The day couldn't have been better: there wasn't a cloud in the sky; the rector in his joy preached for two hours* is ambiguous because the reader can't be sure whether the opening clause introduces both the following clauses or just the first. The day might have been better if the rector had been shorter-winded, after all. A dash instead of a colon would be better at least for American readers, who expect a colon to introduce the entire remainder of the sentence, not just the next clause.

Those who use the colon in the British way should often not follow Rule 2-15, but sometimes they should. If the colon is being used as a kind of dash—not just separating clauses but indicating a logical connection between them—then the word after the colon should not be capitalized even if what follows is a grammatically complete sentence. If it is being used as a colon pure and simple—as in *He wrote as follows: Pay or else!* or *You have two choices: You can pay or die*—Rule 2-15 applies.

2-16   Do not use a colon to introduce words that fit properly into the grammar of a sentence without the colon.

The forbidden activities included: smoking, drinking, and smiling should not have the colon. The colon actually violates Rule 2-4; there should be no punctuation separating the verb *included* from its object.

However, mild beer was permitted in: one's own quarters, the back kitchen, and the sacristy should not have the colon. There should be no punctuation separating the preposition *in* from its object (again, Rule 2-4).

The abbot later added to the list of proscriptions: lechery, blasphemy, and murder should not have the colon: this is also a violation of Rule 2-4. The intervening adverbial phrase *to the list of proscriptions* makes no difference.

The colon often is needed with phrases such as *the following. The forbidden activities included the following: smoking, drinking, and smiling* is correct; if the colon is removed, the words that follow do not fit properly into the grammar of the sentence. Sometimes the colon takes the place of phrases such as *for instance* or *namely. Some unanticipated misbehavior occurred in the first week: lechery, blasphemy, and murder* is the same as *. . . in the first week, namely, lechery, blasphemy, and murder.*

DASH

The dash is almost excessively versatile. It can interrupt the grammar of a sentence in the same way a colon can, and in a few other ways as well. A pair of dashes can enclose a parenthetical construction, as a pair of commas or parentheses can. It can separate independent clauses, as a semicolon can. And it can do some things that no other mark of punctuation can. Any castaway who is allowed only one mark of punctuation on his desert island could do worse than choose the dash (it might even be useful for spearing fish)—but the rest of us should make full use of the other marks of punctuation and not rely excessively on the dash.

The dash is often badly typed. It should be typed as two hyphens, with no space between dash and preceding word or dash and following word, except that there can be a space between dash and following word to indicate the beginning of a completely new statement rather than the resumption of an interrupted statement.

2-17   Don't overuse the dash; consider using other marks of punctuation.

We've been spending the summer pretty much as usual—partly in Vermont—partly on Long Island—usual problems with jellyfish out there—and it's been a cold summer in Vermont—but that must make you New Yorkers laugh—or cry—we certainly don't have much to complain about— This letter could continue indefinitely with no punctuation but dashes; it probably would end with *that's about all the news—see you soon— Love—*

There is really nothing wrong with a heavy use of dashes in casual correspondence. The dashes make such correspondence like friendly conversation: disjointed and elliptical, but easy and even pleasant to absorb. Many of us are fussier about our letter-writing style, but few of us are offended by someone else's dashed-off letter.

Not all writing, however, is friendly correspondence; writing that is not casual should not be casually punctuated. Dashes have a place in even the most formal writing, but they should not displace other marks of punctuation that are more appropriate.

Appropriateness is often a matter of judgment. The following discussion of specific uses of the dash reflects my own judgment, which is harsher than my self-discipline; I tend to overuse the dash myself.

Dashes for parenthetical constructions

He was seen—not for the first time—in the bar downstairs before eleven o'clock could be punctuated with either commas or parentheses instead of dashes. Commas would make the sentence blander, giving *not for the first time* about the same importance as the rest of the sentence. Parentheses would tend to make *not for the first time* seem less important than the rest of the sentence. The dash is a very emphatic mark of punctuation, so the pair of dashes emphasizes *not for the first time*. In a given context, the emphasis might be appropriate or inappropriate.

It was obvious—could there be any question?—that he had a serious problem could be punctuated with parentheses instead of dashes, but not with commas; commas cannot enclose a grammatically complete sentence as parentheses and dashes can, and in any case a comma should not be used after a question mark (see Rule 2-21). Since the intrusion of a complete sentence, and a question at that, in the middle of another sentence must be a sharp break in thought, dashes are usually better than parentheses.

The dash to connect independent clauses

I felt I had to speak to him—he was setting a bad example for the other salesmen could be punctuated with a semicolon instead of a dash. It could also be punctuated with a colon (see the exceptions to Rule 2-15), but this is an unusual use of the colon in American writing, and a looser use than is usual in British writing; the first clause does not lead to the second, but instead the second clause explains the first. In fact, what the dash is actually doing is taking the place of the word *because* or *for*, and it is slightly obscuring the real grammar of the sentence. It isn't two independent clauses at all, in thought, and it would be better to supply *because* or *for* and make it one independent clause with a dependent clause: *I felt I had to speak to him, because he was setting a bad example for the other salesmen.* The original sentence is not wrong, but it is lazy and loose.

It is by no means always poor to connect independent clauses with a dash. *I called him into my office before lunch—he had just reappeared* is quite all right; the dash is not substituting for a word, the clauses are truly independent, and the dash is probably better for this sentence than a semicolon, which doesn't have the added-on, parenthetical effect of the dash. The second clause could be enclosed in parentheses instead of connected with a dash, which would have the effect of making the second clause seem relatively unimportant.

The dash to connect a phrase to the rest of a sentence

Tardiness, insolence, and drunkenness—these are the things a manager must nip in the bud could have a colon instead of a dash, but the dash is far more common. The connected phrase may come at the end of the sentence too: *There are certain things a manager must nip in the bud—tardiness, insolence, drunkenness*. In this situation the colon may have a slight edge over the dash, since introducing such a list is one of its precise functions. However, *I was surprised at his manner—open, innocent, friendly* seems better with the dash, perhaps because the list of adjectives directly modifies the word preceding the dash, and a colon would make too great a separation. The dash is, in effect, substituting for *which was*: *I was surprised at his manner, which was open, innocent, and friendly*. The colon can sometimes replace words (see Rule 2-16), but it is not as versatile in this respect as the dash.

Usually it's possible to save the employee—with firm enough action does not use the dash to connect the ending phrase—no connection is needed, since the ending phrase fits into the grammar of the sentence without the dash—but to separate it and hence emphasize it. This is a special and useful function of the dash; no other mark of punctuation can have the same effect.

The dash to indicate interruption

"I must speak to you about your midmorning boozing," I began politely. "We can't put up with—"
"But I don't drink," he interrupted.
"I—" I stopped, at a loss.
The dash is properly used to show interrupted dialogue, whether another speaker does the interrupting or the original speaker cuts himself off abruptly. Some writers use points of ellipsis—three dots—to indicate such interruptions, but points of ellipsis are better used to show pauses in midsen-

tence or sentences that trail off; they are not emphatic enough to indicate interruption. Points of ellipsis should not be used to show an interruption in the middle of a word; dashes are better. *"But this morning you were obser—" I began to say.*

Dashes to set off material within a quoted sentence that is not part of the quotation

"I don't drink, but I do sell insurance," he went on. "And if you don't like the way I sell it"—now his face was flushed, but with anger, not shame—"I'll tear up this million-dollar policy I've just sold the bartender downstairs." Some writers use commas instead of dashes in this situation, just as they would for an attribution such as *he said* (see Rule 2-11), but usually dashes are better. In the example, adding *and* would make the commas acceptable: *. . . I sell it," and now . . . anger, not shame, "I'll . . .* The commas tend to slow down the sentence; the dashes speed it up.

Note the position of the dashes in the example above in relation to the quotation marks. Sometimes one of the dashes belongs within the quotation: *I said, "Even if you don't drink—and I'm not saying I believe you—" I was pretty angry myself now—"you're fired for insolence."* The punctuation is a somewhat clumsy compromise; usually the construction should be avoided.

Dashes—dashes—dashes—dashes—

As may have been noted, the examples throughout this rule make up a story. Each use of the dash, except the questionable use in the example of the dash to connect independent clauses, is correct, and some of the uses are better than any alternative punctuation. However, try reading all the examples consecutively. There are just too many dashes, even for this casual, informal story.

A worthwhile general principle is to avoid using more than two dashes in any given sentence. *The next time I saw him he was drinking, all right—somehow I knew he was lying about that—but he wasn't mourning, he was celebrating, because he'd taken that million-dollar policy—the one he'd sold the bartender—across the street to Liberty Unilateral and gotten himself another job—at a guaranteed ten grand more a year.* Too many dashes.

It is also wise to avoid using too many sentences with dashes in the same paragraph. Useful as the dash is, it is basically an interrupting mark of punctuation and is always something of a hitch for the reader, bringing him up short, jabbing him in the ribs. A paragraph should have an overall smoothness; it shouldn't repeatedly interrupt itself.

The dash with other marks of punctuation

In modern practice, the dash is not used with the comma, the semicolon, the colon, the parenthesis, or points of ellipsis. It can be used with the question mark (Rule 2-21), the exclamation point (Rule 2-22), and the quotation mark (Rule 2-24).

PARENTHESES AND BRACKETS

Parentheses have the obvious function of isolating some words from other words within a sentence, or some sentences from other sentences within a paragraph. They usually have the effect of making the material they enclose seem less important than the rest of the sentence or paragraph; they imply that what they contain is incidental or digressive and could almost be skipped by the reader.

The most common problem with parentheses is not how or when to use them but how to use other punctuation—commas, periods, question marks—with them. This is covered in Rule 2-18.

Brackets are sometimes used within parentheses when the parenthetical material itself contains parenthetical material. I have not included a rule about this use. (It is obvious enough [at least to most of us] and in any case should usually be avoided.) Usually it is better to use a pair of commas or a pair of dashes within parentheses rather than brackets. However, aside from their use with parentheses, brackets do have certain necessary uses, and these are explained in Rule 2-19.

2-18 Put parentheses in the proper position when they are used with other marks of punctuation, and don't use other marks of punctuation in some circumstances.

The word "proper" in the rule above is quite accurate. The placement of parentheses is governed by their function and is entirely logical. For example, a comma can never directly precede either an opening parenthesis or a closing one, and a comma can never directly follow an opening parenthesis, because there can be no logical function for such placement.

When parentheses enclose an entire sentence

The Smiths were giving a loud party. (We hadn't been invited.) At about two o'clock I began to get annoyed. The enclosed sentence is independent of the sentences before and after. It requires a period, which must go within the closing parenthesis. It begins with a capital letter.

I called the police (they've heard from me before about the Smiths) and made a complaint; not too long afterward (it's a good precinct), a cruiser appeared. Each pair of parentheses encloses a complete sentence, but the enclosed sentences fall within another sentence, so no periods are used within the parentheses. The enclosed sentences begin with a lower-case letter, not a capital. Note the position of the comma after the closing parenthesis of the second pair. Dashes could be used instead of parentheses; if they are, the comma must be eliminated, because dash and comma should not be used together.

Both policemen got out (why should it take two for a little complaint?) and went up to the house. If the enclosed sentence requires a question mark or an exclamation point, it gets one even when it falls within another sentence. Dashes could be used instead of parentheses, and the question mark would remain.

When parentheses enclose more than one sentence within another sentence

The policemen knocked on the door awhile (someone had started playing the bongos. I don't know how the policemen thought anyone could hear the knocking) and then banged on it with their nightsticks. There is a period between the two sentences enclosed by the parentheses, but no period after the second. Dashes should not be used; only parentheses or brackets can make two or more sentences parenthetical.

It is clumsy, and obviously unnecessary in the example, to put more than one sentence within parentheses that are within another sentence. In a passage on a more complicated topic, however, the clumsiness may be preferable to any alternative.

When the material enclosed by parentheses comes at the end of a sentence

Someone finally answered the door (after at least ten minutes of banging). The period is outside the parentheses, since it's the period for the whole sentence, not just the part in parentheses. An exclamation point could be inserted between *banging* and the closing parenthesis, however. If the enclosed material is a question, a question mark should usually be inserted, though sometimes it is optional: *I don't know what the Smiths had to celebrate (and who cares).* If the enclosed material ends in an abbreviation, there can be a period both before and after the closing parenthesis: *I almost called my lawyers (Noyes, Dynne and Co.).*

When there is parenthetical material within parenthetical material

The next day, I hear—I had to go to work (it was a Sunday, but I'm a clergyman) and didn't see it for myself—they found the cops sleeping it off outside in the cruiser is correct, and so is *The next day, I hear (I had to go to work—it was a Sunday but I'm a clergyman—and didn't see it for myself), the police chief found the cops sleeping outside in the cruiser.* The parentheses and dashes are interchangeable.

Note that in the first example there is no comma after the terminal dash, because the comma should not be used with the dash; but in the second example there is a comma after the terminal parenthesis, because the whole word group from *I hear* to *myself* is actually parenthetical and requires commas to enclose it. We have parenthetical material within parenthetical material within parenthetical material.

In the second example, brackets could be used instead of dashes, but the dashes are far smoother. Brackets are rarely necessary except in scholarly writing and for the uses explained in Rule 2-19.

When parentheses are used with quotation marks

The cops didn't have much of an explanation (all they said was "We were keeping an eye on the Smiths' party"). The parentheses enclose the entire quotation, so the quotation mark goes inside the closing parentheses. Note that there is no period after *party*, and there is a terminal period after the parenthesis.

According to the newspaper, "A strange illness overcame the Smiths and their guests last Saturday evening (a form of food poisoning, Smith surmised)." The parentheses enclose only the last part of the quotation, so the quotation mark goes outside the closing parenthesis (and outside the period as well; see Rule 2-24).

When the material within parentheses is a source note following a quotation

Emerson said, "I hate quotations" (Journals, *May 1849*). There is no period after the quotation, even though Emerson put a period there. There is a period outside the closing parenthesis of the source note.

As Dickens put it, "I don't believe there's no sich a person!" (Martin Chuzzlewit). If an exclamation point or question mark ends the quotation, it is retained, but there is still a period outside the closing parenthesis.

There is some disagreement about this rule—a few handbooks advise putting the terminal punctuation wherever it would go if there were no source note, then using just parentheses and no period for the source note. I have used the

Chicago University Press's *A Manual of Style*, which is particularly useful when principles of punctuation and conventions of typography overlap, as my authority.

2-19   Use brackets primarily within a quotation to enclose material that is not part of the quotation.

Parentheses within a quotation enclose material that is part of the quotation. Brackets are the only mark of punctuation that can make it clear that the enclosed material is not part of the quotation. It is a nuisance to insert brackets, because most typewriters don't have them and the insertion must be done by hand—but they should be used in the cases below.

The mayor said, "John is my choice for treasurer" may not be clear unless more of what the mayor said or more about the circumstances in which he said it is supplied. *The mayor said, "John [Smith] is my choice for treasurer"* uses brackets to give the surname.

The mayor said, "He is my choice for treasurer" is more apt not to be clear. *The mayor said, "[John Smith] is my choice for treasurer"* replaces the pronoun *He* with the bracketed material. It could also be *"He [John Smith] is . . .* but it is rarely necessary to hold the reader up this way; it is usually better just to omit the pronoun.

Smith said, "The Bard of Amherst [Emily Dickinson, 1830-86] is my favorite poet" uses the brackets after *The Bard of Amherst* rather than in place of it, because the writer does not want to lose the epithet Smith used but does want to explain it.

The mayor said, *"Smith [who is now out on bail] may not seem the obvious choice"* uses brackets to supply material that may not be essential to clarify what the mayor said but that the writer thinks will be of interest to his readers.

The mayor said, "I base my oratorical style on that of Pliny the Elder [actually, Pliny the Younger; the elder Pliny was a naturalist] and count on overwhelming the electorate with my eloquence" uses brackets to enclose a correction. Such bracketed corrections are apt to seem snide and often are snide—which is all right if the writer is being frankly derisive, but not all right just to slip in a little dig that the writer thinks will make him seem superior to the person he's quoting. The overuse of *[sic]* indicates such a smart aleck—*[sic]* is useful when it is important to point out an error, but it should not appear after every minor error of diction; minor errors should either be allowed to stand for the reader to notice for himself or else be quietly corrected, except in works of literary, historical, or legal significance in which such correction would be a violation of the text.

Scholarly Uses

The hand-printed first edition contained the epigraph "Vulnera[n]t omnes, ultima necat" ("All things wound, the last thing kills") uses brackets to enclose a single letter mistakenly left out of the Latin tag. A scholar discussing the epigraph would not want either to let the error stand or to correct it without comment, so he would use the brackets. Otherwise several extra words would be required to point out and correct the faulty Latin.

Sometimes several letters of a word are supplied in brackets, as to complete names that are given partly in initials in a quotation: *Smith claimed, "Chekhov was not seriously influenced by A[leksey] K[onstantinovich] Tolstoy."* Note that the periods that would follow the initials in the original quotation are omitted.

Brackets have special uses in various areas of learning. For example, in mathematics they enclose material that already has parentheses—$b = [a + (bc)]$ a—which is just the opposite of their relationship with parentheses in English punctuation. Anyone in a special field of study needs a special handbook of usage within that field.

QUESTION MARK

The question mark is probably the most clearly heard of the marks of punctuation. The voice rises to it. But it is dangerous to insert question marks only by sound—quite often the voice rises but the question mark is wrong in writing.

The question mark usually indicates a full stop, like a period—the end of a sentence. However, occasionally it is used as an internal mark of punctuation: *Whatever it was*

that drove him—honor? envy? greed?—he was a man driven.
It is also used within parentheses to express doubt about a
word or a fact: *Chaucer's dates are 1340(?)-1400*. This use
within parentheses is overdone by amateurish writers; *The
beds in the grand hotel (?) had no mattresses* unnecessarily
uses the question mark to underline the irony. Another
amateurish habit is doubling or tripling quotation marks:
What do you mean???

Aside from amateurish misuses, errors with question
marks are usually either from failure to distinguish between
direct and indirect questions (Rule 2-20) or from failure to
position them properly when they are used with other marks
of punctuation (Rule 2-21).

2-20 Use the question mark after direct questions but not after indirect questions.

Do you like zucchini? is a direct question, and the question
mark is used following it. This is the basic function of the
question mark; all its other uses depend on this one.

"Do you like zucchini," she asked? is an error, because the
question mark should follow *zucchini*, not *she asked*, which
is merely the attribution: *"Do you like zucchini?" she asked*.
The error may be made partly because when the words are
read aloud, the voice does tend to rise on *asked*; it takes a
conscious effort to keep it from rising, and hence some effort
to avoid the error in writing.

She asked if I liked zucchini? is an error, because the
sentence is a statement, not a question; it merely contains an
indirect question. Here the sound of the sentence is reliable;
the voice does not rise. The sentence should end with a
period, not a question mark.

Usually an indirect question is phrased slightly differently
from a direct question: *He asked, "What is zucchini?"* is
direct; *He asked what zucchini was* is indirect. However,
sometimes the phrasing is the same: *What is cooking? I wonder what is cooking*.

Does he like zucchini? she wondered is correct; there are
no quotation marks because the question is not voiced but
thought, but the question is still direct. *The question was,*

Did he like zucchini? is also correct; the past tense of the question may seem to make it indirect, but it does not. (If we use quotation marks, the tense changes: *The question was, "Does he like zucchini?"*)

Exceptions

Often an instruction or command is politely phrased as a question, but no question mark is used: *Would you please attend to this immediately.* The absence of the question mark can be heard; when the "question" is really an order the voice does not rise.

Does he like zucchini, I wonder? is in principle an error, because the question ends with *zucchini: Does he like zucchini? I wonder.* However, when the sentence is made to follow the rule, we can't tell if it's one sentence or two, since *I* is capitalized in either case. Similarly, *Does he like zucchini? Mary wondered* may be one sentence or two. *Does he like zucchini? she wondered* does not have this problem, since if two sentences were intended, *she* would be capitalized. I advise breaking Rule 2-20 and putting the question mark at the end of the sentence when following the rule creates the one-sentence-or-two problem, but only if it is important that the sentence be understood as a single sentence rather than two; sometimes it doesn't really matter and the rule might as well be followed.

You thought I might not like zucchini? is not a true question, but the question mark may be appropriate to show a rising tone that expresses incredulity or surprise, or perhaps even anguish.

How can I thank you for the zucchini! is phrased as a question, but uses an exclamation point instead of a question mark to indicate that it is an exclamation rather than a real question.

2-21 Position question marks properly when using them with other marks of punctuation.

The position of the question mark is always logical, though sometimes a compromise is necessary to avoid two question marks close together.

The question mark should never be used with a period, except in some circumstances with points of ellipsis (see Rule 2-27) and, of course, after a period indicating an abbreviation: *Is the proper form Ms. or Mrs.?*

The question mark should not be used with the comma, even when it seems both marks are needed: *The title of the poem, "Why Me?," was suggested by the poet's mother* should not have the comma after the question mark. If the comma omission bothers the writer, he must recast the sentence: *The poet's mother suggested the title of the poem, "Why Me?"* Now there is an omitted period, but it's less noticeable than the omitted comma. See also Rule 3-21.

The use of the question mark with the exclamation point— either *?!* or *!?*— is usually frowned on as childish.

The question mark with the dash

He told me—who would have expected it?—that he had married again logically puts the question mark within the dashes that enclose the parenthetical question.

But do you suppose—? is an acceptable use of the dash and question mark, to indicate a question that is cut off unfinished. However, usually the dash alone is sufficient.

The question mark with the parenthesis

I think the company is bankrupt (who can think otherwise?). The question mark is part of the parenthetical question, so it goes within the closing parenthesis. Note the terminal period outside the parenthesis.

Are we bankrupt (as these figures suggest)? has the question mark outside the parenthesis, since the whole statement is a question; the material within the parentheses is not a question at all.

Are we bankrupt (do these figures lie?)? is permissible—a question mark for the parenthetical question and another for the whole sentence—but the clumping of punctuation is ugly and should be avoided when, as here, there are better alternatives: *Are we bankrupt, or do these figures lie?*

Are we bankrupt (or do these figures lie?), and if we are, what now? shows the question mark followed by a parenthesis and a comma; this grouping is correct, but the question mark should not be directly followed by a comma except in certain scholarly, legal, or other special contexts.

The question mark with the quotation mark

They raised the question "Are we bankrupt?" puts the question mark inside the closing quotation mark, where it logically belongs. Notice that no period is used; there should be no period outside a closing quotation mark (see Rule 2-24), and a period should not be used directly after a question mark, so the period is just omitted.

Did they officially announce, "We're bankrupt"? puts the question mark at the end of the whole sentence, outside the closing quotation mark; the material within the quotation marks is not a question, so it would be illogical to put the question mark there.

Did they ask the question "Are we bankrupt"? and *Did they ask the question "Are we bankrupt?"* are both correct; some handbooks of punctuation advise one, some the other. Most do not permit *Did they ask the question "Are we bankrupt?"?* The *?"?* clumping is even uglier than the *?)?* clumping in the preceding section of this rule.

The chairman warned, "Don't you think the stockholders will ask, 'Are we bankrupt?'" could also be punctuated *'Are we bankrupt'?"* but the former looks better to my eye, possibly because *Are we bankrupt?* is a stronger question than the question it is part of. Since authority can be found for either, we can use our own judgment in any given sentence.

The question mark with points of ellipsis

The committee's report then raised several questions: "What is the present status of the company? . . . When does the treasurer plan to return from Paraguay?" puts a question mark before the points of ellipsis to indicate that something has been omitted following the completed question that ends with the word *company*. If we make it *"What is the present status of the company . . . ? When does the treasurer plan to return from Paraguay?"* the points of ellipsis preceding the question mark indicate that part of the question has been omitted; it did not originally end with the word *company* but went on. See also Rule 2-27.

EXCLAMATION POINT

The exclamation point is essentially an indicator of emotion—anger, pleasure, surprise, strong resolve. When it is used too frequently, it loses its force and is annoying to the reader.

The principles governing the position of the exclamation point when it is used with other marks of punctuation are almost the same as those governing the position of the question mark (Rule 2-21).

2-22 Position exclamation points properly when using them with other marks of punctuation.

The exclamation point with the dash

He told me—we could have expected it!—that he had married again logically puts the exclamation point within the dashes that enclose the parenthetical exclamation.

But—! is acceptable to indicate an exclamation that is cut off short. It is more functional than the question mark after a dash to indicate a cut-off question (Rule 2-21); the phrasing of a question usually indicates that it is a question, so the question mark is unnecessary, but there is nothing in *But—* to indicate any exclamatory quality.

The exclamation point with the parenthesis

I think the company is bankrupt (and it is!). The exclamation point is part of the parenthetical exclamation and thus goes within the closing parenthesis, with a terminal period outside the parenthesis.

I think we're bankrupt (these figures prove it)! puts the exclamation point at the end of the sentence, since the whole sentence is intended to be exclamatory.

I think we're bankrupt (these figures prove it!)! is possible, but aside from the ugly clumping *!)!* it is clearly an excessive use of the exclamation point.

I think we're bankrupt (these figures prove it!), and we'd better decide what to do shows the exclamation point followed by a parenthesis and comma; this is correct, but the exclamation point should never be directly followed by a comma except in certain scholarly, legal, or other special contexts.

The exclamation point with the quotation mark

The chairman shouted, "We're bankrupt!" puts the exclamation point inside the closing quotation mark, where it logically belongs. Note that there is no period to end the sentence; a period should not be placed outside a closing quotation mark (see Rule 2-24) and should not be used directly after an exclamation point, so it is just omitted.

They just announced, "We're bankrupt"! puts the exclamation point at the end of the sentence, making the whole sentence exclamatory.

Other uses with the quotation mark similar to those described for the question mark in Rule 2-21 should be avoided with exclamation points. Question marks often cannot be avoided, but exclamation points almost always can be, and should be if using them produces clumps of punctuation.

The exclamation point with points of ellipsis

One stockholder was furious and wrote the chairman: "I want my money! . . . Get that treasurer back from Paraguay!" The points of ellipsis following the exclamation point indicate some omission after the completed exclamation ending with *money*. If we make it *"I want my money . . . !* the points of ellipsis preceding the exclamation point indicate that part of the exclamation has been omitted; it did not originally end with *money* but went on. In this latter case the exclamation point can often be omitted, with just the three-dot ellipsis remaining or, if the fragment is a grammatically complete sentence, as here, a fourth dot added: *"I want my money. . . . Get that treasurer back from Paraguay!"*

QUOTATION MARKS

The rules that follow cover the most common and most obvious uses of quotation marks—to enclose words or sentences that are quotations or that are borrowed in some similar way from a source outside the writer's own composition.

There are a number of other uses of quotation marks, such as to enclose the titles of short musical and literary works. These uses are covered in Chapter 3 (see Rule 3-21).

2-23   Use quotation marks for direct quotations, but do not use them for indirect quotations and paraphrases.

Samuel Johnson wrote, "Language is the dress of thought." This is a direct quote of the simplest kind. Note that the period falls within the quotation mark.

When Samuel Johnson wrote that "language is the dress of thought," it was in reference to Abraham Cowley, not Aleister Crowley. When *that* is used to introduce the quoted words, they become part of the grammar of the writer's own sentence, and so there is no comma (see Rule 2-8) and the first word of the quotation is not capitalized even though Johnson began his own sentence with it. Even if Johnson's words had been *I believe that language is the dress of thought*, the word *that* should not be within the quotation marks; it is an essential part of the writer's sentence to introduce the quotation and is just by coincidence the word preceding the words the writer wants to quote.

Some writers are very skillful at working quotations into the grammar of their own sentences. *Johnson criticized even Shakespeare, claiming that though "we owe everything" to Shakespeare, Shakespeare "owes something to us," for although some of our admiration for him is well deserved, some is also "given by custom and veneration"; we consider only Shakespeare's "graces," not his "deformities," and we overlook "what we should in another loathe and despise."* All the words within quotation marks in the passage above are exactly Johnson's words. A less skillful writer may encounter terrible problems because the tenses and diction within the quotations don't fit his own grammar, and he may be tempted to corrupt Johnson's text just a bit to make it fit: *Johnson was aware of his debts to earlier writers; he said he "owed everything" to Shakespeare.* This is dishonest quoting, and it may accompany, as it does in this example, a willingness to corrupt the thought as well as the text of the quotation; Johnson was certainly not expressing a feeling of personal debt to Shakespeare in the passage the quotation is from, though he may well have felt indebted.

Direct quotations of more than one paragraph

When a direct quotation runs more than one paragraph, no closing quotation mark is used at the end of the first paragraph, but an opening quotation is used at the beginning of the second paragraph. This pattern continues; the closing quote occurs only when the quotation finally ends.

In nonfiction, long quotations of written material can also be presented without quotation marks by indenting them a few spaces in from the left margin of the regular text. (In books, such quotations are usually set in smaller type than the regular text as well.) Indenting sets off long quotations better than quotation marks do, and so it is a service to the reader.

Quotations from more than one speaker or source

In fiction, the standard American convention is to have no more than one speaker in a paragraph; each time a different person speaks, there should be a paragraph break. The convention can be relaxed occasionally: *The usual squabble was going on in the playroom. "Give me that!" bellowed Amy; "It's mine!" countered her brother. "It isn't!" "It is!" "It isn't!" "It is!"*

The crowd began to turn ugly, and angry shouts were heard: "Come on out and fight!" "You dirty skunk!" "Give us our money!" Random shouts from a crowd can be in the same paragraph. Note that each shout requires its own enclosing quotation marks; otherwise it would appear that only one person in the crowd was shouting or that the crowd was shouting in unison.

In nonfiction, especially scholarly nonfiction, quotations from several properly identified sources may occur in the same paragraph. The main function of paragraphing in nonfiction is to organize the writer's argument or narrative, not to separate quotations from different sources. However, if there are passages of dialogue in the nonfiction, they usually should be paragraphed in fiction style, with a new paragraph for each change of speaker.

Indirect quotations and paraphrases

"Have I made myself clear?" he asked is a straightforward direct quote, correctly punctuated. *"Had he made himself clear?" he asked* is not correctly punctuated. The question *Had he made himself clear?* is a direct question (see Rule 2-20) and deserves the question mark, but it is not a direct quote and cannot have quotation marks. Both the tense of the verb and the person of the pronoun are different from what they are in the direct quote *"Have I made myself clear?" Had he made himself clear? he asked* is correct.

He said he hoped he'd "made himself clear" is also wrong. *He said he hoped he'd "made myself clear"* is correct in principle, but the switch from third person to first person is annoying and quite unnecessary. The quotation should be made an indirect quotation, without quotation marks: *He said he hoped he'd made himself clear.* It could also be made a straightforward direct quotation: *He said, "I hope I've made myself clear."*

If "language were the dress of thought," as Samuel Johnson claimed it is, your speech would be threadbare indeed should not have the quotation marks, because *language were the dress of thought* is not a direct quote—Johnson's words are *Language is the dress of thought*—but a paraphrase. A paraphrase is a writer's rewording or recasting of someone else's words to suit the requirements of his own sentence, or sometimes to simplify a difficult passage. Paraphrases are legitimate and very useful, since they free the writer from the grammar and diction of the actual quotation, but the writer must be careful not to distort the meaning.

Exception

I told the judge yes, you said maybe, and the policeman said no does not require the *yes*, *maybe*, and *no* to be set off as direct quotations, even though that is what they are. These short words of agreement, indecision, or disagreement can function as part of the sentence without any surrounding punctuation—though they can also, of course, be treated as regular quotations: *You said, "Maybe."* Often they may be a kind of indirect discourse: *I told the judge yes, I had stopped at the light* indicates that it is indirect discourse by the tense of the verb *had stopped*; and *The policeman said no, I hadn't* indicates indirect discourse not only by the tense but by the person of *I hadn't*—the policeman must actually have said *he didn't*.

2-24 Position quotation marks according to typographical conventions, even though these conventions sometimes violate logic.

With parentheses, question marks, and exclamation points, quotation marks are placed where they logically belong (see Rules 2-18, 2-21, and 2-22). They are also placed logically with semicolons, colons, dashes, and points of ellipsis, as will be explained below. But they are not placed logically with commas and periods, which are the marks of punctuation most often associated with them.

The quotation mark with the comma and the period

He said, "I have to go home now." The punctuation happens to coincide with logic; the period ends the quotation and is inside the closing quotation mark. Suppose we put the attribution *he said* after the quote: *"I have to go home now," he said.* The quotation is separated from the attribution by a comma, as required by Rule 2-11. But why is it inside the closing quotation mark? Certainly the comma is not part of the quotation; the speaker naturally ended his sentence with a period. The answer has nothing to do with logic. In the days of hand-set type, supposedly, printers discovered that a period or comma hanging out at the end of a sentence after a quotation mark was easily knocked awry, and they solved the problem by putting the period and the comma within the closing quotation mark regardless of logic. Now this arbitrary positioning of the quotation mark is the universal American convention.

I'm not sure what is meant by "fail-safe". This is logical punctuation, but it's wrong; it should be *I'm not sure what is meant by "fail-safe."* It isn't logical, it's just the way it is. Commas and periods always go within a closing quotation mark.

The quotation mark with the semicolon and the colon

He keeps using the word "fail-safe"; I'm not sure what it means puts the semicolon after the closing quotation mark; *He gave me a definition of "fail-safe": a system of safeguards that hasn't failed yet* puts the colon after the closing quote. This is logical, since the semicolon and colon are punctuation for their respective sentences, not for the quotations within the sentences; neither a semicolon nor a colon can have any legitimate function at the end of a quotation, since the one is supposed to connect what precedes to what follows and the other is supposed to introduce what follows—and nothing follows. The only way the semicolon or colon can be used with the quotation mark is outside a closing quotation mark; neither should ever be within the closing quotation mark.

This is true even if there happens to be a semicolon or colon at the point where the quotation ends. If something to be quoted reads in full *I didn't like World War II; it was dull* and the writer wants to quote only the first clause and then follow with a clause of his own, it should be *The duke wrote in his memoirs, "I didn't like World War II"; he found it dull.* If it is important—as it might be in a study of a literary classic—to preserve the semicolon and indicate that the quoted sentence continued, it can be done by inserting points of ellipsis: *The duke wrote in his memoirs, "I didn't like World War II; . . ."; he found it dull.* However, the clumping of punctuation is ugly; in the example it would be better to make *he found it dull* a separate sentence instead of tacking it to the quotation with a semicolon.

The quotation mark with the dash

The dash goes either inside or outside a closing quotation mark, whichever is logical. Several examples are given in Rule 2-17.

The quotation mark with points of ellipsis

". . . regardless of the precedents," read the Chief Justice's dissent, "a wrong is not being righted." Points of ellipsis (three dots) can be used after an opening quotation mark to show the omission of the first part of a quoted sentence. However, often the points of ellipsis are unnecessary (see Rule 2-27).

The dissent continued, "The failure of this Court to address the basic injustice dismays me. . . ." Points of ellipsis (a period plus three dots here, because the quotation is a grammatically complete sentence) are used before a closing quotation mark to show the omission of the last part of a quoted sentence.

It concluded, "This is worse than 'blind justice.'. . . It is a callous averting of our eyes." The single quotation mark follows the period here, to indicate that the internal quotation ends with a period at that point; the points of ellipsis follow the single quotation mark to indicate an omission before the next sentence.

Exceptions

The British usually position quotation marks logically even with commas and periods: *He keeps saying "fail-safe", and I'm not sure what it means; I'm not sure what is meant by "fail-safe".* Here the quotation marks are being used not to set off a specific direct quotation but to set off a term that is being discussed rather than used as an ordinary word in the sentence. However, the British do put the comma inside the closing quotation mark before an attribution: *"I'm going to ask what it means," he said.* The British are likely to use single quotes instead of double quotes; see also the exceptions to Rule 2-25.

In certain scholarly and scientific disciplines, American

practice is closer to the British. Those who write within such disciplines need an appropriate specialized handbook.

2-25   Use single quotation marks only within double quotation marks.

The Ayatollah said, "I well remember the words of your Western philosopher Nietzsche: 'Distrust all in whom the impulse to punish is powerful.'" This is the standard American punctuation for a quotation within a quotation. Note that the single closing quotation mark follows the same rules that the double quotation mark does (Rule 2-24)—it goes outside the period.

As reported in one newspaper, "The ambassador was heard to mutter, 'Who can trust the quotations of those whose Prophet advises, "Whatever verse we abrogate or cause to be forgotten, we bring a better or its like"?'" This is the standard American punctuation for a quotation within a quotation within a quotation. The alternation of double and single quotation marks could go on indefinitely. Note that the question mark is positioned where it logically belongs within the collection of closing quotation marks, as required by Rule 2-21.

Exceptions

The British usually, but not always, use single quotation marks first, then double quotation marks, the reverse of the American sequence.

Many British writers (even some who customarily use double quotation marks for regular quotations) and some American writers use single quotation marks when the words they enclose are not dialogue or regular quotations from some specific written source but words that are set off for other reasons, such as those discussed in Rule 2-26: *The expression 'What's up, Doc?' is a vulgar, leporine Americanism; America may claim to be 'number one', but number one what?* In the second example, note the logical rather than conventional position of comma and quotation mark (see exceptions to Rule 2-24); those who use the single quotation mark in this manner are also likely to follow the British practice of positioning the quotation mark according to logic rather than convention.

Certain scholarly disciplines have assigned special functions to single quotation marks. In linguistics, a word that is being discussed is italicized and its meaning follows directly after in single quotation marks, with no other punctuation:

> *Cleave* 'to adhere' and *cleave* 'to split' are the same in English but have different derivations.

In philosophy and theology, terms of special significance are commonly enclosed in single quotation marks, with other punctuation following the British logical pattern: *There is some question whether 'nonbeing' can have an 'essence'.* Those who write within such a special discipline need a specialized handbook of usage for the discipline.

2-26   Avoid excessive use of quotation marks for purposes other than to enclose dialogue or quotations from specific written sources.

The setting-off function of quotation marks is often indispensable. However, sometimes no setting off is necessary, and sometimes other means of setting off are preferable.

Quotation marks following *signed, marked,* and similar words

I signed the letter just "Gloucester," since *I happen to be a duke* is correct. However, note that *I signed the letter sincerely his, Gloucester*—admittedly a quirky way of putting it—has no quotes, since *sincerely his* makes it an indirect quotation; the actual words would have been *Sincerely yours*.

The crate was stenciled "This side up" is correct. However, usually stenciled words are in capitals. Most book publishers would prefer to use small capitals and no quotation marks: *The crate was stenciled* THIS SIDE UP. On the typewriter, of course, only full capitals could be used.

The copperplate inscription read "For meritorious service" is correct; certainly we would expect *read* to be followed by quotation marks. However, an inscription is likely to be in script, and certainly a copperplate one would be in script. A book publisher might well use italics for the quotation, with no quotation marks:

> The copperplate inscription read *For meritorious service*.

On the typewriter, italics are indicated by underlining.

When capital letters or italics are used for a quotation, the quotation marks may be used as well, but they are usually superfluous; the distinctive typography sets off the quotation adequately. The advantage of capital letters and italics is that they make the words more vivid for the reader; they indicate not just their meaning but their appearance. They can be, overused for this purpose, too; a page spotted with too many capitals and italics (or typewritten underlines) is unattractive.

Quotation marks for words under discussion

The word "grammar" has different meanings in different contexts and to different people is the conventional American way of setting off words under discussion. *I don't think "grammar" is quite the right term here; "diction" or "usage" might be better* is a similar example; the word "word" doesn't have to appear before the word to justify the quotation marks.

Words such as "grammar," "diction," "usage," "syntax," and "inflection" are defined in the Glossary/Index shows the occasional problem that occurs when quotation marks are used for words under discussion—there are so many quotes that a passage may look as if grass were growing on it. We cannot get away with just an opening quotation mark before *grammar* and a closing quotation mark after *inflection*; each term is independent and needs its own enclosing quotation marks. If this problem can be expected to come up frequently in a given written work, it is wiser to use italics (underlines on the typewriter) rather than quotation marks:

Words such as *grammar, diction, usage, syntax,* and *inflection* are defined in the Glossary/Index.

I have chosen to use italics for the words and sentences used as examples in this book, except when this convention doesn't work, as directly above, where I am discussing italics themselves. Once the writer has decided which convention to use, he should usually stick to it throughout the written work. However, if one chapter of a long book has the string-of-quotes problem but the others do not, the difficult chapter might use italics and all the others might use quotation marks.

Note that when a word under discussion is made a plural, it may be better not to use either quotation marks or italics: *This writer uses too many buts and maybes and ifs.* This obviates the annoying problem of deciding whether or not to italicize the plural *s* as well as the word itself, or the necessity of including the *s* within the quotation marks even though the *s* is not logically part of the quotation (*"but"s* is logical but impossibly awkward).

Quotation marks for unfamiliar terms

Ideally, the curve of a suspension bridge's main cable is a "catenary curve," the shape formed by a flexible chain or cord loosely suspended from both ends is a typical use of quotation marks to set off an unfamiliar term. The meaning of the term should either be clear from the context or, as in the example, explained as soon as possible. Subsequent uses of the term should not have quotation marks, unless there is a long stretch until the next use and the writer judges that the term needs redefining.

Quotation marks for this purpose are adequate when unfamiliar terms are few and far between. However, such terms may come up very frequently in technical material of various kinds, in which case italics (or underlines) are preferable. Italics make it much easier for the reader, who may be having trouble following the material, to fix the unfamiliar terms in his mind and, if necessary, to skim back over what he has read to find a previously defined term that he has forgotten. Textbooks, for example, are likely to use italics for such terms.

Quotation marks should not be used following such expressions as *so-called, termed,* and *known as,* because the expressions have the same function as the quotation marks would: *The cable's shape is a so-called catenary curve.* However, italics can be used, if the writer's policy is to italicize all such terms.

Quotation marks for nicknames and epithets

"Joe" Louis is a thoroughly unnecessary use of quotation marks. *"Jersey Joe" Walcott* is not quite so unnecessary a use, but it certainly isn't necessary either; quotation marks are superfluous when a nickname is very well known.

Admiral William Halsey retired after more than forty years of service. "Bull" Halsey is best remembered for his part in the South Pacific campaign in World War II. This is a desirable use of quotation marks for a nickname. If the nickname is used again as the passage continues, however, the quotation marks should be dropped; they are needed only when the nickname is introduced.

William "Bull" Halsey retired in 1947 is the standard method of giving both a first name and a nickname. If both first and middle names are given, the nickname follows the middle name: *Charles Dillon "Casey" Stengel was born in 1891.* Once the nickname has been supplied this way, if it occurs again without the first name no quotation marks should be used.

Alfonso the Chaste, grandson of Alfonso the Catholic, sired no successor shows the invariable form for royalty, great conquerors, and similar historical figures. No quotation marks are used. Whimsical modern epithets based on the same pattern, but sometimes with modern word order and often with the last name instead of the first name, don't ordinarily need quotation marks either: *Jeeves the Inimitable; the Magnificent Montague.*

Epithets without given names or surnames, such as *the Iron Duke, the Swedish Nightingale,* and *the Sun King,* may or may not be familiar enough to a writer's readership to get away without quotation marks or explanations. Each case must be decided for itself. *Louis XIV, the Sun King, succeeded to the throne in 1643* may require both the real name and the epithet to be clear to all readers, but it doesn't require quotation marks around *the Sun King* for any reader. On the other hand, *Jenny Lind, "the Swedish Nightingale," earned Barnum one of his great triumphs* may benefit from the quotation marks; they do suggest to the reader who is completely in the dark that Jenny Lind was a person, not a bird. *Wellington, the Iron Duke, was the hero of Waterloo* requires no quotation marks. However, if the epithet is not immediately after the name but is used for the first time in a separate sentence, quotation marks may be advisable: *When he returned from Verona there were further honors heaped on "the Iron Duke."* Yet in a similar situation, *the Sun King* probably shouldn't have quotation marks. The writer must judge for himself; my advice is to lean toward not using quotation marks.

Quotation marks to indicate raised eyebrows

I felt constrained to award a modest "gratuity," though I felt no gratitude is one example, from among a vast range, of foolish uses of the raised-eyebrow quotation mark. The writer is stepping on his own joke; the quotation marks telegraph the bad news that a weak witticism is coming up.

I have gone to some trouble to think up an entirely contemptible example, because raised-eyebrow quotation marks are perhaps the most irritating of all mannerisms in written English, even though there are times when they are inoffensive and even useful.

After the bellboy left I inspected the "bathroom." It was a hole in the floor with a neat concrete footprint to east and west. The quotation marks telegraph the coming irony, but at least the bathroom is not really a bathroom but a privy and thus has some right to the quotation marks.

The "dining facilities" turned out to be a greasy counter off the lobby where deep-fried pig innards were available.' The quotation marks here might be defended as not just indicating that the writer's eyebrows are aloft but implying that the phrase *dining facilities* occurred in a guidebook, advertising brochure, or spoken description of the hotel. Still, they are hardly indispensable.

The "desk man" turned out to be female—or at least decorated with mascara, nail polish, and sequins—and to have more intimate functions than merely handing over one's mail. Perhaps, perhaps—but the writer has dishonestly set up his archness by choosing the term *desk man*; if he had used one of the more common terms he had available, such as *desk clerk*, the quotation marks would be completely, not just largely, pointless.

I have several times in this book written sentences such as *The comma in this construction can be "heard."* The quotation marks in my sentence are akin to raised-eyebrow quotation marks; they indicate that *heard* is not being used in its literal sense. Each of us must judge for himself when raised-eyebrow quotation marks are genuinely useful, when they are pointless, and when they are offensive; my advice is to be a harsh judge.

POINTS OF ELLIPSIS

Points of ellipsis have two main functions: to indicate the omission of words within something that is being quoted, and to indicate lengthy pauses. They tend to be overused for both functions.

Points of ellipsis look, of course, exactly like periods. However, they are not periods; a period is the mark that indicates the end of a declarative sentence. I call points of ellipsis "dots" in this section to emphasize the distinction.

2-27   Use three dots to indicate ellipsis at the beginning or in the middle of a quoted sentence. Also use three dots to indicate ellipsis at the end of a quoted sentence if the quotation is neither a grammatically complete sentence by itself nor a grammatically complete sentence in conjunction with the words that precede the quotation.

Use a period plus three dots to indicate ellipsis at the end of a quoted passage if the quotation is either a

> grammatically complete sentence by
> itself or a grammatically complete
> sentence in conjunction with the words
> that precede the quotation. Also use a
> period plus three dots to indicate an
> omission within a quotation between a
> grammatically complete sentence and
> another complete or incomplete
> sentence.

I apologize for this very long rule. Fortunately it is easier to understand points of ellipsis than it is to explain in compact fashion the principles governing them.

The following quotation, given in full (that is, without ellipsis), is from an essay by Lionel Trilling. It is used throughout this discussion for examples.

> Matthew Arnold was born in 1822, on the 24th of December. He was the son of a remarkable father. Thomas Arnold was at this time a young clergyman of the Church of England, who, in the little village of Laleham on the upper Thames, made a modest livelihood by taking young gentlemen into his home and preparing them for the universities. He was not long to remain thus obscure. In 1827, at the age of thirty-two, he was elected headmaster of Rugby School, an ancient but much deteriorated foundation. The story of Thomas Arnold's reform of Rugby, of his raising it from the shabby slackness in which he found it to the position of one of the most famous and influential of schools, has become one of the legends of Victorian England, and even today people who do not know another name in the long history of scholastic education know the name of Dr. Arnold.

Ellipsis at the beginning of a quoted sentence

Trilling writes, ". . . even today people who do not know another name in the long history of scholastic education

121

know the name of Dr. Arnold." Except in very formal writing it would also be correct to begin *Trilling writes that "even today,* with the points of ellipsis omitted; the running in of the quotation by *that* and the lowercase *even* suggest, though they do not unmistakably indicate, that Trilling's sentence did not begin with *even.* In relatively informal writing it would be correct to begin *"Even today," Trilling writes, "people who,* with *even* capitalized to suit the requirements of the writer and no suggestion at all that there is an ellipsis.

A writer must decide how important it is in a given piece of writing to indicate ellipsis, then make a policy for himself and hold to it.

Ellipsis in the middle of a quoted sentence

"Thomas Arnold . . . made a modest livelihood by taking young gentlemen into his home and preparing them for the universities," Trilling writes. This is the only way to indicate ellipsis within a sentence. Such ellipsis should always be indicated, even in informal writing.

Trilling begins, "Matthew Arnold . . . was the son of a remarkable father." Here the end of one sentence and the beginning of another have been omitted. This is quite acceptable, and it is done just as if the two sentences were one. The danger is that such a double ellipsis will end up distorting the original meaning of the quoted passage, but there is no problem in the example. Note that the ellipsis could have come after *was* instead of before it, since the word occurs both places in the full text. The writer can make his own choice which *was* to omit; here it seems a little better to keep the entire predicate together.

Ellipsis at the end of a quoted sentence

"The story of Thomas Arnold's reform of Rugby, of his raising it from the shabby slackness in which he found it . . ." One wonders if Trilling does not exaggerate the school's decrepitude to increase Arnold's merit. This is a rare method of quoting; usually a quotation that is an incomplete sentence is connected somehow with a sentence of the writer's. However, it does occur frequently in certain kinds of writing—for example, when the writer is making a detailed,

phrase-by-phrase analysis of the material he is quoting. Three dots and no period should be used. In typescript, the first period may be one space from the last word (in printing the compositor inserts a thin space) to indicate that the dot is not a period, but usually it is not so spaced; just the fact that three dots, not four, appear is sufficient indication that there is no period.

"The story of Thomas Arnold's reform of Rugby, of his raising it from the shabby slackness in which he found it . . ." *makes one wonder if Trilling exaggerates the school's decrepitude.* This is almost the same situation. The quotation has been made part of the writer's own sentence, with the whole quotation used as a noun, the subject of *makes.* The points of ellipsis are correct here, and helpful because they make it clearer that the writer is discussing Trilling's choice of words, not incorporating the meaning of those words into his own sentence, as in *"The story of Thomas Arnold's reform of Rugby" is a thrilling one.* The points of ellipsis are not essential to indicate that Trilling's sentence is incomplete; the quotation is quite evidently a fragment without them.

Trilling begins, "Matthew Arnold was born in 1822. . . ." Trilling's sentence has been cut short, but the period plus three dots is used because what is left of the sentence is itself a grammatically complete sentence. There is an argument in favor of omitting the period to indicate that Trilling's sentence, though grammatically complete, is not quoted in full, but the policy of almost all book publishers and the authorities they use—primarily the Chicago University Press's *A Manual of Style* and *Words into Type* (Prentice-Hall)—is to use the period.

Trilling writes that Thomas Arnold's rise to prominence began "In 1827, at the age of thirty-two. . . ." The period plus three dots is used because though the quotation is not a grammatically complete sentence it blends with the writer's words to make a complete sentence. This particular use of points of ellipsis is, however, far too rigorous for anything but very close analysis of the quoted material. In other writing it is better to assume the reader will understand that the quotation is a fragment—what else could it be?—and to omit the points of ellipsis and also lowercase the *In.*

Of Matthew's father, Trilling writes, "He was not long to

remain thus obscure. . . . The story of Thomas Arnold's reform of Rugby . . . has become one of the legends of Victorian England. . . ." The first set of points of ellipsis includes a period plus three dots, because an entire sentence has been dropped between complete sentences. (The second and third sets of points of ellipsis illustrate omissions already covered.) *"In 1827, at the age of thirty-two, he was elected headmaster of Rugby School. . . . The story of Thomas Arnold's reform of Rugby . . . has become one of the legends of Victorian England. . . ."* The first set of points of ellipsis includes a period plus three dots even though only part of a sentence has been dropped, because the part of the sentence that remains is a grammatically complete sentence itself. It is apparent that the reader won't always know exactly what the writer has done to the original full quotation—points of ellipsis can't tell it all.

Ellipsis around obvious fragments

Matthew Arnold's father ". . . made a modest livelihood . . ." as a tutor is obviously an unnecessary use of points of ellipsis; the quotation couldn't be anything but a fragment. Of course, points of ellipsis may still be needed within an obvious fragment, but they aren't needed before or after it.

Ellipsis with the question mark and exclamation point

The question mark and exclamation point are used logically with points of ellipsis. For example, suppose a quoted sentence ends with a question mark, and then there is an ellipsis, and then the quotation continues. The question mark follows the first sentence just as it did in the full text, and three dots follow the question mark. If a quoted sentence is a question and the last part of it is omitted, the part that is quoted is followed by three dots and then a question mark. If there is then a further omission before the quote continues, there are three more dots to indicate it, so one can have the lengthy clumping . . . ? . . . in the middle of a quotation—not attractive but sometimes necessary. Sometimes the question mark or exclamation point can be omitted to simplify the punctuation; it depends how important the writer feels it is to indicate the punctuation of the full text.

Ellipsis at the end or beginning of a paragraph or between paragraphs

Points of ellipsis, with a period if the last quoted sentence is grammatically complete, should appear when the end of a paragraph has been omitted and the quotation then continues with a new paragraph. This is sufficient even if several paragraphs have been omitted, and it is also usually the convention when the end of the paragraph has not been omitted but one or more complete paragraphs have been skipped before the quotation resumes.

Points of ellipsis should appear when the beginning of a second or subsequent paragraph has been omitted. If both the end of one paragraph and the beginning of the next have been omitted, points of ellipsis should appear in both places.

Note that quotations of more than one paragraph or even one paragraph of more than moderate length are usually better set as block quotations—that is, indented and without quotation marks (see Rule 2-23).

2-28   Use points of ellipsis sparingly to indicate pauses, and use them correctly.

"Well, let's see. . . . We have . . . yes, eleven cents. . . . I'm afraid those candy bars are fifty-nine cents, son," the storekeeper said. The period plus three dots is used when a sentence ends before a pause, just the three dots when there is a pause in the middle of a sentence.

"I don't have enough? Well . . ." Three dots without a period are used when a sentence trails off unfinished.

"Yes," the storekeeper said, "you're forty-eight cents short. . . ." A period plus three dots is used when a complete quotation trails off. This use of points of ellipsis is puzzling, however. The points of ellipsis can't indicate a pause, since the quotation doesn't continue. Can a complete quotation really trail off? A sentence may have a trailing-off intonation,

but punctuation usually does not attempt to indicate such minor subtleties of speech. The points of ellipsis in this situation may sometimes indicate a pause before the next speaker speaks, saving the writer the trouble of writing *There was a brief pause* or *About as much time elapsed as it takes to hit the period key three times*.

Some writers of fiction seem to punctuate mostly with points of ellipsis. It's annoying. As an editor I have had to read a lot of ellipsis-strewn fiction; I wouldn't read it except for money.

One side of a telephone conversation

"Hello?. . . Yes, this is he. . . . Oh. . . . No. . . . I'll come right down and get— Shut up a minute. I'll pay for the damn window. . . . Do you know who I am? I'm the health inspector, in charge of food retailers in the city. . . . That's better. If you've even frightened that boy you'll be sorry. . . . Yes, I'll be right there. Goodbye."

There are several ways of presenting one side of a telephone conversation. The above is what I advise. The unheard side is represented by a period plus three dots, even if the heard side is not speaking in complete sentences. An interruption is indicated by a dash, followed by a space.

When both sides of a telephone conversation are given, it is presented as ordinary dialogue. Italics, or switches from roman for one speaker to italics for the other, are unnecessary.

APOSTROPHE

Strictly speaking, the apostrophe is not a mark of punctuation but a part of the spelling of a word; it occurs as part of a word, not as something between words. Its primary functions are to indicate the possessive case and to indicate contractions and dropped letters.

Errors occur frequently when plurals are confused with possessives and when plurals are possessives. Other errors, such as misplacing the apostrophe in a contraction, are frequent in careless or hasty writing.

Certain special uses of the apostrophe are discussed in Chapter 3; see Rule 3-6.

2-29   Form the possessive case of singular
words, including words ending in *s* or
z sounds, by adding an apostrophe
plus *s*; form the possessive of plural
words ending in *s* by adding the
apostrophe alone.

This is the simplest rule that can be given for forming the
possessive, and still there are a number of common exceptions to it. It is not the only possible rule—some handbooks
of punctuation advise forming the possessive of singular
words that end in *s* or *z* sounds with the apostrophe alone,
some make a distinction according to whether the word ends
in the letter *s* or in another sibilant, such as *x* or *z*, some
make a distinction depending on the length of the word (usually prescribing an *s* after the apostrophe for words of one or
perhaps two syllables but not for longer words), some make
a distinction depending on whether the word ends in a single
s or *ss*, and so on.

Since there is such variation among the authorities about
words ending in *s*, each writer is entitled to make his own
decision about certain possessives, but all writers should try
to have a consistent policy and avoid, for example, inconsistencies such as *Charles's garage is bigger than Miles'
house*.

A generation or so ago, many authorities considered it
improper to use the possessive case with any word that does
not denote an animate thing. Thus one could write (or say)
the dog's dish but not *the dish's contents*; it would have to
be *the contents of the dish*. Why the *of* possessive construction was deemed acceptable is puzzling, since to modern
ears it often shows possession just as clearly as the apostrophe (see also **possessive** in the Glossary/Index). In any
case, the distinction is no longer made except by very fastidious writers; few of their readers have any idea the distinction
is being made, though many may wonder why unidiomatic
phrases such as *a vacation of a week* occasionally appear.

Singular and plural possessives

The candle's glow and *the candles' glow* show the simplest possessive situation; in the first phrase there is one candle, in the second more than one.

The boss's office and *the bosses' salaries* show the use of the apostrophe plus *s* that I advise for singular words ending in *s* and of the apostrophe alone for plural words (which are usually formed by *es* when the singular ends in *s*). There are very few common nouns in English that end in a single *s* in the singular; those that do exist are apt to be more or less direct borrowings from other languages, such as *catalysis*, from the Greek *katalysis*. These words are apt to have special plurals but usually form the possessive plural in the regular way—*catalyses* is the plural, and *catalyses'* is the possessive plural. However, there are many common nouns that end in *x* or *z*, such as *jinx* and *buzz*, and these words can follow the same pattern as *boss* for the possessive: *jinx's*, *jinxes'*; *buzz's*, *buzzes'*.

The children's room, the people's choice, and *women's rights* are examples of an important exception to Rule 2-29. Some of the most common nouns in English are many centuries old, adopted before the added *s* became the standard method of forming plurals. These so-called irregular plurals that don't end in *s* form the possessive in the same way singular words do, by adding an apostrophe plus *s*. *The childrens' room, the peoples' choice*, and *womens' rights* are wrong, yet one sees them frequently—I think usually they are typographical errors rather than ignorant ones.

Another exception is also too important to leave till later: personal pronouns. Personal pronouns have special possessive forms that do not use the apostrophe. The singular forms are *my* and *mine*; *your* and *yours* (and the same for the plural); *his*; *her* and *hers*; *its*. The plural forms are *our* and *ours*; *their* and *theirs*. Errors such as *your's* and *her's* occur surprisingly often—and I think that unlike *childrens'*, they are often ignorant errors. They are certainly bad errors.

Smith's house means a house owned or occupied by someone named Smith, who is either the sole owner or the head of the family, or possibly is just the only person under discussion. *The Smiths' house* means a house owned or occupied by a family named Smith; the surname is made a plural by adding an *s*, and an apostrophe is added to make the plural possessive.

Curtis's house is correct, meaning a house owned or occupied by a person named Curtis. The problem starts with the Curtis family. More often than not one sees *the Curtis's house*, which is wrong. The plural of the surname *Curtis* is *Curtises*, so it must be *the Curtises' house*. One sees plurals and plural possessives of names ending in *s* or *ss* formed wrongly more often than one sees them right. *Mr. Jones, Jones's house, the Joneses' house*; *Mr. Cross, Cross's house, the Crosses' house*—there is no other way to form the plural and plural possessive.

Individual possession and joint possession

Smith's and Brown's cars are in the parking lot has an apostrophe plus *s* for each person; each has a car. *Smith and Brown's tennis match was postponed* has an apostrophe plus *s* only for *Brown*; the match "belongs" to Smith and Brown jointly—they were going to play it together. In these examples the plural *cars* and the singular *match* make the logic quite obvious, but sometimes one has to think a bit: *Smith's and Brown's behavior at the office party was disgraceful* is correct if they misbehaved separately; *Smith and Brown's behavior* is correct if they formed a team.

The Smiths' and Browns' parties were on the same night; *The Smiths and Browns' joint party was a success*. Plurals follow the same rules that singulars do for individual possession and joint possession.

This is my and my brother's car does not follow the usual rule but is correct. Personal pronouns are in the possessive case even in joint possession; it can't be *me and my brother's car* or *I and my brother's car*.

Possessives of phrases

The King of Spain's sponsorship, *the Senator from New York's personal fortune*, and *the chief of staff's report* show the standard method of forming possessives of short phrases denoting a single person. *The master of ceremonies' introduction* and *the ambassador from the United States' dismissal* are permissible but awkward; it is better to make it *the introduction of the master of ceremonies* and *the dismissal of the ambassador from the United States*. Phrases denoting inanimate things often look odd with the apostrophe plus *s* except in poetic diction: *the pot of coffee's position on the table* and *the wine from Greece's resinous taste* should be recast, but *I await the door into summer's opening* is permissible in verse or fanciful prose.

Problems are apt to come up with plurals of phrases. *The grandees of Spain's displeasure* is displeasing, *the Senators from New York's disagreement* is disagreeable, *the chiefs of staff's dispute* is disputable, though all are in principle correct. The phrases should be recast: *the displeasure of the grandees of Spain*; *the disagreement between the Senators from New York*; *the dispute among the chiefs of staff.*

She is the man who was knighted yesterday's wife is unacceptable; possessives should not be formed with word groups that contain dependent clauses, except possibly for very well-known word groups: *The boy who cried wolf's problem was getting people to believe him.*

Possessives with *Jr.* and *Sr.*

Jr. and *Sr.* cause problems: (1) *John Doe, Jr.'s, wife*; (2) *John Doe Jr.'s wife*; (3) *John Doe's, Jr.'s, wife*; (4) *John Doe, Jr.'s wife*? *Jr.* and *Sr.* should by convention be set off by commas, unlike *II*, *III*, and so on. Yet at least in spirit they are not parenthetical but defining (see Rule 2-1); they indicate which John Doe is meant. I advise the rule-bending (4), and as a second choice (1); the smoothest is actually (2), but readers might then notice that *Jr.* is set off with commas elsewhere in the passage and be disturbed by the inconsistency.

Piled-up possessives

That's my brother's wife's sister's daughter's cat's leash is correctly punctuated, but such piled-up possessives should be avoided except for humorous effect. *That's the cat of my brother's wife's leash* cannot be correctly punctuated and must be avoided—we can't make it *cat's of my brother's wife's*, because *cat's* is adjectival, since it is possessive, and adjectives cannot be the subject of an *of* phrase, only nouns and pronouns can.

Compound nouns with possessives

Many compound nouns are formed of two nouns with the first one in the possessive case: *bull's-eye, baby's breath, monk's cloth*. If a compound is unfamiliar, we have to use a dictionary to determine whether there is a possessive, whether the possessive word is singular or plural (usually it's singular), and whether the compound is all one word, hyphenated, or two words, because the language is quite inconsistent. For example, *goat grass, goatweed, goatsbeard*, and *goat's rue* are the forms given in the Merriam-Webster unabridged dictionary for four different plants.

Hyphenated compounds can be a problem in the plural. *My brother-in-law's house* is fine in the singular, but *my brothers-in-law's houses*, though correct, should be avoided.

Possessives of words ending with a silent s

Descartes's work, Des Moines's police force, Arkansas's governor, the Chablis's taste. The fact that the *s* is silent does not affect the rule; the possessive is formed as usual.

Exceptions

Names from the Bible and from classical history and legend that end in *s* often take only the apostrophe to form the possessive: *Jesus', Moses', Aristophanes', Hercules'.* Adding the *s* is not wrong, but the convention is to omit it, and in many cases when it is added it looks odd, especially with long names: *Aristophanes's.*

Most handbooks of punctuation advise dropping the *s* in certain common phrases, especially with *sake*: *for convenience' sake; for conscience' sake; for goodness' sake.* The intent is to avoid a succession of *s* sounds. I have rarely seen any of these forms. I usually make it *convenience's sake* and *conscience's sake*, and forget the possessive completely and make it *goodness sake*—that's the way I pronounce the phrases—but I haven't found any support for these personal preferences.

Official names of companies, organizations, and institutions follow no rules; one simply must find a reliable authority for the proper form of a given name. Often an apostrophe that seems necessary or desirable isn't there; one would expect Columbia University's subdivision to be Teachers' College, but it is Teachers College—the plural noun directly modifies *College*, without being made a possessive. According to the *Los Angeles Times* book of style and usage, Childrens Hospital is the Los Angeles institution, even though *childrens* isn't a permissible English formation. The Bricklayers, Masons and Plasterers' International Union of America follows the joint-possession rule given above, the International Longshoremen's and Warehousemen's Union doesn't. The Textile Workers Union of America, like many unions and like Teachers College, doesn't bother with the apostrophe at all.

2-30   Don't overuse contractions; when you do use them, put the apostrophe in the proper place.

Contractions such as *don't* for *do not* are natural and convenient in speech. They are also natural in writing—in fact, they come too easily, for when they occur frequently they give the written work an informality greater than may be intended. Judging where to draw the line is very much a question of using one's own ear and eye. It is important to read over any written work, except the most casual letter or note, for many reasons, and one of the most important reasons is to check for excessive use of contractions and other flaws that distort the intended tone.

The contractions *don't*, *won't*, *wouldn't*, *aren't*, and others based on the combining of a verb with *not* are often incorrectly spelled *do'nt*, *would'nt*, and so on.

The contraction *it's*, meaning *it is*, is sometimes misspelled *its*, which is the possessive of the pronoun *it*. The opposite mistake is much more common—using *it's* for the possessive.

The contraction *who's*, meaning either *who is* or *who has*, is often misspelled *whose*, which is the possessive of the pronoun *who*.

The contractions *should've* (meaning *should have*), *I'd've* (meaning *I would have*), and others formed by contracting *have* to *'ve* are often misspelled *should of*, *I'd of*, and so on. Usually the mistake is from ignorance; the writer just does not know the correct form and is misled by the similarity in sound of *'ve* and *of*. Some writers who know better make the mistake deliberately in dialogue or when writing in the first person to add flavor; *should of* and *I'd of* have a drawled look that the more clipped *should've* and *I'd've* lack. Ring Lardner and John O'Hara often used *of* for *'ve*, and it is unlikely that either did it out of ignorance. However, I have noted the error outside dialogue in O'Hara's writing, and it makes me wonder.

Contractions to indicate substandard speech

"I'se goin' to town fer feed; won' be back till mornin'. Anything is possible in dialogue, and almost anything is permissible. Note that *won'* drops the *t* of *won't*, so the apostrophe is doing double duty.

Twenty years ago I thought that if an author had a character drop his *g*'s, that character had to drop the *g* every time he used an *ing* word. I no longer believe that; it can be very tiresome. Just an occasional dropped *g* in the right place, and the avoidance of any glaring inconsistency such as the same word two ways in the same sentence, is more effective and easier to read than a rigorous consistency. It takes considerable judgment to use just the right amount of contraction and no more—that is why some writers are much better at this kind of dialogue than others. Anyone who wants to write substandard dialogue well should make a close study of some writer he admires.

Certain contractions are puzzling. Writers of Westerns are fond of *th'* for *the*, as in *"Gimme th' gun, Luke—you ain't goin' outta th' house."* The contraction *th'* may indicate that the speaker did not stretch out *the* to *thee*, as might an Anglican preacher pausing while waiting for the felicitous word to descend to his brain, but the reader would not need to have this pointed out. (The same writers like to use *bin* or *ben* for *been*, even though almost all Americans, not just those in spurs, pronounce it *bin* or *ben* rather than *bean*.) Since contractions can be annoying anyway, there is certainly no point in using them when they're meaningless.

Some writers prefer to drop the apostrophe for contractions, perhaps hoping to make them less annoying: *"We allus goin, goin, never get noplace. Jus runnin in place like a lil tree owl wit mouse shortnin bread on his mine."* Sometimes it works, sometimes it doesn't.

One could do worse than study Mark Twain's *Huckleberry Finn*. Contractions and other devices to show substandard speech are heavy in dialogue—very heavy in Jim's speech, quite heavy in Huck's, absent in some characters'. Contractions are light in the narrative, even though it is recounted in the first person by Huck. Twain must have thought a great deal about his contractions; he wanted to reproduce speech faithfully but didn't want to annoy the reader. For young children he may not have succeeded completely—they have trouble with the book, though most will plow through it somehow rather than leave it unfinished—but for most of us he did.

HYPHEN

Most marks of punctuation serve in some way to separate words from one another (comma, semicolon, colon, dash, parenthesis) or sentences from one another (question mark, exclamation point, period). The hyphen is the only mark of punctuation that has the specific function of joining words together.

Almost all words containing a hyphen are compound words—that is, words formed from two or more base words. A few are compounds not of one word with another but merely of a prefix or suffix that is not a word in itself with a base word; usually such compounds are written as one word (see Rule 2-31). When there is a hyphen, it serves mainly to make the pronunciation and meaning apparent. *Co-worker* contains a hyphen, unlike many similar compounds such as *coauthor* and *coheir*. Perhaps this is because if it is written as a solid word, *coworker*, it is apt to be momentarily misread as a compound of the meaningless *cow orker*, closed up like the apparently similar compounds *cowpoke*, *cowpea*, *cow-*

man, and *cowlick*. But many *co* words that are not hyphenated are just as easy to misread. There are no hard-and-fast
rules governing the appearance of the hyphen in words such
as *co-worker*; one has to rely on a dictionary.

There are some general principles governing the hyphen in
compounds formed of two words, such as the noun *break-in*,
but one frequently still needs the dictionary. For example,
Webster's New Collegiate Dictionary and its parent, *Webster's Third New International Dictionary*, list *break-in* and
breakout as nouns. Why hyphenate one and not the other? I
think a writer working on something that requires constant
use of two terms that his dictionary treats inconsistently
should often make an exception to the dictionary for that
particular piece of writing, to avoid puzzling the reader.
(Surely some other dictionary somewhere would support
him; dictionaries vary considerably on compound words.)

The British make different uses of the hyphen than we
do—they are apt to use it when we would not, as in their
compound noun *dining-room*, and not to use it when we
would, as in their adjective + participle compound adjective
good looking. Their use of the hyphen is so at variance with
the best American use that I have not followed my usual
practice of listing British uses as exceptions to the rules.

Most of the following rules are concerned mainly not with
the kind of compound words discussed above, which can be
found in the dictionary, but with so-called temporary compounds—words that may be compounded because of the role
they play in their sentences but that normally stand alone.
Some of them do appear in dictionaries, but only the most
common ones; there are countless thousands of possible
temporary compounds. Therefore one must understand the
principles of compounding, not just rely on the dictionary.

The rules outline a rather rigorous use of hyphens—some
would consider it old-fashioned—that depends on an understanding of grammar and particularly of the parts of speech
and their functions. I cannot pretend that my rules all represent standard American practice; some do more than others.
I do urge the rules on those who use this book, because I
think the hyphen is a valuable, if neglected, asset in English
punctuation and because the best writing, if not the average
American thinkpiece or novel, does follow my rules.

2-31   Don't hyphenate most compounds formed with the prefixes listed below; connect them solidly to the base word.

This list is based on one in *Words into Type* (Prentice-Hall), one of the major guides used in the publishing industry.

anti	intra	re
co	macro	semi
de	micro	sub
hyper	non	supra
hypo	pre	trans
infra	pseudo	un

Antiwar, coauthor, deactivate, hypersensitive, hypoallergenic, infrastructure, intramural—a glance at the dictionary will confirm that these prefixes almost always combine with base words to form solid words, not hyphenated ones.

Exceptions

Alas, an exception can be found for every prefix on the list.

Compounds with these prefixes are often hyphenated to avoid doubling a vowel: *anti-art, co-opt, de-emphasize*, and so on. This exception has exceptions: Merriam-Webster dictionaries list *cooperate*, for example, though some other dictionaries (including older editions of Merriam-Webster dictionaries) use the hyphen, and some list *coöperate*, with a diaeresis over the second *o* to clarify the pronunciation, as an alternative. When using any of these prefixes to form an unfamiliar compound not found in the dictionary, the principle of avoiding doubled vowels is useful.

Sometimes there is a hyphen to prevent a word from being identical with another word of quite different meaning: *I'll re-cover the sofa when I recover from the flu.* One has to be quite alert sometimes. Does *He's going to release the apartment* mean he's going to let it go or lease it again? If the latter is the case the hyphen is needed. Again, there are exceptions

136

to the exception: *I'm relaying the message that the workman is relaying the tiles.*

When any of the prefixes in the list is combined with a capitalized word—that is, a proper noun or a word formed from a proper noun—the hyphen is usually used to avoid a capital letter in the middle of a solid word: *anti-American, un-English,* and so on. Yet again, the exception has exceptions; sometimes the capitalized word is highhandedly lowercased. Almost all modern dictionaries list *transatlantic* and *unchristian,* for example. Rule 2-31 can be followed as a general principle only; one needs a dictionary.

Because of the differences among dictionaries and the inconsistencies in any single dictionary, hyphenation in the situations discussed in Rules 2-31 and 2-32 is much more a matter of judgment than are most matters of punctuation. Actually, the uses of the hyphen discussed in these two rules are matters less of punctuation than of spelling, and there are many words that can be spelled more than one way. Nevertheless, those who study Rules 2-31 and 2-32 will improve their judgment even if they don't find firm answers to specific hyphenation problems.

2-32 Hyphenate compounds with the words *all* and *self* used as prefixes, and many compounds with the words *great* and *half* used as prefixes.

This rule is fairly reliable for *all* and *self*: *all-around, all-American; self-confidence, self-examination.* However, it can be stated only vaguely for *great* and *half,* because there are so many exceptions: *great-aunt, great-grandfather; half-life, half-truth;* but *greatcoat, greathearted; half brother, halfhearted.*

The rule can be taken as a general principle for forming new compounds with *all* and *self. Great* is often just an ordinary adjective, as in *great ape* and *great circle,* but when it has something to do with kindred, as in *great-aunt,* it should usually be hyphenated: *Old North French is one of the English language's great-ancestors.* Compounds with *half* are extremely unpredictable in the dictionary. Those that aren't in the dictionary are often clearer with the hyphen—*half-pound*, *half-kilo*, and so on—especially when they are pronounced in a run-together fashion rather than as two distinctly separate words. Like other marks of punctuation, the hyphen can usually be "heard."

2-33 Don't hyphenate adjectival combinations of adverb + adjective or adverb + participle unless the adverb does not end in *ly* and can be misread as an adjective.

Since the function of adverbs is to modify adjectives and verbs, and since participles are merely forms of verbs that act like adjectives, the combination of adverb + adjective or adverb + participle is just a simple case of one word's modifying another, and no hyphen is needed to show the relationship.

An appropriately-red bridal gown and *a completely-confused groom* are errors in American English; there should be no hyphens. (The British often do hyphenate such compounds, however.) Some writers are misled by three-part compounds, such as *a completely broken-down neighborhood*, and insert an unneeded hyphen between *completely* and the properly hyphenated *broken-down* (which is a participle + adverb combination, discussed in Rule 2-35).

Note, however, that *a scholarly-looking person* is not an error. *Scholarly*, *leisurely*, and a few other adjectives end in *ly*, which is the standard ending for adverbs, but they are still adjectives, and the combination of adjective + participle, as in *scholarly-looking*, should be hyphenated (see Rule 2-34).

Adverbs that do not end in *ly*

An ill-clothed baby is not an error, even though *ill* is an adverb and the combination is adverb + participle. The reason for the hyphen is that *ill* can be misread as an adjective, meaning *sick* and directly modifying *baby* rather than the participle *clothed*. The hyphen links *ill* to *clothed*. Even though it is rare that the omission of such a linking hyphen causes real confusion, I recommend the hyphen; it does suggest the run-together spoken delivery of the compound and speeds the reader along. It is impossible to give rules for hyphenation of such compounds that cover every case, but here are some general principles.

Most adverbs that do not end in *ly* can also be adjectives. *Well*, *better*, and *best* are common examples. Other examples are *slow, little,* and *long.* These six and some others should be routinely followed by a hyphen when they are used in adverb + participle compounds that come before the modified word: *well-dressed parent*; *better-clothed baby*; *best-written book*; *slow-moving train*; *little-used car*; *long-awaited speech.* Many such compounds are so common that they occur in dictionaries as hyphenated compounds; they can therefore be considered permanent hyphenated compounds and the hyphens can be left in even when the compounds come after the modified word: *The groom was well-bred and the bride was well-heeled; she was also well-rounded, so the wedding was well-timed.*

Much, *more*, *most*, and *least* can be either adverbs or adjectives. However, they rarely appear in ambiguous constructions, and therefore I do not usually hyphenate them when they are combined with participles or adjectives: *a much loved baby; a more comprehensive report; a most loving parent; the least forgivable sin.* Nevertheless, ambiguities do occur with these adverbs and sometimes a hyphen can help. *We need more comprehensive reports* could mean either that we need more reports that are comprehensive or that we need reports that are more comprehensive. *We need more-comprehensive reports* could have only the second meaning.

Too, *very*, *almost*, and a few other common adverbs do not end in *ly*, but they cannot be adjectives either, and so I do not hyphenate them in most compounds: *too loving parent*; *very comprehensive report*; *almost forgivable sin.* (There are, however, complicated compounds that do require hyphens to unify them: *too-many-cooks situation.*) *Always*, *never*, *ever*, and *seldom* cannot be adjectives, yet I do hyphenate them in most compounds that come before the modified word: *always-loving parent*; *seldom-comprehensive report*; *never-forgivable sin.* My not hyphenating compounds with *too*, *very*, and *almost* is in line with standard prescriptions in handbooks of punctuation. My hyphenating of compounds with *always*, *never*, and *seldom* is in agreement with some handbooks, disagreement with others; hyphenation cannot be codified completely.

When an adverb + participle compound follows the modified word, the hyphen is often not used, because the word order alone makes it impossible or at least highly unlikely that the adverb will be misread as an adjective: *A baby ill clothed is a distressing sight*; *The child was better dressed than most*. However, as pointed out above, some compounds are so common that they occur in dictionaries as permanently hyphenated compounds, such as *well-bred*; these compounds tend to look odd without the hyphen and should therefore retain it even when they follow the modified word.

Some adverb + participle combinations can be momentarily confusing even after the modified word unless they retain the hyphen: *Some executives are hard-driving because their neuroses are deep-seated*. *Hard* and *deep* are genuine adverbs in the example, as they are in *He played hard and swam deep*, but are too easily misread as adjectives if the hyphen is omitted. *Well*, *ill*, and a few other adverbs are so commonly found in compounds after the modified word that they are unlikely to be confusing, and so the hyphen should usually be omitted, but I recommend retaining the hyphen in any doubtful case.

2-34   Hyphenate compounds formed with adjective + participle or noun + participle, except compounds that have already become one word.

A high-powered executive may be soft-shelled. An adjective + participle compound should be hyphenated whether or not it occurs before the word it modifies. Note that *powered* and *shelled* are somewhat unusual participles; they are really just nouns with *ed* added to make them look like participles. That is why the compounds are formed with adjectives rather than with the adverbs *highly* and *softly*—the compounds are based on the phrases *high power* and *soft shell*, which are nouns modified by adjectives. Other such compounds are *able-bodied* and *blue-eyed*. Some adjective + participle compounds are formed with genuine participles, as in *dark-painted house* and *lazy-seeming man*, but usually the participle is artificial, based on a noun rather than a verb.

Is that heart-stopping freckle-faced girl the tot, mischief-loving and dimple-cheeked, who used to live next door? The noun + participle combinations should be hyphenated, both before and after the words they modify. Again, some of the participles are fuzzy; neither *cheeked* nor *faced* is formed from a true verb (though both *cheek* and *face* can be verbs with meanings quite different from those intended here)—they are both nouns with an artificial participial ending.

Some handbooks advise not hyphenating adjective + participle and noun + participle compounds unless there is a real possibility of confusion; some say specifically not to hyphenate such compounds when they occur after the modified word, since confusion is unlikely then. However, this leaves it up to the writer to foresee every possible misreading—and almost all writers find it difficult to see their own ambiguities, since they themselves know what they mean. I advise using the hyphen; even when it is not really necessary to prevent misreading, it helps show the relationship of words within the sentence and is thus a service to the reader. In addition, the hyphen is usually "heard" in these combinations—the words are run together—so one might as well indicate the close connection.

One-word compounds

Many adjective + participle and noun + participle combinations are so common that they have become one word, such as *kindhearted* and *towheaded*. Some noun + participle combinations are one word because they are participial forms of compound nouns or compound verbs that have become one word, such as *watchmaking* and *brainwashing* (these compounds usually can function as gerunds—that is, *ing* or *ed* forms of verbs that are used as nouns). Such compounds are not wrong with the hyphen, and some dic-

tionaries have them hyphenated, but those who want to follow the practice of a specific dictionary will look them up.
The more common a compound is, the more likely it is that it
has become one word.

2-35 Hyphenate adjectival compounds formed with participle + adjective, participle + adverb, noun + adjective, and adjective + adjective when they occur before the word they modify, and in some cases when they occur after.

Burning-hot soup is a participle + adjective combination.
The hyphen is unnecessary if the modifier follows the
modified word: *The soup was burning hot.*

Stirred-up soup is a participle + adverb combination. *The
soup was stirred up* requires no hyphen, because *stirred up*
can be taken as merely a verb + adverbial preposition (see
Rule 2-37), but when such a compound must be adjectival, it
should be hyphenated even after the word it modifies: *The
soup, hot and stirred-up, scented the kitchen.*

Ice-cold soup is a noun + adjective combination. *The
soup was ice cold* is permissible, but often it is better to
retain the hyphen when the noun + adjective modifier follows the word it modifies. A hyphen is usually clearly heard
in speech with noun + adjective combinations—that is, the
compound is run together. I routinely hyphenate them
whether they occur before or after the modified word: *He
was razor-sharp*; *He was girl-crazy.* I advise using the
hyphen, though many handbooks do consider it dispensable
when the compound follows the modified word.

Dark-blue soup is an adjective + adjective combination.
The soup was dark blue. Adjective + adjective combinations seem usually to involve color, sometimes more than
one color: *bluish-green soup.* Many handbooks advise not
using the hyphen with compounds involving color on the
ground that misunderstandings are highly unlikely. How-

ever, ambiguities can occur: *You take the light brown suit-case and I'll take the heavy one.*

2-36   Hyphenate adjectival compounds formed with adjective + noun and noun + noun.

Note that the rule includes the word *adjectival*. When these compounds are not used as adjectives, they should not be hyphenated.

A *hard-science teacher* (adjective + noun used as modifier) is one who teaches one of the hard sciences—that is, a science such as physics rather than one such as sociology. A *hard science teacher* is, or at least is apt to be understood as, one who is hard on his students; *hard* modifies *teacher*, not *science*. The hyphen makes the distinction; if we don't use it, we can't avoid ambiguity.

A *teacher-shortage problem* (noun + noun used as modifier) means a problem caused by a shortage of teachers. A *teacher shortage problem* could mean a number of things—perhaps in a snack bar shared by faculty and students the teachers are granted credit but are not paying their tabs, and so there is a shortage problem caused by teachers. Probably, of course, it does mean *a teacher-shortage problem*, but only the hyphen can make this meaning unmistakable.

Note that ordinary compounds of adjective + noun and noun + noun are not hyphenated when they are not adjectives: *He taught the hard sciences*; *The school suffered a teacher shortage*. Some noun + noun compounds, however, are hyphenated to show that the nouns are of equal value: *city-state*, *soldier-statesman*, and so on. The first noun does not modify the other so much as combine with it to make a new word with the meanings of both original words. The commonest such compounds are in the dictionary; the same principle should be applied to many compounds a writer invents for a specific use, such as *poet-thief*. Often, however, the meaning is adequately clear without hyphenating, as in *gentleman thief*, in which the hyphen is optional.

The helpless hyphen: clumped compound modifiers

It was decided to postpone the hard science replacement teacher shortage problem discussion. We could hyphenate the six-part modifier. In fact, we could hyphenate it in several different ways, which is why it is not worth hyphenating; hyphens can't really cope with the relationships among the words in the modifier, and the reader will have to figure it out without help.

Many fields of study or interest—education is a good example—have vocabularies that abound in noun clumps of two, three, four, or more words that are not customarily hyphenated in the literature within their field. Thus *slow student techniques* and *teacher training requirements*, though at least the first might be ambiguous to someone not in the field of education, would not be apt to be hyphenated within the field. Then one clump is used to modify the other: *Slow student techniques teacher training requirements should not be relaxed this year.*

This clumping of modifiers, which is discussed as a fault of composition in Rule 4-11, is perhaps more responsible than any other single fault of diction for the difficulty laymen have with works on education, sociology, politics, philosophy, and other wordy fields. The writer, who is presumably familiar with the parlance of his field, or else a strict editor who knows as much about the field as the writer should protect the reader from clots of multipart modifiers by rephrasing and recasting. Certainly nouns can modify nouns; the construction helps make English as powerful and flexible as it is. But a writer who is addressing laymen should not let his words coagulate into clumped compounds.

Exceptions

There are, of course, some compounds that are so common as nouns that hyphens are hardly necessary when they are used as adjectives: *science fiction*, *grammar school*, and so on. Yet even the most familiar compounds can be ambiguous in the right—that is, wrong—context: *a public school meeting* could be either a school meeting that is public or a meeting about public schools, and in a carelessly written newspaper account the ambiguity may be real, not just momentary. Nevertheless, it is wise to omit the hyphen from familiar compounds when all it will do is puzzle readers who, though they can be expected to respond properly to helpful uses of the hyphen, don't know the rules governing hyphens and have no interest in seeing those rules followed with rigorous elegance: *Science fiction has greatly changed since the days of early science-fiction writers Jules Verne and H. G. Wells* should omit the hyphen, since few readers will understand that the compound is first a noun and then an adjective but many may be bothered by the apparent inconsistency. Each writer must decide for himself what adjective + noun and noun + noun compounds he must hyphenate when they are used as adjectives and what ones he shouldn't hyphenate to avoid puzzling his readers.

Phrases of two or more words that denote animals or plants and are used as adjectives should not normally be hyphenated: *Douglas fir forest*; *great horned owl scat*. Many such phrases, however, have hyphens even as nouns— *adder's-tongue*, for example—and retain the hyphen when they are used as adjectives.

Especially within a specific field, phrases that are the essential vocabulary of the field may not need hyphenating when used as adjectives. Thus in chemistry, *a sodium-sulfide solution* has an unnecessary hyphen; like *a science-fiction writer* it would just puzzle most readers. In a work not for chemists but laymen, an incidental use of *sodium sulfide* as an adjective may benefit from the hyphen, however.

2-37   Hyphenate adjectival compounds that are prepositional phrases or are formed with participle + prepositional phrase when the compounds occur before the word they modify but not normally when they occur after the word they modify.

Prepositional phrases

An off-the-wall report modifies *report* with the prepositional phrase *off the wall*. *An in-the-bag situation* modifies *situation* with the prepositional phrase *in the bag*. These are standard uses of the hyphen when prepositional phrases are used as adjectives and precede the word they modify.

The out-of-order motion came from the floor and *The from-the-floor motion was out of order* illustrate the difference between a prepositional phrase used as an adjective before the modified word, one used as a standard adverbial modifier, and one used as an adjective after the modified word. In the first sentence, *from the floor* modifies the verb *came*. In the second sentence, *out of order* is an adjectival phrase linked to the noun *motion* by the verb *was*. These phrases are not hyphenated. But when the phrases act as adjectives preceding the modified noun, *motion*, they are hyphenated.

The man in the gray suit contains the prepositional phrase *in the gray suit*. Similarly, *the man with the small child* contains the prepositional phrase *with the small child*. The phrases follow the word they modify—*man*—and so no hyphens are used.

Participle + prepositional phrase

A worked-out problem does not actually include a participle + preposition modifier, because prepositions—*out*, *in*, *under*, *by*, *from*, and so on—are actually adverbs when they modify the meaning of a verb and do not have an object (in *Come in the house*, the words *the house* are the object of the preposition *in*). Thus *a worked-out problem* really has a participle + adverb modifier, and the reason for the hyphen is covered in Rule 2-35.

When we have a participle + prepositional phrase, however, the situation is a little different. In *a bounced-off-the-wall preliminary report*, *off* is a true preposition, part of the prepositional phrase *off the wall*. The hyphen should occur between *bounced* and *off*. The other hyphens are there because the prepositional phrase *off the wall* is being used as an adverbial modifier, modifying the participle *bounced*, and is combining with *bounced* to form the adjectival modifier *bounced-off-the-wall*; the hyphens connect the four words to show that they form a single modifier.

The problem was worked out contains no hyphen not because the prepositional phrase follows the noun but because there is no prepositional phrase at all—*was worked out* is just a verb (not a participle but a true verb, in the passive voice) with the adverbial modifier *out*.

The problem was off the wall, however, does have a prepositional phrase, *off the wall*, acting as an adjective modifying *problem*, to which it is connected by the linking verb *was*. It is not hyphenated, because in its sentence it follows the word it modifies. (Some prepositional phrases, such as *out-of-date*, are so common that they are given, with hyphens, in dictionaries, and it cannot be considered an error to leave the hyphens in when such a phrase follows the modified word: *By the time it was passed, the law was out-of-date*. Usually it is nevertheless better to omit the hyphens.)

A serious error: hyphenating verb + adverbial preposition

We hammered-out a compromise and *O'Neill tried to shoo-in the bill* are errors committed by those who know that sometimes *hammered out* and *shoo in* are hyphenated—*the hammered-out bill*; *The bill was a shoo-in*—but don't know what hyphens do. It is a very common error, and shows the depths to which the hyphen has fallen; the schools have given up trying to teach its proper use because the teachers don't know what that is, and publishers have given up because their editors don't know either.

If some of those who use this book choose to use hyphens less frequently than I advise, they are merely following a path of least resistance well trod by both well-educated and uneducated writers. But I hope the discussion in this and the preceding rules will at least preserve them from *We worked-out a compromise* and similar near-illiterate misuses.

There are occasions when the same phrase can be either hyphenated or not, depending on the meaning. *The cabin's floor was pine and the bunks were built-in* means the cabin had a pine floor and built-in bunks. *The cabin's pine floor was laid and the bunks were built in* means someone laid the floor and the same person or someone else built the bunks in. Omitting the hyphen in the first sentence may just be from the common fear of hyphens and reluctance to use them.

Supplying a hyphen in the second sentence can only be a sign of ignorance.

2-38   Use the hyphen properly—or in some cases don't use it at all—in the miscellaneous situations discussed below.

Phrases with numbers

A ten-year-old girl; a ten-year-old; The girl was ten years old. Not *a ten-year old girl* or *a ten-year old* or *The girl was ten-years-old*.

A five-dollar bill (or *a $5 bill*); *the bill was five dollars*. Not *a five dollar bill* (or *a $5-bill*) or *the bill was five-dollars*.

An eighteenth-century (or *18th-century*) *philosopher; a philosopher of the eighteenth century*. Not *an eighteenth century philosopher* or *a philosopher of the eighteenth-century*.

Ranges of numbers

The hyphen can be used to indicate a range of numbers: *The children were 12-14 years old* is acceptable, as a kind of shorthand, for *The children were from 12 to 14 years old*. However, if the first word of a phrase pair such as *from . . . to* or *between . . . and* is given, the hyphen should not be used as a substitute for the second word of the pair: *They were between 12-14 years old* and *They were from 12-14 years old* are incorrect. Similarly, *in the years 1941-1945* is correct, but *in the years from 1941-1945* is incorrect. *In 1941-1945* is generally accepted but is really excessively compact for most written work; *in the years 1941 to 1945* is better.

Compounds that must be separated and recompounded

Schoolboy is a noun + noun compound found in almost all dictionaries as one word. *A private schoolboy* is, or seems to be, a shy boy who goes to an unspecified kind of school. It could be *private school boy*, separating *school* from the compound, or, better, *private-school boy*, forming a new hyphenated compound and making the meaning unambiguous—*private* modifies *school*, not *boy*. Similar examples are *aircraft*, *heavier-than-air craft*; *taxpayer*, *excise-tax payer*.

Professional and businessmen requires separation without recompounding: *professional and business men*. It could also be *professional men and businessmen*, but this has the disadvantage of an extra word and seems somewhat tedious.

Adjectival compounds with capitalized words

A French Canadian canoe means a canoe from French Canada. *A Spanish American revolution* means a revolution in Spanish America. But *the Spanish-American War* means a war between Spain and America, not just a war that happened in Spanish America; it requires the hyphen. Similarly, *an Italian-American family* requires the hyphen.

Except for such combinations of nations and nationalities, proper nouns—that is, capitalized ones—and adjectives formed from them normally do not require hyphens when they are used as adjectives, because their capitalization makes it clear that they are a unit: *a Department of Defense spokesman, a Wall Street firm, a North Atlantic Treaty Organization general meeting.*

This dropping of hyphens sometimes carries over to book and article titles and similar capitalized phrases, where it is not justifiable; an article title such as "Factors Relating to the Eighteenth Century Drop Off of Currency Control Regulation in Long Occupied Countries" breaks several rules, and the capitalization, which exists only because it is conventional to capitalize main words in titles and not because there are any proper nouns, does not help untangle the relationship of the words to one another.

Suspended compounds

I bought ten- and twenty-year bonds shows the standard form for a suspended compound, with a space after the suspended hyphen. Suspended compounds can get too complicated: *The article attacks the myth of the kitchen-, church-, and children-oriented woman and the fame-, achievement-, and money-oriented man* is correctly punctuated but would be much smoother if rewritten to avoid the compounds.

Foreign phrases

It has to be a something-for-something deal hyphenates the modifying phrase, *something for something*, but *It has to be a quid pro quo deal* does not. This holds true whether or not the writer chooses to italicize *quid pro quo* (see Rule 3-23). The foreignness of the phrase is assumed to be enough to set it off as a unit. However, there are times when foreign phrases can be momentarily misread: *I don't believe in absentia voting should be permitted* is confusing because *believe in* is such a common combination. The confusion should be watched for when foreign phrases are used; this one could be eliminated by inserting *that* after *believe* or, of course, by italicizing the foreign phrase (underlining it on the typewriter).

Time of day

It was twelve-thirty; *It was twelve thirty-five*. When a time is rounded to the nearest ten-minute interval, a hyphen joins the hour and minute designations. When the minute designation has a hyphen itself, the hyphen between the hour designation and minute designation is dropped.

3

HOW TO STYLE WRITTEN ENGLISH: MISCELLANEOUS MECHANICS

By using *style* as an infinitive rather than as a noun in the title of Chapter 3, I hope to make it clear at once that in this book the word does not have its usual broad meaning—the way an individual writer or speaker combines diction and manner to express himself.

To professional writers and to editors, the noun *style* means how such elements as numbers are treated (that is, whether in figures or spelled out) and how mechanics of English such as capitalization and italics are used in a specific piece of writing or when writing for a specific publication. The word can be used as a verb, as in *The editor styled the manuscript*, or as an adjective, as in *The manuscript contained style inconsistencies*. Sometimes the term includes matters covered in Chapter 2, such as whether a comma is used before a conjunction in a series of three or more items (see Rule 2-6).

Style is basically a matter of consistency. Poor style can make writing that is otherwise acceptable look shabby and amateurish:

The Company's[1] performance was judged relative to that of its major competitors, the Fulsome company, Flabbergast Inc., and Farfetch Company International Incorporated.[2] Our chairman of the board, Mister Shaw,[3] obtained figures for these companies with the help of a private Cybernetics[4] consultant who asked to remain unnamed in this Report.[5] Our Secretary-Treasurer,[6] Mr. Sleet, with the help of his Mother,[7] Mrs. Vedanta Sleet,[8] well-known as a Necromancer,[9] adjusted the raw data by means of a formula too complicated to explain in this stockholders' report. The results, shown in table three and Chart 2,[10] can be quickly summarized. Over the past twelve months (figures for the past 3 months are estimates) the company increased its gross net by eight and a half percent, while corresponding figures for Fulsome, Flabbergast, and Farfetch range from 2-6%.[11]

[1] It is common for *company* to be capitalized when a company refers to itself in a publication such as a stockholders' report, though the capitalization is undesirable in most other contexts (see Rules 3-12 and 3-13). However, if it is capitalized here, it should be capitalized in the last sentence in the passage as well.

[2] The treatment of the three named companies is inconsistent, ranging from informal to abbreviated to formal.

[3] *Mister* should almost always be abbreviated unless it stands alone as a form of address, and in any case it is abbreviated in the next sentence, so the style is inconsistent.

[4] Capitalizing *cybernetics*, a field of science and technology, would be correct only if it meant a specific department of a school or unit of an organization's staff (see Rule 3-12).

[5] The word *report*, like *company*, could be capitalized when a report refers to itself, but if it is, *stockholders' report* in the next sentence should certainly be capitalized too.

[6] In a company's report, the title *Secretary-Treasurer* can be capitalized, though it usually shouldn't be elsewhere (see Rule 3-14). But if it is, surely the superior title *chairman of the board* in the preceding sentence should be capitalized.

[7] Kinship titles such as *mother* are often capitalized in direct address, but shouldn't be capitalized in this context (see Rule 3-16).

[8] *Mrs. Vedanta Sleet* would have been considered unacceptable a generation ago—*Mrs.* should be used only with the husband's given

name, not with the wife's—but this usage is now quite common, especially for divorced women who have retained their married surnames. Nevertheless, the usage still seems inelegant to many. Just *Vedanta Sleet* would be preferable here—if she is well-known, it is probably as Vedanta Sleet, not Mrs. Vedanta Sleet.

[9] *Necromancer* should not be capitalized (see Rule 3-12).

[10] Charts and tables should be referred to in some consistent way, such as *Table 3 and Chart 2*.

[11] There are several inconsistencies in treatment of numbers in this sentence (see Rule 3-1, especially the exceptions, and Rule 3-7), and the writer should decide between *percent* and %.

Good style is usually unnoticed by the reader, which is as it should be—it is only when style is inconsistent, unusual, or convention-flouting that it is noticed. Good style makes writing easy to absorb; it doesn't call attention to itself but unobtrusively serves the interests of the writer's meaning and the reader's comprehension.

Style is less a matter of right and wrong than a matter of good judgment and poor judgment. A styling may be poor because it is needlessly unconventional, such as spelling out a year (*nineteen hundred and eighty-two*), or because it is inappropriate for a given kind of writing, such as using figures for all numbers in a novel full of dialogue (*"I want to be number 1," he said*). Therefore, there are many styles. Books on etiquette and manuals for secretaries prescribe quite different styles for correspondence. Large newspapers have their own stylebooks (smaller newspapers are apt to use *The Associated Press Stylebook and Libel Manual*). Most book publishers use *A Manual of Style* (University of Chicago Press) or *Words into Type* (Prentice-Hall), and some have supplementary stylesheets of their own. Most magazines have a so-called house style so that stories or articles by different writers in the same issue will not have conspicuously different styles. Technical journals have quite elaborate style manuals that may be accepted as the preferred style not just for a given journal but for all writing within a given technical field.

The rules given in this chapter are intended to assist those writing on general subjects. Not all of them are in complete agreement with any other guide; they do reflect the prescriptions of a number of guides as well as my own experience in styling many hundreds of books. They do not cover all the style problems a writer may encounter—only the most common ones—but they do show what considerations are brought to bear when making style decisions, and thus they can serve as a model for decisions a writer with unusual style problems has to make for himself. They are full of qualifications and exceptions, because I have tried to foresee the problems writers inevitably encounter when they try to follow generalized rules in specific situations. Anyone who uses this chapter as a guide and finds a rule in it he doesn't like is probably right to break it—as long as he keeps to a consistent style of his own and as long as his judgment is good.

NUMBERS

Numbers are very commonly mishandled. Numbers style can vary a great deal, but except in special circumstances it should not vary within a given written work, whether the work is a single sentence, a paragraph, an article, a book, or a multivolume encyclopedia.

3-1   When numbers occur infrequently, spell out numbers from 1 to 100 and round numbers beyond 100, except for certain exceptions noted below.

This is the basic rule for general writing. Editors of newspapers and many magazines and journals are more likely to spell out numbers only from 1 to 9 and use figures for all the rest, both to save space and because in a publication that includes a variety of items it is better to force figures on items that don't contain many numbers than to force spelled-out numbers on items that do contain many. Writers in any field that relies heavily on numerical information may use figures for all such enumeration, even between 1 and 9.

A round number can be considered one that can be spelled out in no more than two words: *two hundred*; *fifty million*; but *110*, since spelling out *110* would require several words:

one hundred and ten. One has to decide whether to consider hyphenated numbers one word or two—*2,500* or *twenty-five hundred*—and the decision will depend on which style is less conspicuous.

Very large numbers are often expressed with a combination of figures and a spelled-out word: *20 million people*; *$168 billion*. Decimals can be used: *2.5 billion*; *$3.2 billion*. This style is convenient, compact, and easy to read.

Exceptions

Year dates, days of the month, page numbers, street address numbers and sometimes the numbers of streets themselves, route numbers, percentages, and similar familiar uses of numbers are exceptions to the rule. In dialogue, numbers are usually spelled out for some of these uses too; the writer has to decide which to spell out and which to leave as figures. For example, *John said, "It was in June 1980—the twentieth or twenty-first, I think"* uses figures for the year but spells out the days of the month, which is a reasonable compromise.

A written work may include precise and frequent enumerations for some categories of things but only occasional enumerations of other categories of things. For example, an article on building birdhouses would probably contain precise numbers for measurements in inches of birdhouse designs, less precise numbers for some other units of measurement, and various miscellaneous numbers. The writer may decide to use figures for all units of physical measurement: *When we inspected the martin house thirty days later—from about 20 feet away through binoculars—we estimated a population of ninety-eight birds, all in a volume of 1½ cubic feet (12 inches wide, 12 inches long, and 18 inches high). A farmer 4 miles away complained that the martins had deserted their former nests on his 80 acres of scrub woodland.* Or he may not like having to use figures for imprecise and incidental enumerations such as *about 20 feet*, *4 miles*, and *80 acres*, and so he may decide to use figures only for birdhouse dimensions and otherwise follow Rule 3-1.

When numbers both below 100 and above 100 are used close together to enumerate the same things or very similar things, the numbers should either all be in figures or all be spelled out: *There were 70 women and 108 men at the meeting*. Usually it is better to make all the numbers figures rather than spell them all out. This principle applies always within the same sentence, usually within the same paragraph, and often within a passage of several paragraphs dealing with the same subject. However, the principle should not be followed blindly: *We have 3 children—1 boy and 2 girls—which would seem laughable to my great-grandmother, who had 13 children of her own and a total of 134 great-grandchildren when she died* lets *134 great-grandchildren* force all the other numbers to be figures, which is poor judgment. It would be better either to spell out *134* or to let it remain a figure but spell out all the other numbers; the inconsistency is the lesser annoyance.

With Rule 3-1 as a basis, the writer can make a list of exceptions that will tailor his numbers style to what he is writing. He should try to avoid too complex a style; the simpler the style, the easier it will be to follow and the less obvious it will be to the reader. It is better to have a simple style and violate it for occasional exceptional reasons than to have a complex style that allows for all special circumstances but puzzles the reader throughout.

3-2   Spell out numbers that begin a sentence, except for years.

One hundred and twelve people attended this year, compared with 128 last year and 142 the year before. This does violate the principle of treating similar enumerations the same way (see exceptions to Rule 3-1), but the spelled-out number beginning the sentence should not be allowed to force every following number to be spelled out. Usually it is easy to avoid the problem by recasting: *This year, 112 people attended . . .*

1980 was the last year of his term. Figures denoting years can begin a sentence. Even *'80 was a good year for Chardonnay* is permissible, though it would be better not to abbreviate the year.

The conclusion was obvious: 121 members of the state

legislature were foul-mouthed begins a sentence, or at least an independent clause following a colon, with a figure, but the colon permits it; the figure does not annoy the eye the way it would if it began a truly independent sentence.

3-3   Use figures for numbers accompanied by abbreviations.

Abbreviations used with numbers usually are for units of measurement: *lb.*, *in.*, *mm*, *mph*, *hrs.*, *rpm*, and so on. Writing that contains such abbreviations is very likely to make heavy use of numbers anyway, and thus to require some special style rules in addition to Rule 3-1; perhaps the rule can be a simple one, such as to use figures for all units of measurement, or perhaps it has to be more complicated.

Exception

Occasionally an abbreviation is spoken—that is, used in dialogue. However, usually it is better to avoid figures in dialogue (Rule 3-4). Therefore, when an abbreviation is spoken, Rule 3-3 is not followed: *"It begins to knock at about four thousand rpm," he said*; *"Give her ten cc's now and ten more in an hour," the doctor said.*

3-4   Spell out numbers in dialogue unless they are excessively awkward.

"You owe me one hundred and fifty-five dollars," he said is preferable to *"You owe me $155," he said.* Numbers, and also the dollar sign and percent sign, somehow do not look right in dialogue, although we do accept them in quotations in newspaper accounts; newspapers do not follow Rule 3-4.

"The materials were $122.36, the labor comes to $88.50 plus $43 for overtime, and payoffs were $1,250 to the city and $10 for the doorman, giving us a grand total of $1,413.86," he said would be very tedious if all the sums were spelled out. They could be spelled out if the writer

wants to stretch them out for effect, but they are easier to absorb as figures and most readers would be much less put off by the figures than they would be by *one hundred and twenty-two dollars and thirty-six cents*.

Exception

The only general exception is years—they are always in figures in dialogue unless the writer wants them said in an unusual way: *"It was in nineteen-ought-six," he said, "and long before anyone foresaw the ruckus that came in nineteen and fourteen."* Depending on the requirements of what he is writing, a writer can decide to make any exceptions he chooses. *"We're expecting the probe to be closest to Titan at exactly 2236 hours"* and *"Don't use this stimulant if the temperature is below 96.5 or above 101.5"* could both spell out the numbers without excessive awkwardness, but if military time occurs constantly in the context of the first example and body temperature occurs constantly in that of the second, a writer may justifiably decide to use figures.

3-5   Always spell out time of day with o'clock and phrases such as *in the morning*; in general, use figures with A.M. and P.M.

The meeting was held at eight o'clock; *The meeting was held at 8:00 A.M.* Some stylebooks recommend *8 A.M.* for on-the-hour times; either is permissible, but *8:00 A.M.* is preferable if there are nearby times that are not on the hour: *The meeting was scheduled for 8:00 A.M. but didn't get started till nearly 8:30.* Since a writer may not be able to tell in advance whether times on the hour and not on the hour will be close together, he might as well always make it *8:00* and be assured what he's writing will be consistent throughout in this respect.

"Be here at eight A.M. sharp," he said is all right; see the exception to Rule 3-3.

When neither o'*clock* nor A.M. or P.M. occur with the time

Most books, stories, articles, and other written works have a natural leaning toward either figures or spelled-out numbers for specific uses, such as for time of day. The direction of the leaning isn't always determined by the type of writing—a disaster novel that employs minute-by-minute fictitious reportage to heighten dramatic effect will probably require figures for times of day, and a scientific treatise in which time of day is mentioned only incidentally—the time when the guinea pigs were customarily fed, the times the dedicated researchers arrived in the morning and went home at night—may be better off with spelled-out numbers for times of day: *On the morning of the critical experiment, Dr. Smith arrived at seven-thirty and had scalpel in hand by seven thirty-five.* (Note the use of the hyphens; *seven-thirty-five* is also acceptable but is slightly harder for the reader to make immediate sense of. See Rule 2-38.)

If *A.M.* and *P.M.* occur frequently with times in a given work, the writer might as well use figures for all times and make sure *o'clock* and *in the morning* and similar phrases don't occur directly following a time of day; times should still ordinarily be spelled in any dialogue, however. If *A.M.* and *P.M.* occur infrequently or not at all and there are frequent times in dialogue, the writer may choose to spell out times without *A.M.* and *P.M.* and perhaps even to eliminate these abbreviations in favor of *in the morning* and *in the evening*, so all the times of day can be spelled out.

3-6   Don't normally use the apostrophe to form the plural of a number in figures.

The 1890's is an unnecessary use of the apostrophe; the plural number is just as clear without it: *the 1890s*. The apostrophe with the plural is necessary in a few situations—for example, to form the plural of lowercase letters, as in *p's and q's*—but not to form the plural of numbers.

Plurals of numbers usually can follow Rule 3-1—that is,

numbers to 100 and round numbers beyond 100 can be spelled out: *He was in his fifties; He started counting heads but gave up somewhere in the two hundreds.* Sometimes plurals of numbers have to be spelled out, even in work that uses figures whenever possible: *One bacillus dividing under optimum conditions can number in the thousands in a matter of hours.* We cannot say *in the 1,000s*, which would be read *in the one thousands.*

3-7   In an inclusive range of numbers, don't use the hyphen when the word *to* or *and* is called for, and adopt a style to handle the second element consistently.

The range was from 2-6% is poor style; it should be *from 2 to 6 percent* or *from 2% to 6%*, depending on whether the writer has chosen to spell the word *percent* or use the symbol. Since the symbol is so short, if it is used there is no reason to drop it after the first number; it makes the range a little clearer. The *to* is required to go with *from. The range was 2-6%*, dropping the *from*, is all right, especially in writing in which many percentages occur and the reader must be expected to understand compact ways of giving them.

Inclusive dates within the same century can be in the form *1922-1925* or *1922-25*; they should be treated consistently. Page numbers can be in the form *122-125* or *122-25*; some publications use the shortest possible form, *122-5*, except in the teens—*114-17*—because it would be peculiar to say *114-7*. Again, *from 1922-25* and *from pages 122-25* are wrong. When *from* does not introduce the inclusive numbers, the hyphen is correct: *He was headmaster, 1922-25.* It is frequently seen with *in*: *He was headmaster in 1922-25.* This seems to be accepted by most publications, but in principle is not correct; *in* should be used only for a specific single year, single decade, single century, and so on.

DATES

Dates are simple, straightforward items of information, but

enough different ways of expressing them exist to make inconsistent or inappropriate style very common.

3-8 With dates including month, day, and year, use commas to set off the year; with just the month and year, don't use commas.

The September 15 payment is due; *The September 15, 1982, payment is due*. When the year is given, it is treated as a parenthetical element (see Rule 2-1) and enclosed in commas. *The September 15, 1982 payment is due* is a common error.

The September 1982 payment is due does not require the parenthetical commas, because *1982* has more of a defining, restrictive function when only month and year are given than it does when all three elements are given. Nevertheless, it is permissible to make it *The September, 1982, payment is due*, and many publications do use this style. I advise dropping the commas just because they are unnecessary, and a sound general principle of punctuation is to avoid using it unnecessarily.

When the order of the three date elements follows the British and Continental practice—*15 September 1982*—there are no commas.

3-9 In general, use cardinal numbers for days of the month (*June 3*), not ordinal numbers (*June 3rd, June third*), except in dialogue.

We are much more likely to use ordinal numbers for days of the month in speech—*"We're going to Florida on December twenty-third," she said*—though occasionally we do use cardinal numbers. In writing that is not dialogue, however, the convention is to use cardinal numbers, except in wedding invitations and similar special material. *The school will open for registration on September 10th, 1981* has an amateurish look.

Exceptions

Certain holidays are customarily expressed with ordinal numbers, which are spelled out and capitalized: *July Fourth*; *the Fourth of July*.

When the month does not occur in the expression of a date, an ordinal number must be used: *He was hired as a clerk on May 17, and on the 24th he was appointed to the board of directors.*

ABBREVIATIONS

Abbreviations, like other matters of style, should be handled consistently. If a somewhat unfamiliar abbreviation occurs throughout a passage, it is often a good idea to spell the term out the first time it is used, with the abbreviation following in parentheses, and then use the abbreviation thereafter: *The silicon chip measured a mere 4 square millimeters (mm²), later reduced to 2.5mm².*

Most dictionaries give proper forms for abbreviations. Everyone knows the most common ones—*Mr., Dr., oz.*—but not everyone knows that the abbreviation for *kilohertz* is *kH* and that for *megacycle* is *Mc*; we have to look them up. The United States may be in for a period of some confusion about abbreviations as the metric system takes over.

3-10   Don't use periods with most abbreviations made up entirely of initials; do use periods with most other abbreviations.

It is cumbersome and unnecessary to use periods in such abbreviations as *CIA* (name of an agency), *UAR* (name of a country), *ILGWU* (name of a union), *UNESCO* (name of an international organization—and pronounced as a word), *NW* (name of a compass point—and written out as a single word, *northwest*, except in Britain and sometimes in Canada), and so on. Periods should be avoided even with the initials of people, unless part of the name is spelled out: *JFK, J.F. Kennedy*; *Old GS was at the party, and Bill C. was there but Bill M. wasn't.*

There are a few initial-type abbreviations that do require periods. *U.S.* always has periods, to avoid momentary confusion with the word *us*, but *USA* rarely does. *U.K.* (United Kingdom) usually has periods, perhaps to avoid the infelicitous result of trying to pronounce the abbreviation as a word. The abbreviations of academic and professional degrees— *B.A.*, *D.D.S.*—always have periods; some of them, of course, are not made up entirely of initials: *Ph.D.*, *Litt.D.* Initial-type abbreviations of state names have periods— *N.Y.*, *R.I.*—but not when they are used with ZIP codes: *NY 10036*. The ZIP code style was established by the U.S. Postal Service.

Other abbreviations almost always have periods. *Saint* is abbreviated *St.*; *Mister* is abbreviated *Mr.*; *Lieutenant Commander* is abbreviated *Lt. Comdr.* Exceptions are mainly very common abbreviations for units of measure. The preferred forms are still *lb.*, *oz.*, *ft.*, and so on, but *lb*, *oz*, and *ft* are commonly seen and are accepted—unlike *in* for *inch* or *gal* for *gallon*, which can too easily be misunderstood. Periods are not used with metric abbreviations: *cc*, *mm*, *kg*, and so on.

Enough exceptions to Rule 3-10 exist to make a dictionary essential in doubtful cases, but the general principle of the rule should be sufficient for abbreviations not found in the dictionary.

3-11   If a comma occurs between a proper noun and an abbreviation, and the sentence continues, use a comma after the abbreviation as well.

Oliver Wendell Holmes, Sr. was a medical man is a punctuation error, because *Sr.* has to be handled as a parenthetical element (see Rule 2-1) and enclosed by commas. Similarly, *John Smith, Ph.D., LL.D. gave the address* is an error; there should be a comma after *LL.D.* This is the only case in which a period and a comma can occur together—though actually the little round mark is not a period at all. It may look like one, just as points of ellipsis look like three periods in a row, and a typesetter as well as the rest of us would call it one.

But in the strictest sense, a period is a full stop—the mark to show the end of a declarative sentence.

The parenthetical commas are somewhat cumbersome, and they are rarely heard in speech. In some contexts both commas can be omitted: *Holmes Sr. was a doctor, and Holmes Jr. was a jurist* is acceptable, though it might be better to spell out *Sr.* and *Jr.* in such a case. The commas cause special problems with *Jr.* and *Sr.* when the name is being used as a possessive: *Oliver Wendell Holmes, Jr.'s, father* is one of several alternatives, none completely satisfactory (see Rule 2-29 for more discussion of this).

The comma may not occur between the proper noun and the abbreviation: *the Macmillan Co.*; *Dynamic Learning Corp.* When the abbreviation is *Inc.* or *Ltd.*, the practice of the company itself should be followed; *National Notions Inc.* may have no comma in its official letterhead name, but *Regional Regimens, Inc.* may have the comma and thus require one after *Inc.* as well. (It does not have the second comma in the preceding sentence because I have italicized it to indicate that it is an example rather than a normal part of the grammar of my sentence. Similarly, *"The Noble Gerbil, Man's Most Prolific Friend" was the winning essay* does not have a comma following the appositive because the words in quotation marks are a title, not part of the grammar.)

GENERIC TERMS

Most of the rest of the rules in this chapter require, in one way or another, an understanding of what a generic term is and how it should be styled—capitalized or lowercased, in italic or roman type, and so on—when it occurs with or is substituting for a term that is not generic.

3-12   Learn to distinguish generic terms from proper nouns and adjectives formed from them.

A generic term is merely one that is not the name of a specific thing and not a trademarked name but instead the name of a general class of things. Thus *river* is a generic term, appropriate to refer to any river in the world. But *Mississippi River* is not a generic term; the term *river* has become part of a specific geographical designation and thus part of a proper noun phrase, and so it is capitalized.

Specific terms often become generic terms in time. Thus *sherry* is lowercased in most dictionaries, but in previous centuries was usually capitalized, presumably because it had not been forgotten that the term is a corrupted pronunciation of *Jerez*, the Spanish city the wine came from. One often sees *Burgundy* and *Bordeaux*, wines named for the regions in France that produce them, lowercased, especially in reference to wines of the same general type that are produced elsewhere; and *burgundy* meaning a color is almost always lowercased. There are many other examples. The word *utopia* is lowercased in most dictionaries even though it comes from Sir Thomas More's sixteenth-century book *Utopia*, about an imaginary country of that name. The word *Olympian*, used in reference either to the Olympic Games or to the ancient Roman gods, is capitalized, but *olympiad*, meaning the four-year interval between Olympic Games, is not. One needs a dictionary as well as common sense to determine whether a capitalized specific term has become a lowercased generic one.

Trademarked terms sometimes become generic terms— usually to the distress of those who own the trademark—and they can be special problems for the writer, because only the most common trademarks are found in dictionaries. The term *kleenex* is often used for any face tissue, though the manufacturers of Kleenex retain the trademark and attempt to protect it. The manufacturers of Coca-Cola used to send book, newspaper, and magazine publishers form letters of complaint whenever they found the registered trademark *Coke* lowercased. Many terms, such as *mimeograph* and *mason jar*, were once trademarks but have established themselves solidly as generic terms. Many others seem to be on their way; it is a surprise to most people to discover that they are actually trademarks: *Styrofoam*, *Formica*, *Lucite*, just to stick to the plastics industry. Some terms are generic sometimes and trademarks sometimes; a *jeep* is a military vehicle of the GP (general-purpose) type first used in World War II, and a *Jeep* is a somewhat similar nonmilitary vehicle sold under that trademark, as in *Jeep station wagon*.

The *Trade Names Directory* (Gale Research Company), available in many libraries, is a useful listing when it is important to style a term correctly. The United States Trademark Association, 6 East 45th Street, New York, NY 10017, will send anyone who asks for it a collection of useful stylesheets listing hundreds of trademarks. Common sense may be even more important than correctness in some cases. It always bothers me to see *Ping-Pong* and *Jell-O* in figurative contexts such as *The Ping-Pong of international diplomacy reduced the ambassador to Jell-O*—but the words are trademarks. When I find such a trademark lowercased in a book I am editing, I am apt to pretend I don't know it should be capitalized, though I can't conscientiously recommend such dishonesty to anyone else.

TITLES OF OFFICIALS AND NAMES OF THEIR OFFICES

Capitalization style for titles and offices varies somewhat from publisher to publisher and from stylebook to stylebook, and modifications of a given style must often be made for specific works. However, the following rules are a sound general style, and I have included instances of desirable modifications of the basic rules.

3-13   Capitalize formal titles of most specific offices and organizations, but in some cases distinguish between federal and state bodies, major and subordinate bodies, and so on.

Names of governmental and judicial bodies such as *Senate, House, Finance Committee, State Department, Supreme Court, Fourth Circuit Court of Appeals*, and *Juvenile Court* are usually capitalized when they refer to specific bodies. However, many such terms can be generic terms as well: *The country's legislature has no senate in the usual sense*; *The circuit-court system was changed considerably in 1912.*

Most of the states have governmental bodies with names identical to those of the corresponding federal bodies—the states have senates, houses of representatives, supreme courts, and so on. In a book dealing entirely with politics and history within a state, it would probably be appropriate to capitalize the names of state bodies. However, in a work dealing with regional or national politics and history, and also in works on general topics that make occasional mention of federal or state governmental bodies, it may be better to capitalize only the names of specific federal bodies: *The Arizona supreme court's decision was challenged unsuccessfully in the federal courts of appeal but was eventually reversed by the Supreme Court.*

Similarly, *Chamber of Commerce* should normally be capitalized to refer to the organization in a specific town, but in a work on the activities and functions of chambers of commerce throughout the country, it might be better to capitalize the term only when it refers to the central organization—the Chamber of Commerce of the United States, to which all local chambers of commerce belong—and to lowercase it elsewhere: *the Buffalo chamber of commerce.*

Some phrases are so strongly generic that they should not be capitalized standing alone even if they are the formal name or part of the formal name of a specific office, organization, or government body: *police department*; *criminal court*; *post office*; *customhouse.* However, some such terms may be capitalized when they refer to a specific building: *The town hall was an important institution in Brattleboro*, but *His office is in the Town Hall*; *He is a judge in the criminal court*, but *I'll meet you on the steps of Criminal Court.*

Ordinarily when the proper name of an organization is cut back to nothing but a generic term, it is lowercased: *the Department of Defense*; *the department.* There are a few common exceptions: *the House of Representatives*; *the House.* Often *the Court* is capitalized when it means the U.S. Supreme Court. It is also capitalized to mean the judge who is presiding in a given court: *If the Court pleases* means if the judge pleases, not if the courtroom or the court as a judicial institution pleases.

In the past decade or so, following a trend toward lowercasing, many newspapers and magazines have begun lowercasing some generic terms even when they are used with proper nouns or adjectives formed from proper nouns: *Democratic party*; *Republican national convention*. I prefer to consider such phrases unified proper nouns and to capitalize all the elements. However, the lowercasing is preferable to excessive and meaningless capitalizing, which begins to make English look like German: *We went to the Museum and then through the Park to the Conservatory*; *We stopped at the Bank on the way to the Beach*.

3-14   Don't capitalize titles of most officials unless the title occurs directly before a name, and sometimes not even then.

Titles such as *president*, *prime minister*, *king*, *senator*, *judge*, *governor*, *mayor*, *general*, *pope*, *archbishop*, *chairman*, and *professor* are all capitalized when they occur before a name—*President Reagan*, *Professor Waggoner*, and so on—but are all also generic terms, and there is no need to capitalize them when they stand alone.

Other titles are really not titles but simply descriptive terms: *clinical psychologist*; *head nurse*; *foreman*; *author*. The magazine *Time* adopted the eccentric style decades ago of capitalizing such terms—*Clinical Psychologist John Smith*—and the magazine has been around so long that the style now looks right to many people, but it's not. (*Time* was deliberately flouting convention to achieve a snappy, important look.) It should be *the clinical psychologist John Smith*; the word *the* can be dropped, though this tends to make sentences seem hurried and telegraphic.

Note that *Doctor of Laws*, *Knight of the Garter*, and similar phrases are not titles in the sense discussed in this rule; academic distinctions and noble orders should be capitalized.

Titles used in address

Phrases such as *Mr. President* and *Madam Chairman* (or, unhappily, *Chairperson*) are always capitalized, but there is no need to capitalize titles without *Mr.*, *Madam*, or similar introductory polite forms. However, see modification 4 below. Forms of address are discussed at greater length in Rule 3-15.

Modifications of Rule 3-14

There are many possible modifications of the basic lowercase style of Rule 3-14. Here are a few.

1. Capitalize titles of federal officials and their foreign equivalents; lowercase lesser officials. This is a common and sensible modification made by a great many writers and imposed by many editors, and it is quite easy to apply. *The President approached U.S. Steel through its president* is an apparent inconsistency, but readers are so used to the principle behind it that they do not notice it and are probably unconsciously aided by it. One does have to decide just where to draw the line—for example, secretaries of cabinet rank, members of the House and Senate, and Supreme Court justices might be capitalized, but not those below them in the federal hierarchy. Also, applying this style may result in anomalous indications of comparative importance: *The Congressman from Utah met with the governor of New York.*

2. Capitalize titles that are used throughout a work as a substitute for a person's name. This modification makes sense when a real person or fictitious character is referred to frequently as *the Judge* or *the Major* or *the Senator*. The titles become more nicknames than actual titles. The style runs into trouble when the Judge runs into another judge, the Major calls on a general, and the Senator gets a call from the president. Sometimes these problems can be avoided by using modification 3, below; sometimes it's better to return to the basic rule and not capitalize any titles.

3. Capitalize all titles when they refer to specific people. Thus a sentence could be styled *Major Smith found the usual collection of colonels and generals between him and the bar, and an admiral kept sloshing his drink on the Major's freshly pressed sleeve.* Again, it seems anomalous to capitalize the lesser rank and lowercase the others. Also, one has to decide just when a character or real person has been sufficiently

identified to deserve the capital. This is a difficult modification to apply successfully.

4. Capitalize all titles used in direct address. This is a common modification and generally works well. Since a word used in direct address has a special significance within a sentence, the reader generally will not notice the alternate capitalizing and lowercasing of the same terms: *"Tell me, Major," said the tipsy admiral as the major pointedly wrung out his cuff, "who told you you could play in this sandbox?"* However, there is usually no good reason for this capitalization, any more than there is for capitalizing *buddy*, *sir*, *young lady*, or any other term used in address as a substitute for a person's name.

5. Capitalize titles when they are used with the capitalized name of a political division, the name of a governmental body, or a similar term that completes the meaning of the title. This is often a sensible modification and is usually easy to apply: *the king, the King of England*; *the senator, the Senator from Maine*; *the chief justice, the Chief Justice of the Supreme Court*; *the archbishop, the Archbishop of York*; *the ambassador, the Ambassador to the Court of St. James's*. The completely lowercase style of Rule 3-14 may seem too extreme for a work in which titles are frequent and important, and then this modification is useful. Also, a work full of such titles as *the earl of Darlington*, used essentially as substitutes for names as in modification 2 above, may be better styled by modification 5: *the Earl of Darlington*; *the earl*.

6. Capitalize titles that would otherwise be ambiguous. This is a sensible modification on the face of it—it is always sensible to avoid ambiguity. Thus *O'Neill, the speaker of the House* could be unclear, especially to a young reader; even if *senator* and *president* are not capitalized, *Speaker of the House* often should be, and stylebooks that prescribe equivalents of Rule 3-14 often make this title an exception. Similarly, *General of the Army*, a specific rank above four-star general, would often be ambiguous if lowercased.

7. Capitalize all titles. This is going all the way to the opposite extreme and can result in a great many capitals. However, it may be a sensible style in a work for young readers or any others who can be assumed to be unfamiliar

with the titles mentioned; the capitals help the reader absorb the titles and learn them.

FORMS OF ADDRESS

Many forms of address are not titles in the sense that the terms discussed in Rule 3-14 are. The tendency is to capitalize too many of them or to capitalize them inconsistently.

3-15   Don't capitalize *doctor*, *madam* or *madame*, *sir*, *my lord*, and similar forms of address unless they occur directly before a name.

There is no reason to capitalize terms denoting professions or terms of polite respect when they occur alone as forms of address. When they are used to preface given names or surnames, they are considered part of the name and are capitalized: *Doctor Smith* (or usually *Dr. Smith*); *Madame Bovary*; *Sir Walter*; *My Lord Castlereagh* or *Lord Castlereagh*.

The same rule applies when the form of address is in a foreign language: *monsieur* or *m'sieu*, *signore*, *señor*, *effendi*, *tovarich*, and similar foreign words do not require capitalization. The German *mein Herr* is an exception; *Herr* is always capitalized, because all nouns are capitalized in German. Note that none of these quite common foreign terms require italics (underlines on the typewriter) if they are used within an English sentence; they are italicized here only because they are used as examples.

Exceptions

Some major stylebooks that advise lowercasing *my lord* and *his lordship* nevertheless capitalize *your honor*, *your grace*, *your highness*, *your eminence*, *your excellency*, and their third-person equivalents *his honor*, *his grace*, and so on. I pass this exception along, but I do not understand it and usually do not make it. These terms of respect are not different in principle from *sir*, *ma'am*, and other polite forms, and certainly not different from *my lord* and *my lady* (which are the correct forms for addressing marquesses, earls, viscounts, and barons and their wives; *your grace* is used for dukes and their wives and for Roman Catholic archbishops).

A form of address that is used frequently throughout a work as a substitute for a person's name may be better off capitalized as a kind of nickname (see Rule 3-14, modification 2): *It was now six in the evening, and Madame was well into the sherry.* Similarly, shortened versions of forms of address such as *Doc* and *Rev* can be considered nicknames and capitalized.

3-16   Capitalize *mother*, *grandma*, and other kinship terms for preceding generations when they are used in direct address, but don't capitalize *brother*, *son*, and other terms for the same or succeeding generations.

When his mother and his son appeared, he greeted them, "Look, Mother, I've bought a new motorcycle—hop on the back, son." The first time *mother* occurs in the example, it is as an ordinary generic noun; the second time it occurs it functions as a name and is treated as one. *Mama, Mommy, Maw,* and similar terms follow the same rule: *"Where's your mommy?" "There's Mommy."* The word *son*, however, is not capitalized, because it is no more a proper name than *buddy* or *miss*. A person would normally address a brother or sister, a son or daughter, or a nephew or niece by his or her given name; the use of the kinship term as an alternative to the name does not make it a substitute for a name in the same way *Mother* is.

Uncle and *aunt* are often lowercased in address when they stand alone, though they are capitalized just about as often. Since they usually occur with a given name—*Uncle John*, Aunt Mary—they are not quite as much substitutes for names as *Mother* is.

Some stylebooks, including the University of Chicago Press's *A Manual of Style*, prescribe lowercasing all kinship terms except directly before a name, as in *Uncle Ed*; many others are in essential agreement with Rule 3-16.

When kinship terms occur with names

Rule 3-16 can be applied when kinship terms are used with names as well as when they are used alone: *Mother Hubbard, Grandma Moses*, and *Uncle Charley*; but *brother Bill, sister Mary*, and—though such a phrase would be rare—*nephew John*. However, *Cousin Pete* is better than *cousin Pete* if the combination is treated as a nickname: *Come here, Cousin Pete, and meet my cousin Jane*.

Kinship terms for priests, nuns, and friars and others who are not kin

In such forms as *Father William* or *Father Smith, Brother John*, and *Sister Elizabeth*, used either to address or to refer to a priest or member of a religious order, the kinship term is capitalized. When the terms are used without a given name or surname, usage varies. I prefer to lowercase the terms when they stand alone; they are then basically terms of respect, like *sir*, not substitutes for names.

Look out, dad—make way for the younger generation and *Excuse me, mother— I didn't mean to step on your goiter* are examples of kinship terms used rudely or politely to address older people who are not kin; I advise lowercasing them.

PLACE NAMES

The correct forms for geographical features and political divisions are listed in atlases and gazetteers, and the most common ones are in most dictionaries, either in an appendix or with the general vocabulary. Style problems may occur when these terms are made adjectives and when generic terms that are normally used with them are used alone or are used in the plural.

3-17 Capitalize names of specific political divisions and subdivisions and the names of geographical regions and features; in most cases, also capitalize adjectives derived from such names.

The names of countries, states, provinces, counties, cities, towns, and villages are obviously capitalized, though sometimes a decision has to be made about generic terms that may occur with such names. *New York City* is an official name and *Kansas City* is the only name; there is no question that *city* is capitalized in these examples. But *Washington state* and *Washington State* both occur, to distinguish the state from the District of Columbia; and *New York state* and *New York State* both occur, to distinguish the state from the city. A workable rule with *state* is to capitalize it when it follows the proper noun but not when it precedes: *the state of Washington*. Canadian provinces, however, have the official form *Province of Quebec, Province of Ontario*, and so on.

The names of continents, oceans, rivers, lakes, islands and island groups, mountains, canyons, and similar geographical features are also capitalized, but again there may be some style problems when there are accompanying generic terms.

Adjectives derived from place names are capitalized when the place is still an important part of the meaning: *Roman history, French literature, Brussels lace*. Many lose the capital when the place is no longer a significant part of the meaning: *roman numeral*; *french window*; *brussels sprouts*. Sometimes even the original nouns lose the capital: *morocco* (leather); *plaster of paris*; *china*. Check the dictionary when in doubt.

Generic terms used alone

Except for a few terms, such as *the States* for the United States, *the Union* for the United States or the Union of South Africa, *the Dominion* for Canada, and, when the term is clear in context, *the Channel* for the English Channel, generic words used without proper names for political divisions and geographical features are lowercased. Some capitalized terms, such as *the Coast* for the West Coast, are somewhat slangy and, though common, may not be understood by everyone; they are certainly appropriate in novels, especially in dialogue, but may not be appropriate and usually will not be preferable to standard terms in nonfiction.

Here are some examples of complete terms and generic words used alone: *the Fifth Precinct*, *the precinct*; *the Twenty-first Congressional District*, *the congressional district*; *the Massachusetts Bay Colony*, *the colony*; *the Roman Empire*, *the empire*; *the United Arab Republic*, *the republic*. Sometimes exceptions are made in special circumstances. For example, *the Federal Republic* might well be used to underline the distinction between the Federal Republic of Germany (West Germany) and the German Democratic Republic (East Germany); otherwise the writer might feel it necessary to repeat the entire name each time it is used, since the names of the two Germanys are similar.

Occasionally a writer will capitalize a generic term to give it special significance. Thus *the Mountain* may be appropriate if a particular mountain looms large in a novel or in a work of popular nonfiction.

Generic terms in the plural with two or more proper names

Kings County capitalizes the generic word *county*, but *Kings and Queens counties* lowercases its plural. Similarly, *the White River* capitalizes the generic term, but *the White and Connecticut rivers* lowercases it. A plural generic term following two or more proper names is lowercased. One would not lowercase the generic term in *Rocky Mountains*, since the plural word is part of a single geographical term, but it should be lowercased in *the Catskill and Adirondack mountains*, even though *Mountains* is the proper term when either the Catskills or the Adirondacks are mentioned separately.

When the generic term precedes two or more proper names, it is usually capitalized—*Lakes Erie and Superior*; *the Rivers Styx and Lethe*—but sometimes lowercased; either is acceptable.

Geographical regions: some complications

Terms for regions within the United States are usually capitalized: *the East*, *the West*, *the East Coast*, *the Far West*, *the Southwest*, *the Midwest*. Stylebooks are divided on whether to capitalize the corresponding adjectives— *Eastern*, *Midwestern*, and so on—and related nouns such as *Easterner*. I prefer to capitalize them, because if they are lowercased an occasional ambiguity will inevitably occur.

Similar terms for larger regions, such as hemispheres, are also usually capitalized: *the East* (that is, the Orient), *the Middle East*, *the Continent* (Europe). Again, there is disagreement over capitalizing the corresponding adjectives; I capitalize them.

Generic words used with names of geographical entities may or may not be considered part of the name and thus may or may not be capitalized—a dictionary, almanac, atlas, or gazetteer may be needed. *The Indian peninsula* uses an adjective derived from the name of a political division, India, to identify an enormous geographical feature that is not normally thought of as a peninsula, and the generic word is lowercased. *The Arabian Peninsula* uses an adjective derived from a historical political division that is frequently thought of as a geographical feature—a peninsula—and contains several modern nations. Sometimes one can think of a possible reason for the distinction, sometimes one cannot; the safest practice is to consult a reference book.

Terms such as *Atlantic Coast* and *West Coast* are capitalized only if they refer to regions on land, not if they refer to offshore waters or the actual junction of land and water: *The Atlantic Coast is heavily populated*; *The Atlantic coast of the United States is heavily fished*. The word *seaboard* refers only to the land along a coastline, not to the water; it is usually capitalized with *Atlantic* and *Pacific* but lowercased with other terms, as in *Florida's Caribbean seaboard*.

**3-18   Never capitalize *east*, *west*, and
similar terms when they indicate a
direction rather than a region or**

location, and don't invariably
capitalize them even when they do
indicate a region or location.

He traveled nine miles East is a very common error. Here
the word *east* is merely a compass point or direction; there is
no reason to capitalize it. *He left the East in 1849 and followed the Gold Rush west, but found the West a disappointment and headed east again* is correct, and though the apparent inconsistency in capitalization may seem glaring
when attention is called to it, it would go unnoticed by most
readers, who are accustomed to the distinction between region and direction.

Capitalizing terms such as *the North*, meaning the Northeast and part of the Midwest of the United States during the
Civil War, a somewhat larger area of the United States today, or the North of England, depending on the context, is
helpful. However, such capitalization is not helpful if a convention for capitalizing the term has not been well established. *In southern Nebraska the growing season is longer
than in the North* is apt to distract the reader, who, even
though he may understand what is meant, can't help but
think of irrelevant contexts in which he might expect the
capitalized word—the Yukon, the U.S. Northeast, or wh"at-
ever. When writing about a region unfamiliar to most
readers, a writer can establish capitalization conventions
that are appropriate to the region, but he must do so carefully, making sure the reader can follow and is given immediate significant information to associate with the
capitalized terms: *The region from the capital to the coast—
the North—has been called ·the country's breadbasket. The
South is almost entirely nonarable, though it is well
populated.*

TITLES OF PUBLICATIONS AND WORKS OF LITERATURE, WORKS OF ART, MUSICAL COMPOSITIONS, AND OTHER WORKS

Style conventions governing the use of capitals, quotation
marks, and italics (underlines on the typewriter) for the

kinds of titles discussed in this section are basically quite simple, though complexities can occur. The rules given here are well established, but they are not universally observed; many publications have variant styles, and many fields of scholarship and research, particularly in the sciences and social sciences, have detailed styles of their own. A publishing house or publication will usually routinely impose its own style variants on work it publishes. A writer in a field with its own style will need a specialized stylebook.

This book does not cover title citations in footnotes and bibliographies. There are some general rules that could be given because they apply within a great many fields, but a number of fields have their own styles, and a writer within any specific field must make himself familiar with the style preferred in that field.

3-19   Use italics (underlines on the typewriter) for the names of newspapers and periodicals.

A very simple rule—and as long as the writer confines himself to mentioning newspapers such as *Women's Wear Daily* and magazines such as *Outdoor Life* he will have no problems. But should it be *The New York Times*, the *New York Times*, or the New York *Times*? Should it be *The Kiwanis Magazine* or the *Kiwanis Magazine*?

Some writers find some more or less official guide to use when deciding how much of a periodical name to italicize and whether or not to capitalize *the*. A common guide is the annual *Literary Market Place* (R. R. Bowker Co.), which is available in most libraries. I know one book editor who, over many years, has stuffed a file with front-page logos and mastheads clipped from newspapers all over the country so that he can be certain what a newspaper's own preference is. I think this is going too far, and those who use authorities such as *Literary Market Place* or personal files are forced into such annoying inconsistencies as the *Chattanooga Times* in one sentence and *The Cleveland Daily Banner* in the next.

It is easier and better to adopt simple general principles, perhaps making exceptions to them in difficult cases. The principles below are supported by the stylebook most used in book publishing, the University of Chicago Press's *A Manual of Style*, but not by some other major stylebooks.

Newspapers

Do not consider *the* part of a newspaper's name, but do consider a city, town, or village part of the name:

the *New York Times*
the *Shelter Island Reporter*

Those who prefer not to consider city, town, or village part of the name must still consider other place names part of the name:

the *Arizona Star*
the *Wall Street Journal*

Those who prefer to consider *the* part of the name must still consider it not part of the name when the newspaper's name is used as an adjective and *the* goes with the following word, or else the newspaper's name has to be made a possessive:

the *New York Times* account
The New York Times's account

Periodicals

Do not usually consider *the* part of a periodical's name:

the *American Historical Review*
the *Kiwanis Magazine*
the *Hillside Journal of Clinical Psychiatry*
the *New York Times Magazine*

However, the word *the* in the names of some periodicals is, or at least once was, an essential part of the meaning of the name. In some cases the original significance of *the* is retained strongly, in others only weakly, and the writer has to use his own judgment to decide whether the word should be considered part of the name. The following are examples of my own judgment:

the *New Yorker*
the *Living Church*
the *Commercial Fish Farmer*
The Nation
The American West

The last two do not seem right to me unless *the* is part of the title, but I cannot explain exactly why. They are not the same: I would say or write "I read an article in *American West* the other day" but not "I read an article in *Nation* the other day." Yet if *the* precedes the title *American West*, I would capitalize and italicize it as part of the title.

It may be a publication's own preference to capitalize and italicize *the* as part of its name—for example, *The New Yorker* is the magazine's own style—and a writer can choose to follow such preferences when he is aware of them. However, the effect of this may be to create an apparently inconsistent style that annoys the reader.

3-20   Use italics (underlines on the typewriter) for the titles of books; independently published poems; plays and movies; musical compositions except single songs or short instrumental pieces and those known by generic titles; and paintings, sculptures, and similar works of art.

Many newspapers and periodicals use quotation marks for the titles listed in the rule, but many others follow the rule and virtually all book publishers do.

Books

A Tale of Two Cities and *The Way of All Flesh* are typical examples. *A*, *the*, and any other word that is in the title is considered part of the title and is accordingly italicized, and capitalized if it begins the title or is a major word (see Rule 3-22).

When a book is part of a series, its own title is treated like any other. The series title may or may not be treated like a book title, depending on the type of series and the conventions within the field in which the writer is writing. Donald R. Dudley's *The Romans: 850 B.C.–A.D. 337* is part of the series The History of Human Society, edited by J. H. Plumb. Peter Gay's *The Enlightenment: An Interpretation* is a multivolume series that includes the book *The Science of Freedom*. Here we can draw the obvious distinction that in the first case the book is part of a series of books by various authors, and in the second case the series is the work of a single author—all the books in it make up a single work. However, the romances of Sir Walter Scott are usually collectively called the Waverley Novels, or sometimes the Waverley novels, even though they are all his work. (Sometimes they are called the *Waverley* novels, a reasonable enough style, since the first novel in the series was titled *Waverley*.) Perhaps we could make the distinction that in this case the collective term was not Scott's but was imposed by literary historians.

Poems

Milton's *Paradise Lost* is a long book; the title is italicized. T. S. Eliot's *The Waste Land* is much shorter—434 lines—but was independently published, so again the title is italicized. Whitman's "Song of Myself" is more than twice as long as *The Waste Land* but it is part of the large collection *Leaves of Grass*; it was not published independently, so the title is not italicized but instead is in roman type and within quotation marks (see Rule 3-21). In works mentioning a great many titles, all poem titles are sometimes put in italics for consistency and to avoid troubling the reader with a distinction based on mere publishing history, which may be irrelevant. Nevertheless, the best style is to use italics only for independently published poems.

Plays and movies

Titles of plays, even short one-act plays, and of movies are italicized: *Oedipus Rex* (or, depending on the edition or production, *Oedipus Tyrannos* or *Oedipus the King*); *Star Wars*.

When a play is part of a series, the series may or may not be italicized too, like a series of books. There are two other plays in Sophocles' *Oedipus* series—or Oedipus Trilogy or *Oedipus* trilogy, whatever style one chooses. The miracle plays of late-medieval England are grouped in cycles—the Wakefield Plays, the Chester Plays—the names of which are usually not italicized, but sometimes they are.

Television and radio programs

Style for television and radio programs varies considerably from publication to publication. I advise italicizing the name of a regular feature or a series: *Imus in the Morning*; *Quincy*. When an episode in a series has a title of its own, I advise not italicizing it but setting it off with quotation marks.

Musical compositions

Titles of musical compositions are more complicated than other titles, because sometimes they are entirely made up of generic terms, which are not italicized; sometimes they are real titles, like book titles, and are italicized; and sometimes they are mixtures. Also, short compositions are handled differently from longer ones (see Rule 3-21 for short compositions).

Here are examples of long compositions with titles that are entirely generic terms:

> Beethoven's Symphony No. 9
> Beethoven's Ninth Symphony
> Haydn's Concerto in E flat for Two Horns and
>   Orchestra
> Bach's Mass in B Minor
> Bach's B-Minor Mass
> Bach's Passacaglia and Fugue in C Minor for Organ
> Copland's Duo for Flute and Piano

Here are examples of long compositions with titles that contain no generic terms:

> Mozart's *Magic Flute*
> Rossini's *The Barber of Seville*

Handel's *Messiah*
Gershwin's *Porgy and Bess*
Bernstein's *Trouble in Tahiti*

Some compositions are well known by both a generic name and a specific title, such as Schubert's String Quartet in D Minor, which has the specific title *Death and the Maiden*. Here are examples of mixtures:

Beethoven's *Pathétique* Sonata (or Sonata No. 8 in C Minor)
Haydn's *London* Symphony (or Symphony No. 104 in D Major)
Rossini's *William Tell* Overture
Chopin's Variations on a Theme from *La Cenerentola*

When a generic term is a true part of a specific title rather than merely descriptive, the whole title is italicized:

Liszt's *Hungarian Rhapsodies*
Mussorgsky's *Songs and Dances of Death*
Britten's *Gemini Variations*

It is apparent from all the above that one must often know something about a musical piece to style it properly. It is permissible to adopt some much simpler style, such as italicizing all titles of longer compositions whether they include generic words or not. However, the best style is that shown here.

When problems come up, general encyclopedias and encyclopedias of music are helpful, but their styles often vary. One very handy guide is the *Schwann Record and Tape Guide*, which is issued monthly; for purposes of checking titles an old issue will do as well as a new one. It is surprisingly scholarly and complete. It does have typographical conventions that must be interpreted. Major keys are indicated by capital letters, minor keys by lowercase letters. A strange symbol like a long, thin comma indicates a flat key, a regular sharp sign a sharp key, and the absence of a symbol a natural key. No italics are used; specific titles of compositions both long and short are enclosed in quotation marks if they occur with a generic title and are not distinguished in any way if they occur alone, so one must decide some things for oneself.

Paintings, sculptures, and other works of art

There are few problems with these titles:

> Gainsborough's *Blue Boy*
> Rodin's *The Thinker*
> Duchamp's *Fountain* (a urinal displayed as sculpture)

Some works of art, especially drawings and etchings, are grouped in a series, in which case both the title of the series and the title of the individual item in it are italicized. Thus Hogarth's *The Innocent Country Girl* is the first plate of his six-plate series *The Harlot's Progress*.

Titles ending in marks of punctuation

Titles such as *Annie Get Your Gun!* and *Whither Goest Thou?* contain marks of punctuation that are integral to the title. If they occur in a series, they cause a problem, since ordinarily the comma shouldn't occur with the exclamation point or question mark. When the series is of titles that are italicized or underlined, as are those discussed in this rule, I advise bending the rule and using the comma:

> *Annie Get Your Gun!*, *Whither Goest Thou?*, and *Outrageous!*, the last rather tattered, were the only works in the piano bench.

However, I advise not using the comma when the titles are in quotation marks; see Rule 3-21.

3-21   Use roman type, enclosed by quotation marks, for titles of parts of books; poems unless independently published; short stories, essays, and articles and features in periodicals; and individual songs and short instrumental compositions or parts of longer compositions.

This rule causes few problems.

Parts of books

Leslie A. Fiedler's *Love and Death in the American Novel* is divided into parts and chapters. Part III is titled "Accommodation and Transcendence," and within that part Chapter 13 is titled "*The Scarlet Letter*: Woman as Faust." The titles of the part and the chapter are both in roman type and set off by quotation marks. (Note that *The Scarlet Letter* is nevertheless italicized as part of the title of Chapter 13, because it is the title of Hawthorne's novel.) However, parts of a book that are merely generic words, like *index* and *preface*, are usually lowercased and not in quotation marks.

Poems

Subdivisions of long poems are handled the same way as parts of books. For example, T. S. Eliot's *Four Quartets* contains four moderately long poems—"Burnt Norton," "East Coker," "The Dry Salvages," and "Little Gidding."

Any poem that has not been independently published, whether it is short or long, should be in roman type within quotation marks, not in italics. Thus in general, any short poem's title is apt to be in quotation marks, but longer ones may be tricky; Whitman's "Song of Myself" is long enough to be a book but in fact was only part of the collection *Leaves of Grass*.

Sometimes all poem titles in a work that gives a great many will be either in quotation marks or in italics to avoid troubling the reader with a technical distinction that may be irrelevant; nevertheless, careful writers do make the distinction.

Short stories, essays, and articles and features in periodicals

Hemingway's story "My Old Man," Pedro Arrupe's article "Marxist Analysis by Christians," and William Safire's column "On Language" are examples. Names of some features may not be in quotation marks; the *New York Times*'s op-ed page often appears with neither capitals nor quotation marks, as a mere descriptive term rather than a title. Usually when a feature is by a specific person the quotation marks are used, but even this is not invariable; magazines may have a Publisher's Page, for example. However, titles of short stories and essays are always in quotation marks.

Songs and short compositions

"Greensleeves" and "A Hard Day's Night" are individual songs; their titles are in roman type and within quotation marks. Titles of short instrumental compositions such as "Fiddle-Faddle" are treated the same way.

Titles of cantatas and arias from operas are in roman type and within quotation marks, but in one other respect they are handled differently: They do not have normal title-style capitalization (see Rule 3-22) but capitalize only the first word, unless some of the words are normally capitalized anyway. These titles are actually just the first few words of the song or cantata. Bach's cantata "Ihr werdet weinen und heulen" and Puccini's aria "Che gelida manina" from *La Bohème* are examples. Sometimes English titles of well-known cantatas do follow normal title-style capitalization; Bach's "Jesu Joy of Man's Desiring" is usually so styled.

Titles ending in marks of punctuation

Titles such as "Whales Weep Not!" and "Why Should Not Old Men Be Mad?" that end with marks of punctuation cause problems when they are used in a series, because ordinarily the comma shouldn't occur with the exclamation point or question mark and shouldn't be outside a closing quotation mark. For italicized titles, I advise using the comma anyway (see Rule 3-20), but I advise not using it for titles in quotation marks, because the combination of exclamation point or question mark, comma, and closing quotation mark is too awkward. The problem has no really good solution, but using the semicolon instead of the comma will at least get the quotation mark in the middle, making the clump less awkward to my eye:

> His favorite poems were Lawrence's "Whales Weep Not!"; Yeats's "Why Should Not Old Men Be Mad?"; and Graves's "Down, Wanton, Down!"

In a given series that presents this problem there is usually some alternative phrasing or punctuation or both, but it may create other problems, such as an awkward repetition of *and*:

> His favorite poems were "Whales Weep Not!" and "Why Should Not Old Men Be Mad?" and "Down, Wanton, Down!"

Some carefully styled publications, including the *New Yorker*, do use the comma; anyone to whom this seems the best solution is in respectable company. My own dislike of the clumped *!,"* and *?,"* may be excessive.

3-22   Capitalize the main words in a title and the first and last word, but do not capitalize *a, the, to,* or prepositions and conjunctions of fewer than five letters when they occur in the middle of the title.

This rule applies to all capitalized titles discussed in Chapter 3, not just the kinds that are the subject of this section. I have chosen to put the rule here because errors are most frequently made with titles of literary and artistic works.

The Bridge Of San Luis Rey is such an error; *of* should not be capitalized, because it is a preposition. *The Rape Of The Lock* is worse; both the preposition *of* and the article *the* should be lowercased. *The Moon is Down* is an error; *is* is a short word, but it is an important one, a verb, not a mere preposition or conjunction, and it must be capitalized.

Travels With Charley is wrong; the preposition *with* should be lowercased. *Clock Without Hands*, however, is right; the preposition *without* has more than four letters. *They Came By Sea* is wrong; the preposition *by* should be lowercased. *The Parade Passed By and the Music Died* is not wrong, however—here *By* is an adverb modifying *Passed*, not a preposition. This is a tricky one that fools most people. Faulty capitalization in titles may result from insufficient understanding of the parts of speech; the writer who is not sure when a word that is often a preposition is actually an adverb is at a disadvantage. In the hope of helping such writers anyway I have made Rule 3-22 somewhat redundant by specifying that the last word of a title should be capitalized. Titles are unlikely to end in conjunctions (though titles such as *I Tried, But . . .* are possible), and when they end in a word that looks like a preposition the word is almost always functioning as an adverb (though occasionally there are titles such as *A Place to Come Home To*) and thus should be capitalized anyway.

I Lost Both Ears is properly styled; here *Both* is an adjective. *Life Is both Brutish and Short* is also properly styled, because here *both* is a conjunction—a special type called a correlative conjunction, used in partnership with *and*.

A colon in the middle of a title

The Corporation: A Theological Inquiry is correctly styled. A colon interrupts the title, and any word following it is capitalized just as if it began a new title, which in a sense it does. However, the colon is the only mark of punctuation—except for question marks and exclamation points, which may be used in some wordy titles—that is automatically followed by a capital. If a word follows a semicolon or dash, it also follows Rule 3-22: *The Corporation—a Theological Inquiry*.

FOREIGN WORDS

The basic style for foreign languages is very simple—isolated common words and phrases are treated as English words, and uncommon words and phrases and complete sentences are italicized. However, generic foreign words and foreign proper nouns should be treated differently, and failure to realize this causes many problems.

3-23   Use italics (underlines on the typewriter) for isolated foreign words if they are too uncommon to treat as English words, but not for foreign

**proper nouns and proper noun phrases
except when special emphasis or
clarity is needed.**

Some dictionaries indicate which foreign expressions they consider it necessary to italicize and some don't. Even the writer who uses a dictionary that does include this indication should not rely too much on it but should use his own judgment; *laissez-faire* may be perfectly clear to the probable readers of some works but a mystery to the probable readers of others.

Foreign proper nouns, including the usual nouns denoting persons and places and also noun phrases such as are formed when a title is used with a person's name, do not require italics. Here are some of the problems that occur when such terms are italicized:

> *Ciao, Dottore* Einaudi's latest book . . .
> The *Bundesrepublik Deutschland's Bild-Zeitung*
>   says . . .

Is *Ciao* the title of Dottore Einaudi's latest book, or is the sentence badly punctuated and is *Ciao, Dottore* the title of Einaudi's latest book? Is the *Bundesrepublik Deutschland's Bild-Zeitung* the name of a newspaper, or is it the *Bild-Zeitung*, published in the Bundesrepublik Deutschland (West Germany)? Care in reading punctuation would help (if similar care was shown in writing) in the first example, and a fair store of general information or a knowledge of German (which does not use the apostrophe as it is used in the example) would help in the second, but the possibility of misunderstanding is there—as it often is when legitimate uses of italics, such as for book titles and newspaper names, are mixed with unnecessary uses.

Here are some proper uses of foreign proper nouns:

> Bibliothèque Nationale (French form Bibliothèque
>   nationale)
> Palacio Nacional; the *palacio* (italics optional)
> Rue de la Paix (French form rue de la Paix)
> Oberstleutnant Braun; the *Oberstleutnant* (capitalized
>   as a German noun)

the *canaille* in the Jardin des Tuileries
the duc de La Rochefoucauld (or Duc; see Rule 3-14,
     modification 5)

Note that I have given foreign forms as well as English ones in some cases. When a foreign proper noun is used in English, it is essentially a temporary English word, and I prefer to impose English capitalization on it; otherwise *Bibliothèque nationale* and similar noun phrases may be unclear to readers not accustomed to foreign capitalization conventions. I do nevertheless capitalize German words when they are generic words and are italicized—the italics show that they are being presented as foreign words, and the capitalization conventions of the foreign language should be retained.

Foreign titles of books, paintings, and so on follow Rules 3-20 and 3-21; a title is essentially a proper noun, so it is not affected by being in a foreign language, but is in italics or in roman enclosed by quotation marks just as an equivalent English title would be.

Plurals and possessives of foreign words

When a foreign word is italicized, it is common to add an *s* to make it plural whether or not the foreign language forms its plurals that way:

> The *chador* is no longer required, but at a recent reception I counted thirty *chadors*.

This creates a bastard word—neither English nor foreign. The University of Chicago Press's *Manual of Style* advises making the added *s* roman—*chador*s—but this distinction is almost invisible in printed type and looks odd in typewriter underlining, and it doesn't really make the plural legitimate but just shows that the writer is aware it is illegitimate. Purists would insist on using the foreign plural—whatever it is, in this case. Often the problem can be circumvented by avoiding plural use of the word or by deciding not to italicize the word in the first place. If a foreign word, even a most uncommon one, occurs so frequently in a written work that plural uses are unavoidable, it might as well be considered a temporary adoptee of English and not italicized except on its first mention, when it is defined.

Possessives are often formed in the English manner too:

The *chador*'s folds concealed her form.

The Chicago *Manual of Style* practice—making the apostrophe and *s* roman—seems more acceptable here; because of the separation provided by the apostrophe, the distinction is more apparent in printed type and less awkward-looking in typewriter underlining. But the same objections can be made by purists—a foreign word has been given an English inflection.

I advise not using English plural and possessive inflections for italicized foreign words, but allowing exceptions when avoiding this minor lapse creates awkwardness.

4

BEYOND THE SENTENCE: DICTION AND COMPOSITION

Diction and composition cannot be judged right or wrong in the same way that grammar and punctuation can, but they can be judged appropriate or inappropriate, effective or ineffective. Those of us who have little trouble with grammar and punctuation may still be unsure of our diction and composition.

Diction includes grammar but goes beyond it; it is the choice of words and word relationships that we make whenever we express ourselves, either vocally or in writing, and it can be ineffective or inappropriate even when our grammar is faultless.

Composition is the combination of sentences into larger structures, from paragraphs to books; it is the context within which sentences operate, and it can be ineffective or inappropriate even when each individual sentence is well made.

Diction and composition together give a speech or written work its character. A listener or reader will not be much aware of grammar or punctuation, unless they are faulty enough to make him wince, but he will be aware of diction and composition, for these communicate both the personality of the speaker or writer and the message—and they can be evaluated almost as we evaluate a person and his message: interesting or dull, intelligent or stupid, attractive or repellent.

Good diction and composition are hard to define. Generally we have been exposed to them if we have been effectively instructed, entertained, or persuaded by something we have read or heard—though the dramatic subject of a newspaper account, the luridness of an adventure novel, or the personal importance of a notification from the IRS may hold our attention even when diction and composition are poor. Also, the diction and composition of the best writers and speakers are not easy to analyze; such writers and speakers may break the rules that this chapter discusses, but their diction and composition are in service to an unusual overall talent for expression—expression that can be admired, and can even be learned from, but cannot be dissected without threatening its unique life.

Poor diction and composition, however, are fit subjects for analysis, and ineffective and inappropriate expression should be dissected—it's dead anyway, and maybe the postmortem will make it possible to give life to the next creation. This chapter, like those on grammar and punctuation, concentrates on common errors and suggests routine ways of avoiding them. Its final section, on revision, concerns catching errors that have not been avoided.

OCCASION AND INTENT

Communication is a triad: speaker or writer, listener or reader, and matter. The speaker or writer, with the qualifications discussed in Rule 4-1, can accept himself as a relatively constant member of the triad. The listener or reader is not constant; each one, or each group, represents a different occasion—a conversation with a friendly or unfriendly subordinate or superior at work, a speech before a sober or drunk audience of ecclesiastics or teamsters, an article for an ignorant or knowledgeable readership of taxpayers or economic advisers. Nor is the matter constant; each time we speak or write we have a specific intent—to give or request information, to amuse or alarm, to persuade or dissuade.

We don't have to think consciously about each member of the triad every time we open our mouths or put pen to paper, though doing so more often might keep us out of trouble and make us better company. Such conscious thought does help when either the occasion or the intent is not a familiar one.

4-1 Remember who you are.

Each of us has many aspects—each of us represents a sex, an age, a marital category, an occupation, a type of background, and so on—but each of us is one person. Even a neurotic or psychotic person who is aware of having two or more distinctly different personalities is a single person, if an erratic one, and is so perceived by others. We can change ourselves, and time and circumstances change us, but at any given instant each of us is what he is. Within limits, we can choose to accentuate some aspects of ourselves and conceal others, and this is no more dishonest than changing clothes between cleaning the chickenhouse and going to church, but we should not pretend to be what we are not or not to be what we are.

I do not mean this rule to be a homily on character, yet a prescription of honesty about oneself and with oneself is as close as I can come to a Golden Rule of expression—and specifically of diction, for it is usually ineffective or inappropriate diction that gives the pretentious speaker or writer away.

Pretending to be what we're not

We've all done it and will do it again. Once we did it transparently, as a look at the stories and essays we wrote in school would prove; we aped the suavity and acidity of writers we admired. A story about a preppie written by a preppie: *He arched an eyebrow, then tipped up her chin and kissed her expertly.* A college sophomore's essay on the metaphysical poets: *George Herbert, though occasionally capable of an amusing twist, fell far short of Donne's aesthetically satisfying complexity.*

We may still be embarrassingly transparent when we pretend more knowledge or authority than we have. The junior executive who writes *Let me assure you that such fluctuations are acceptable* in a report intended for his seniors may have forgotten who he is—a young man addressing older ones with considerably more experience with flux—or may be trying to give the impression that he's one of them; in any case, his seniors are apt to be annoyed by his diction rather than reassured. The junior executive probably does know more than his seniors about some matters—the size of the fluctuations, the cause of them, or whatever—and would be justified in writing authoritatively about them, but he should confine his larger judgments to *I believe that such fluctuations are acceptable* or some similar unassertive diction.

Pretense comes in all forms and degrees, and it is often quite unconscious. Sometimes we get away with it; more often at least some of our listeners or readers catch us at it.

Pretending not to be what we are

No one likes being talked down to. The company president who in a newsletter to employees makes jokes about supposed romances between the *boys* who drive the trucks and the *girls* in the office, the headmaster who uses, and probably misuses, his students' slang, the clergyman who laces his instructions to the affianced with mild vulgarities— all are being falsely magnanimous, pretending not to be in the positions of authority that they hold.

We may sincerely want to put aside the trappings of office for a while and to be treated as an equal rather than a superior, and those who perceive our sincerity may oblige us. But in any context in which our authority, experience, or position is relevant, we shouldn't pretend we don't have it. Talking down, after all, is only a form of bullying.

I: the perpendicular pronoun

Sometimes it doesn't matter much who we are—we simply have the job of transmitting information, in an impersonal fashion, to a listener or reader, or we are writing an account in the third person. In such circumstances, *I* can be an intrusion and should be avoided.

Just avoiding the perpendicular pronoun may not be enough. Its shadow may be much in evidence if the speaker's or writer's diction is loaded—that is, if it includes words that indicate the speaker's or writer's opinions and reactions. *The senator slipped still another rider into the bill* suggests that the senator was being sneaky and had already added a sufficiency of riders—which are matters of opinion, not impersonal fact; an *I* must be casting a shadow, and shouldn't be if the context is an impersonal news report.

4-2 Remember who your listeners or readers are.

All spoken expression is intended for a specific audience. Much written expression is similarly intended for specific readers, though a given work of writing may find its own uniquely composed readership among the general public. A speaker whose diction is inappropriate to his audience, whether he is in church or in prison, will often be told so by his audience and may be able to adjust his diction accordingly. A writer has no such immediate feedback; he must start with a good idea of who his readers are, or his writing will be ineffective.

Usually, listeners or readers can be roughly characterized by terms such as the following:

> friendly/unfriendly/neutral
> well educated/average/poorly educated
> knowledgeable/ignorant
> concerned/unconcerned
> serious/relaxed
> young/old/mixed
> male/female/mixed

Diction that is appropriate to listeners or readers who are friendly, poorly educated, knowledgeable about the topic, unconcerned, relaxed, young, and female—for example, the diction a shop steward might employ in a memorandum to cannery workers about the company picnic—would obviously be disastrously inappropriate in a brief to the Supreme Court.

Even a single slip of diction can be disastrous. An ugly example is the phrase *final solution*—the Nazi term for the attempted extermination of the Jews—used casually to mean any drastic measure; in spite of its import the phrase has become common currency among many who are not anti-Semitic (and may be Jewish) and do not mean to offend but are simply insensitive. Offend the phrase does, and the listener or reader it offends may choose to be as unforgiving as the speaker or writer is insensitive. All of us are insensitive to some degree and to some things; all of us should try to be less so.

Inappropriate diction is usually, however, less dramatically off—it is too jocular or too serious for the occasion, it expects too much or too little of those addressed, or it is too colorful or too bland to appeal to a significant number of those addressed; no one may be offended, but few are entertained, informed, or persuaded. We cannot always achieve maximum effectiveness in what we say and write, but we can usually avoid complete ineffectiveness by considering who our listeners or readers are.

4-3   Remember what you intend to express.

Each of us lives with an interior monologue that obeys none of the rules in this book, let alone the rules in this chapter. The monologue may be in words—though not always, at least not always in recognizable words—but thoughts are often unfinished or oddly connected to other thoughts, and attention and point of view shift and evolve. Our stream of consciousness, though we are capable of concentrating it, is in its unconcentrated state as flighty as any animal's.

Thus spoken and written expression is in a sense unnatural. It takes an effort to achieve it—to focus the mind's monologue on a specific task and keep it from wandering. We may merely want to convey an emotion or attitude, such as pleasure, satisfaction, disappointment, grief; we may want to impart information; we may want to persuade. Whatever spoken or written expression we intend, the mind's monologue constantly expands, contradicts, digresses; it must be jerked back to the task by deliberate effort.

This effort is the process of composition. In conversation

and casual public speaking, composition can be very loose and is sometimes modified on the spot as listeners react; often the speaker digresses, following his interior monologue, and has to remind himself of his intent: *Where was I? Oh yes, the gerbil situation.* In less casual public speaking and in writing, composition is less loose and sometimes has to be very tight indeed; a politician can ramble considerably in speaking for a bill on the Senate floor, but the bill itself must be carefully organized and unambiguously expressed or—perhaps—it will go back to committee.

A constant awareness of intent—a persistence in intent—will give some shape to almost any expression and make it more effective, even if all the other rules in this chapter are ignored.

ORGANIZATION

Sinclair Lewis wrote well-constructed novels, but before he hit his stride he must have been familiar with the difficulties that afflict the beginner. In *Babbitt*, his hero sits down one evening to outline a paper he has been asked to deliver before a professional group. The result:

> He had written seven pages, whereof the first
> page set forth:

> The other six pages were rather like the first.

After some days of similar fumbling, Babbitt does succeed: "One evening . . . Babbitt forgot about Style, Order, and the other mysteries, and scrawled off what he really thought about the real-estate business and about himself, and he found the paper written." He even delivers it well: "When he stood on the low platform before the convention, he trembled and saw only a purple haze. But he was in earnest, and when he had finished the formal paper he talked to them, his hands in his pockets, his spectacled face a flashing disk, like a plate set up on edge in the lamplight. They shouted 'That's the stuff!' and in the discussion afterward they referred with impressiveness to 'our friend and brother, Mr. George F. Babbitt.' "

There is much to be said for Babbitt's artless route— above all, that it was the only route open to him; the principles of organization and structure half-remembered from his school days were not enough. However, besides his sincerity, Babbitt had the advantage of a friendly audience of men just like himself, men who could be counted on to like him and his message. We are not always so lucky as Babbitt, and what we have to say or write is not always so close to our hearts that our sincerity alone can make it persuasive.

Sometimes organization is "organic" in the sense that Babbitt's speech presumably was, developing naturally in the actual course of composition and then continuing to grow beyond his written words, but more often at least some conscious thought has to be given to it. In fictional fact, Babbitt's apparently fruitless attempts at conventional outlining may have organized his thoughts more than he knew.

The organization of a speech or written work may be very simple or very complex; it may be reducible to a list of two or three items or may cover pages of detailed outline. This section gives two basic rules that apply to both extremes and everything in between.

4-4   Decide on a beginning thought and an ending thought.

Beyond the simplest sentence, whatever we speak or write should go somewhere. The ending thought is essentially our intent (see Rule 4-3)—the thought we want transmitted to the listener or reader. The beginning thought is the initial link in the chain of thoughts that gets us to the ending thought—and often it is the hardest link to forge.

A beginning thought may be simply a bald statement of intent: *As your new life-tenure president I would like to ex-*

plain some modifications I will impose on our electoral system. This approach is adequate, and usually desirable, when the listener or reader can be assumed to be interested in the matter at hand from the start or, as in newspaper accounts, when the writer wants to expose his topic as concisely and quickly as possible so that his readers can decide immediately whether they are interested.

Often, however, the writer or speaker must connect his first link not just to what follows but to what precedes. The connection may be very obvious in a spoken address—the speaker takes off in some way from a previous speaker's words or from the occasion itself. It is less obvious, but still there, at the beginning of any successful written work; the opening words connect somehow to the reader and his desires, whether those desires are for information or for entertainment. A novel may start by immediately gratifying the reader's appetite for blood: *As the furtive little man who had jostled him disappeared in the crowd, Hamilton looked down incredulously at the machete sunk to the hilt in his breastbone*. What precedes these first words is the reader's appetite and the writer's ability to satisfy it, and the first words are the link. A book or article on a comparatively bloodless subject may begin by doing its best to link the subject with the reader by arousing interest: *John Gant is as obscure today as he was in life, but were it not for his courageous anatomical studies we would all be wearing gloves with no thumbs*.

The first link may be no more than a joining of the writer's perception and literary skill and the reader's willingness to appreciate them. Many novels begin with scene-setting paragraphs that please or intrigue the reader and lead him into the story. An essayist may begin at a tangent to his subject, trying to inveigle readers with a few urbane paragraphs designed, more or less ingeniously, to introduce the true subject and the writer's cast of mind at the same time; this is a somewhat leisurely, old-fashioned approach to an essay, but does survive—the editors of the *New Yorker*, for example, seem to consider it essential for the magazine's longer nonfiction articles.

Even if the beginning thought is at a tangent or apparently unrelated to the ending thought, the speaker or writer should have the connection in mind and should be able to trace it for his listener or reader—the subject of the next rule.

4-5   Connect the beginning to the ending.

Just as the words in a sentence are related by the rules of grammar, the sentences in a paragraph and the paragraphs in a speech or written work are related by the principles of composition. One thought must follow another; each thought must be linked with the preceding one and with the following one.

A simple linear argument may merely trace cause and effect, connecting an opening assertion with a conclusion: *No one seems to have realized that the gun club is responsible for the tick infestation of recent years. The club imported pheasants for its fall shoots a few seasons ago, and soon found it necessary to trap out our local foxes to protect the birds. Our rabbit population has exploded, of course, in the absence of the foxes, and so has the population of the ticks they carry. We must restore the foxes and restrain the gun club.* Gunners, pheasants, foxes, rabbits, ticks, gunners.

A more complicated argument may require several chains of reasoning that eventually link together. Similarly, a narrative may require several story lines that eventually converge. To form the connection between beginning and ending, the speaker or writer needs two things: an outline, whether written or mental; and a sense of when digression is permissible and when it is not.

Outlines

Formal outlines—with main heads I, II, III, subheads A, B, C, subordinate subheads 1, 2, 3, and so on—are often essential, both for the writer and for the reader. Some material must be presented in a systematic, highly structured way. Textbooks are an obvious example; they are intended to organize a field of study, or some aspect of it, for the reader, and the formal outline is the necessary basis of organization.

Formal outlines can be useful even when they are not essential. A speaker or writer, even a practiced one, may not start with an outline—he may not even be sure when he begins how he is going to arrive at his ending thought, and may find himself modifying his ending thought as he speaks or writes—but by the time he finishes, either something like a formal outline will have emerged or he will leave his listeners or readers up in the air and dissatisfied. Therefore he might as well start with one, and avoid the backtracking and filling in that will otherwise be necessary to cover his subject. An outline makes the actual composition much easier, because it keeps the speaker or writer focused on where he is, and aware of the links connecting where he is with where he has been and where he is going.

Some of us simply cannot start with an outline; we end up staring at a jumble of severed heads and insubordinate subheads. Outlining does take practice, as any kind of logical thinking does. It may be easier just to get some words down on paper, letting one thought lead to another without worrying about a final structure. Then it will be apparent, perhaps, what has been left out, what has been misplaced, what has been left hanging—in fact, then it will be apparent what the structure, which is to say the outline, should be. At this point, it may be quite easy to write out a good outline and do a second draft, picking up most of the words from the unorganized first draft.

I favor tight, formal composition for almost any final product, from an "informal" speech to a textbook, and therefore I recommend outlining a speech or written work early. However, especially for the beginning speaker or writer, tightness and formality are not ends in themselves; they are nothing but impediments if they prevent or constrict expression instead of merely organizing it. Those who are impeded by trying to write to an outline—or, indeed, by any of the advice in this chapter—should get some words down, words no one else yet has to hear or read, and then see if those words can be better arranged.

Digressions

The *Where was I?* syndrome has no place in formal speech or writing, but digression itself is often useful and desirable.

A digression can illuminate a point or make it more vivid, or it can serve as a breather between one chunk of complex material and another, or it can—when used skillfully—heighten suspense in the middle of a dramatic passage. A digression that serves no purpose at all, of course, should be eliminated, and therefore a speaker or writer should ask himself a few questions before allowing himself a digression: Will it illuminate the topic? Will it provide a breather, and will listener or reader remember what I've been talking about? Have I actually created enough suspense to carry through a digression, or will listener or reader just forget what it is I'm making them wait for?

An odd feature of amateur public speaking and writing is the digressive ending. The speaker or writer reaches his ending thought—and continues, and continues. Perhaps he is trying to supply something that should have been an earlier part of his composition, and would have been if he had been more careful to link beginning and ending. Perhaps he is afraid of an abrupt conclusion and wants to ease away from it; he is uncomfortable with the role of authority he has temporarily assumed and hopes to reestablish his customary conversational manner. Whatever the reason, the ending should never be a digression—it will just puzzle the listener or reader and weaken the true ending thought.

TONE

This section is an expansion of the advice given in Rules 4-1 and 4-2; the writer or speaker who remembers who he is and whom he is addressing will probably avoid errors of tone. However, an amateur writer or speaker is often a nervous one, or an angry one, or a perplexed and troubled one, and hence may make an unwise choice of tone; and a practiced writer or speaker may have long ago assumed an accustomed tone that serves him poorly. The three rules in this section are intended for both.

4-6 Avoid haughtiness; avoid chumminess.

An army drill instructor, not ordinarily a man of broad or deep intellect, is haughty because part of his function is to humble recruits and make them long for the status of trained soldier that he represents. A critic, not ordinarily a man of much artistic, dramatic, or literary achievement himself, may be haughty because he believes part of his function to be to force improvement, excoriate the shabby, and increase the sophistication of his readers. But few of us stand at such an elevation above those we speak to or write for.

A speaker or writer can, and should, judge the capacities of his listeners or readers (Rule 4-2), but he should not talk down to them or sneer at them; he should treat them civilly. In addressing them he assumes the responsibility of entertaining them, informing them, persuading them, perhaps even rebuking them—but not the privilege of insulting them or sneering at their attention, which he has presumably solicited.

Few of us think we are overendowed with self-esteem, and thus few of us think we are apt to be haughty. But haughtiness is just as apt to result from a defensive, combative attitude as from excessive self-esteem—and a beginning speaker or writer is quite likely to feel defensive, and to defend himself with haughtiness. His listeners or readers, not aware of the quivering creature behind the Oz of his words, respond defensively themselves.

Chumminess, though not as directly insulting to listener or reader as haughtiness, is still something of an insult; it suggests that the speaker or writer thinks he can win over those he addresses with a wink or a nudge in the ribs. As chumminess progresses to clowning and buffoonery, the speaker or writer becomes insulting to himself as well as to his audience.

A writer or speaker does assume a position of authority—granted him by those he addresses—and should assume some dignity along with it. A speech or written work may be friendly and may reveal the personality of the speaker or writer, but it can still be dignified.

4-7 Avoid excessive or false emotion.

Often a writer or speaker wants both to make a statement and to express his feelings about it. If his feelings are strong—whether feelings of anger, humility, sorrow, or some other emotion—he is apt to overdo their expression and obscure the statement. Hyperbole in such expression can be effective and amusing, especially in speech, but it can also be offensive.

Often the stronger the expression of the emotion is, the weaker or more diffuse the result is. Consider the examples below—all of overwritten and rewritten correspondence.

Anger

I have just received your infuriating letter informing me that my assessment has been increased because of the addition of a swimming pool to my property. This moronic missive confirms my fears that when my benighted fellow citizens voted you Republicans in they were tolling the death knell for the town. If I must be taxed—which I do not for an instant concede; I don't have any children in the schools and I was happier before the roads were paved—why does the assessment have to be left up to you nitwits?

This sorehead may eventually make his point, but all he has done so far is insult his addressee. A temperate version:

I have just received your letter informing me that my assessment has been increased because of the addition of a swimming pool to my property. This increase is the result of a misunderstanding that would have been avoided if your assessor had been diligent enough to consult me or at least to inspect the so-called improvement. The body of water in my backyard is not a swimming pool but a collapsed septic tank.

The second version expresses indignation and makes a rebuke, but the rebuke is directed only at the probable culprit, not at all members of the town government, the writer's neighbors, the Republican Party, and the principles of taxation. Its tone of justified annoyance would probably be more effective in getting the wrong righted than the first letter's rabid wrath.

Humility

I probably should not take up the time of anyone who has written such a magnificent book as *Poison Oak Simplified*, especially since I am in no way a botanist but merely the humble owner of an ancient and honorable shade tree now threatened by the dire vine, and I hope you will believe that I do so presume only because I have exhausted not only my own poor store of horticultural lore but also the problem-solving tips contained in your otherwise excellent book.

This mannered opening admittedly has more faults than merely its excessive and insincere humility—it squirms from cliché to cliché, constantly calling attention to the writer and to his satisfaction with his own words, and it ends with an unnecessary criticism of the *otherwise excellent* book. But false humility is apt to be accompanied by an overall fulsomeness of diction; the falsely humble are apt to be false in every way. A respectful but also self-respecting version:

I hope you can take the time to help me with a special problem that I haven't found covered in your excellent *Poison Oak Simplified*.

This straightforward approach is polite, establishes the writer's claim to the author's time (he has bought, or at least borrowed or stolen, the author's book and tried to use it), and avoids seeming to criticize the author and his book (the problem is *special*; the book remains *excellent*; the writer leaves it as a possibility that the information he needs may actually be in the book). The tone is appropriately humble— the writer is asking a better-informed person for his time and advice—but it is not abject or fulsome.

Sorrow

John's passing has left us prostrate. I wish I could think of what to say to comfort you in what must be a comfortless time, with the prospect of dismal years ahead. Your grief must be unbearable, on top of the past months of sadness as John failed so pathetically—months that were hard for us all, for he was much in our thoughts even though we were unable to see him because of our busy schedule. Please let us know if we can help in any way.

Letters of condolence are difficult to write. They may be sincere, written with feelings of genuine sympathy, and yet have a tinge of insincerity—*prostrate* is too strong a word for the emotional condition of one who was too busy to call on the dying man in his last months, though a sincere writer might use it from fear that a milder word would belittle the importance of the death. The writer's perception of the widow's situation may be sensitive and accurate, but it is certainly no comfort to the widow to dwell on it so gloomily. A version that evinces less sorrow but more real concern for the feelings of the widow:

> We were saddened to hear of John's death. Nearly thirty years ago he became an important part of our lives—the cheerful and friendly man who attended our ills and always made a checkup or even an inoculation something of a treat for our children. He was our friend as well as our doctor, and we wish we had seen more of him after his retirement.
>
> I understand that you have had a houseful of guests. May I come over and help you clean up after them, or cook for any that remain? I'll call you later in the week.

I do not offer the second version as a model. A letter of condolence should not follow a pattern but should be governed by a conscientious and self-controlled estimate of what will comfort most and trouble least, and this estimate will vary greatly depending on circumstances and personalities. However, this version does exemplify some useful principles. Implicit in the letter is an assumption that the widow is strong enough to withstand her loss and that her life will go on; explicit in the first version is the assumption that the widow must be, even should be, miserable and without recourse. The second version does not overstate the writer's emotion or seem to ask for sympathy as well as offer it. It evokes thoughts of the dead man's prime, not of the sad immediate past or future, and explains why the writer's family had affection and respect for him. The ticklish topic of failure to call on the dying man, a failure that may genuinely trouble the writer, is not allowed to trouble the reader, though a regret is expressed, in an undefensive way, for failure to keep in touch. The offer of help is explicit and specific, to be followed by a phone call—if the writer is not actually willing to help, no help should be offered.

4-8   Avoid inconsistencies and improprieties of tone.

Variety is desirable for some aspects of diction, such as sentence structure (see Rule 4-11). It is not ordinarily desirable for tone; a speaker or writer should not slip back and forth from formality to informality, from precise to slangy, from assertive to beseeching, from indignant to jesting, from complacent to alarmed.

Admittedly, some good speakers and writers, those who are sure of their effects, can get away with abrupt changes in tone that make a listener prick his ears, a reader widen his eyes. The speaker or writer who can satisfy the suddenly increased attention he has stimulated is justified in stimulating it. More often, inconsistency of tone is pointless and annoying: *The ponderous logographic system employed for so many centuries by the Mesopotamians was retained by some successor cultures but almost completely discarded by others—which is why there ain't no such animal as a vowel in early Semitic syllabaries, although later syllabaries do show tentative vowel indicators.* The jocular substandard diction in the middle of the scholarly sentence is distracting, not amusing.

Progression of tone

Progression of tone is not inconsistency of tone. Antony's speech over Caesar's body begins on a tone of sorrow, passes through irony, and ends with anger, and his listeners follow. A speaker or writer, like a moviemaker or playwright, can use deliberate changes of tone to lead those he addresses from mood to mood. Tone usually should be varied in this way in a speech or written work of considerable length. If the speaker or writer tries to sustain the same mood at the same pitch forever, his listeners or readers will tend to seek relief in random mood changes of their own, usually easing toward boredom; he might as well control and direct the natural volatility of those he addresses by intensifying or changing his tone to fit the course of his words.

Progression of tone does not come easily to a beginner, but it is a device he should be aware of and may find himself capable of using in some circumstances.

Comic relief, ridicule, and black humor

Comic relief is the injection, sometimes inadvertent, of humor in a spoken or written passage that is intensely serious or tragic in tone. It is a clear violation of Rule 4-8, but thoroughly justifiable when it serves a true function—purging for a moment feelings that have become clotted and need relief, so that the listener or reader can return clearheaded to the serious or tragic matter at hand. Inadvertent comic relief in a speech must be accepted; the speaker can only hope his audience will purge itself and return to him and the tone he has tried to establish, as it probably will if he keeps his composure. Deliberate comic relief in either speech or writing is dangerous, because it is difficult to know when it is really needed and when it is merely incongruous, but it is splendid when it comes off.

Ridicule is the use of humor for a serious intent—to destroy someone or something. It is appropriate in conjunction with some tones, such as anger and assertion, but not others. Whether appropriate or not, it should be used sparingly; it is overused by many speakers and writers who are unsure of themselves and their message and consider offense the best defense.

Black humor, laughing at death and disaster, is more an attitude than a tone. Some consider it an inescapable attitude—the only rational response a sensitive intelligence can make to the horrors of a world of contradiction, disappointment, and pain. Others are repelled by it and consider it a kind of sniggering at serious matters, a cowardly refusal to be truly serious and thus to risk being the butt of someone else's black wit. Black humor is in itself inconsistent, being composed of contradictory emotions, but inconsistency is not its danger—rather it encourages too much consistency, a consistently irreverent, wry, uncommitted attitude that is habit-forming. As an occasional device, it has always had legitimate uses, either to heighten emotion or, like comic relief, to purge it. As an unvarying attitude, it is a vice. The addicted black humorist may think that once he has gotten his laugh or easy shudder he has polished off his subject, but for many listeners or readers—most, I hope—he has barely broached it.

REVISION

Revision—derived from Latin *revidere*, "to look back," though the English word means actual changing rather than mere review—is a reconsideration of both the broadest and the tiniest elements of a draft. It may result in no more than a word or punctuation change here and there, or it may involve massive reworking and successive drafts that take far longer than the initial composition. Each of us has different habits of composition and different standards to meet, our own as well as those of the occasion, and consequently the process of revision differs, but "looking back" is always an essential part of it and should never be omitted. Don't overlook looking back. The rules in this section concern what to look for.

Most of the rules earlier in this book are intended to be fault-preventing, but the rules here are fault-finding. There is some danger in any fault-finding approach, because it can be endless. Faults can always be found; anyone who doubts it should read Robert Graves and Alan Hodge's *The Reader over Your Shoulder* (Vintage paperback), which, constructively and with good nature, pillories short passages by exemplary writers such as J. B. Priestley, G. B. Shaw, and T. S. Eliot. If these writers—who are no less admirable because of Graves and Hodge's criticism and are indeed admired by Graves and Hodge—can be reduced to tatters, most of the rest of us cannot expect to grasp the perfection we should nevertheless reach for.

Revision can be excessive and destructive. It is all too easy to revise while in the wrong mood—the mood of despair and self-doubt that so commonly descends after making love, after giving birth, after creating anything. Composition, whether of notes for a short speech or of a long book, can be an intense experience, overloading the writer, and the more intense it is, the worse the hangover. Experienced writers are familiar with the depression that afflicts them at various stages of composition and especially toward the end, and they know enough to avoid revising their work while their mood is negative and hypercritical, or, if a deadline gives them no choice, to make allowances for their mood as best they can.

Revision can be pointless if done in the opposite mood, which is also common—a mood of elation and exultation, even of joy. A writer who revises in this mood will probably do his draft no damage—every word is magnificently right!—but will do it no good either; he is still too absorbed in it to see the flaws his readers will. Revision can be almost as absorbing and intense an activity as composition, but it is a different kind of intensity—intellectual and cool-headed, even somewhat impersonal. Try to do it when you can achieve that mood. If you can't get in the mood, you really need an editor—a professional whose primary skill is revising the words of others.

Revision can be immobilizing to a writer, even a cool-headed one, who just will not stop. There is a point of diminishing returns even in the most carefully wrought work. Don't be obsessed with revision; go on to something else.

4-9   Check for logic and continuity.

This is essentially a check for continuity of thought—for missing links, bent links, or dangling links in the chain that connects the beginning thought and ending thought (Rules 4-4 and 4-5).

Missing links

We know what we mean; we know why one clause or sentence follows from another and leads to the next. The listener or reader doesn't know unless the connection is obvious or explicit. The connection may be obvious, as in *The forecast was for rain; they postponed the picnic.* It may be mysterious, as in *The forecast was for rain; they postponed the waxing of the floor*—the writer knows that waxing is more successful on dry days, but the reader may not, so the writer must make the connection explicit. Sometimes the missing link is as simple as a *but* or *therefore* that will show whether what follows is an opposing statement or a logical conclusion.

The speaker or writer usually knows more about his subject than the listener or reader (see Rule 4-2). *In that winter at Valley Forge, the starving troops were reduced to gnawing at scraps of harness, and their commander, of course, was denied even that fare* would amuse those who know Washington had dental problems and a succession of ivory and wooden dentures, but puzzle or mislead everyone else— some might think Washington's tastes were too dainty. Even a trivial obscurity is annoying, and a major one may make some listeners or readers miss the entire point.

The listener's or reader's memory is shorter than the speaker's or writer's. Whodunit writers take advantage of this by dropping in clues that almost all readers will forget; the rest of us, especially if we are public speakers, should take notice of it, not advantage, and spare the reader or listener puzzlement. This often means repeating information and reinforcing connections. Excessive repetition can be tiresome, but from the standpoint of clarity, too much is better than too little. Heavy repetition can be made a virtue; repetition of key words or key points is a standard device of diction and composition to fix them in the listener's or reader's mind.

Whole paragraphs of linking exposition may never have made it from our mind to the page, and we won't know it unless we consciously look for the connections our listener or reader needs. Or a paragraph may have made it, but too late in the composition; it should be moved to where it belongs. Or an objection to our line of reasoning that many listeners or readers might make may not have been brought up and dealt with. Now is the time to repair all these gaps in the chain of thought.

Bent links

Thoughts may be connected, but some of the connections may be faulty; that is, our logic may be flawed. *All men are mortal, and Socrates is a man, therefore Socrates is mortal* is sound deductive logic. Another syllogism—that is, a three-part argument consisting of a major premise, a minor premise, and a conclusion—may be flawed: *All men are two-legged, and chickens are two-legged, therefore men are chickens.* Or the syllogism may be sound within itself but have a flawed premise: *All two-legged beings are men, and chickens are two-legged, therefore chickens are men.*

There is no room here for any further discussion of logic itself. It is a topic of immense complexity, and in some of its aspects, such as inductive reasoning, a topic that human minds can never fully plumb. However, our logic should be as good as we can make it, unless, of course, our intention is to flummox listeners or readers rather than address them honestly. Therefore, in reviewing a draft for bent links, we must test each one with suspicious questions. Does this sentence really follow necessarily from that one? Is this conclusion really the most reasonable one, or are there other equally reasonable conclusions? Have I conveniently left out some information that would make my conclusion seem less reasonable?

Logic that is based on false information, such as the premise *All two-legged beings are men*, leads to false conclusions, and thus an item of information can be a bent link too. We should be sure of any facts, but particularly of those that are parts of chains of reasoning rather than mere illustrations or window dressing.

Dangling links

We may get so interested in a particular thought in a chain of thoughts that we take off from it, beginning a new chain from it. Then, collecting ourselves, we go back and hitch on to the particular thought again and resume our original chain. This can be a problem for the listener or reader, who is left dangling at the end of the unfinished new chain, trying to see how it connects to the resumption of the old chain.

Dangling links are digressions (see Rule 4-5). They are not necessarily bad. Not every chain of thought has to stretch straight and tense to its conclusion; especially in a speech, there should be occasional times when the logical tension is relaxed and the listener can catch up. However, we must make it clear just when we are dropping a dangling link and where we are hitching back to the main chain: *Gerbils are fascinating little creatures, and I wish I had time to say more about them. But to get back to the Greeks' use of bird entrails for divination . . .*

We may even find ourselves adding a dangling link or two in the course of revision as new thoughts occur to us. Fine—but too many dangling links and long chains of dangling links begin to weigh down the main chain of thought. Part of revision is reconsidering the desirability of such digressions; they may seem acceptable at the slow speed of composition but be troublesome at normal speaking or reading speed.

4-10 Check for rambling.

Rambling is what we do when we're in no hurry and merely want to enjoy the walk. Sometimes rambling is enjoyable in speech and writing too—in friendly conversation, in personal letters, even in periodical features and columns by writers whose personalities are familiar to and enjoyed by their readers, and in books of the reflections of those with interesting minds. It is not enjoyable when the speaker or writer should be proceeding somewhere without unnecessary delay; for the listener or reader it's like walking a dog with infinite interest in every inch of curb.

A common symptom of rambling is very heavy use of coordinating conjunctions—*and, but, or.* Coordinating conjunctions are used to connect words, phrases, or clauses of equal grammatical value: *Dickens was a great novelist, and his best books are still read today, but his life was not a happy one, and he was only in his fifties when he died, or he might have given us still more books.* This rambling sentence covers a fair amount of ground, but doesn't chart a course or take it. The individual clauses—clauses of equal grammatical value—are plopped down one by one, like isolated links still waiting to be formed into a chain. Sentences such as this can go on endlessly, becoming more and more tiresome; a listener or reader will soon get impatient with such a dull ramble and give it up.

Rambling may result from a kind of fear of the brief silence imposed by a period or other strong mark of punctuation, as if the silence might give the listener or reader a chance to interrupt. Some conversationalists speak in endless rambling sentences; perhaps they all come from talkative households in which to end a sentence is to yield the floor. The public speaker and the writer do not have to fear this kind of interruption; they do not have to keep the words coming, using whatever floats to the surface of the stream of consciousness (see Rule 4-3).

One way to get out of the habit of rambling is to try to use stronger conjunctions, such as *although* and *because*, and conjunctive adverbs, such as *however* and *therefore*. These words indicate logical connections between clauses and sentences and form them into a chain. Simply eliminating *and* and *but* and putting in periods may help too, but the result may be a succession of short, babyish sentences that still rambles.

4-11   Check for monotony.

Monotony in speech is the drone that puts us all to sleep no matter how interesting the matter. An unvarying bellow has almost the same effect; it may keep us awake, but our minds go to sleep and we stop hearing the actual words. Avoiding monotony in speech is achieved by variations in delivery—in pitch, volume, pace, and so on—much more than by variations in diction, and is thus a subject outside the scope of this book. Occasionally diction that would be monotonous in written work is not monotonous, or does not have to be, when the same words are spoken; emphasis and variation in vocal inflection can even make a virtue of such diction.

Monotony in writing, despite the derivation of the word from Greek *monotonos*, "having one tone," is not prevented by alternating formal and informal tones, cool and friendly tones, and so on; such alternation is usually a mistake (see Rule 4-8). Nor is it prevented by so-called elegant variation, which is discussed at the end of this rule. It is prevented by varying sentence structure and by avoiding excessive use of either abstract or figurative diction.

Monotonous sentence structure

The basic types of sentence structure are discussed in Rule 2-1—the simple sentence, the compound sentence, and the complex sentence; sentences containing parenthetical or defining subordinate phrases and clauses; and sentences that begin with the main clause and those that begin with subordinate constructions. To these we can add two more types: short sentences and long ones. Above the level of first-grade readers, a written work should be composed of a variety of types.

I have had difficulty varying sentence structure in this book. Almost everything I write seems to require qualification or exception, and consequently many sentences begin with *but* or *however*. Sometimes a sentence containing a *but* clause is followed by a sentence beginning with *however*—every but has little buts upon it, or big buts about to devour it. I apologize to readers who have noted this failing.

I have also made heavy use of the semicolon and the dash, the first because it helps keep expression compact and implies a relationship between the clauses it connects that it would be tedious to write out, and the second because pairs of dashes are such a convenient way to slip almost anything in, including *but* and *however* constructions. The result is that many of my sentences are long and have a compound-complex construction which many readers may find wearing.

I shrive myself here not to disarm critics, though I am not above that intent, but to dissociate my advice on variation of sentence structure from my practice in this book. My variation of sentence structure is not exemplary. I do consider my sentences to be workmanlike and to be a reasonable compromise between easy readin' and scholarly denseness, and they are the best I can do for this book; they will probably strike the rare cover-to-cover reader of such a book as monotonous.

A common monotony is a succession of compound sentences joined by *and* or *but*. *The morning passed slowly, and by noon Mary felt ill. She went to the school nurse, and the nurse told her to go home and get into bed. She woke the next day, and Dr. Smith was bending over her. "You have measles," he said shortly, and the pale ceiling above her went blank.* With some adjustments, this passage could have a certain cadence that would help express the plodding feeling of illness, and the monotonous succession of compound sentences would be a justified monotony contributing to the effect. (If the words are read aloud, a good speaker could bring out their latent cadence without any revision.) But imagine the same structure going on and on—one might as well have the measles oneself.

A succession of short sentences is choppy; it jerks the reader from one subject-predicate combination to another. A succession of long sentences can be overwhelming, with the structure of one complicated sentence imposing itself, like the image of a bright light when we turn our eyes from it, on the different structure of the next. After a long, complicated sentence the reader wants a break.

A succession of sentences that begin with the subject of the main clause seems to hammer at the reader: *France had not yet fallen, and America had not entered the fray. Trench warfare and the Maginot Line had not yet proved to be antique. The policy in all quarters of the globe was to avert the eyes. Roosevelt was one of the few who had even privately made a commitment.* The hammerblows have a cadence, but it turns out to be a spurious one; *France, Trench warfare and the Maginot Line, The policy,* and *Roosevelt* are not closely enough related to support the cadence. Even a practiced speaker would probably have difficulty making the succession of similar constructions sound good; to do so he would have to downplay the similarity of construction and the cadence rather than exploit them.

A succession of sentences that begin with subordinate constructions is tiresome too. *At the end of the year, France had not yet fallen. Despite the advances in armament, the Maginot Line still seemed impregnable. In all quarters of the globe, the policy was to avert the eyes. Across the Atlantic, Roosevelt was one of the few who had made even a private commitment.* The passage, with the pauses required between the introductory constructions and the beginnings of the main clauses, seems to sway like a very slow pendulum. Sleep . . . sleep . . .

Any repetition of the same type of sentence can be monotonous. A skillful writer can sometimes use the repetition to achieve the emphasis of an orator, but usually such repetition is accidental and annoying.

Too much abstract diction

Abstract diction is almost a language by itself, and in certain types of writing is edging out English. It is characterized by heavy use of abstract nouns—that is, nouns that refer to concepts, to classes of objects or beings rather than to objects or beings themselves, and to other things that exist in the mind but not in the concrete world—and by heavy use of nouns as adjectives. Some call it the noun plague. Often the writer abstracts himself as well, avoiding at all costs the use of the personal pronoun, so that instead of a straightforward *we believe* or *we doubt* everything *is believed* or *is doubted*. Here is an example of abstract diction:

> The addition of subject chronological age consideration factors to raw measurements of ideation variety and complexity reveals a modality of progression rate consistency in both variables in the third decade, and measurement repetition over two or more temporal units, in this study one year, can provide sufficient ideation level data to serve as an index of progression rate expectation on an individual basis.

In English:

> Our data show that from age twenty-one to age thirty, thinking tends to increase steadily in both variety and complexity, and that by testing the same subject twice or more at yearly intervals we can predict his rate of progression.

To a social scientist, the first version is probably sufficiently clear, and the second version, though much clearer to laymen, may seem imprecise and even puzzling to him, because it does not use the abstract vocabulary and sentence structure that he is accustomed to. Abstract diction is legitimate in some sciences; it forces the speaker or writer to keep himself out of what should be an impersonal statement about objective reality, and it is meant for those who are interested in the data, not in the expression, and who in any case are used to the special diction of their field.

Abstract diction has been taken up by the "science" of education, which has thereby made itself an easy target. To a student, a parent, or a teacher, education is neither impersonal nor objective, and one is tempted to accuse educationists who use abstract diction of being off in a pretentious and

self-important world of their own far from the classroom.
One might go further; anyone who uses abstract diction excessively in any type of speaking or writing may be hoping
the long words, passive constructions, and complicated sentences will awe the listener or reader.

It is perfectly appropriate to have some abstract diction in
a speech or written work. *It is evident that in some circumstances justice may be served better in a biased court than in
an unbiased one* is an abstract conclusion that is fine if it
follows concrete examples, but if it follows a string of similarly abstract statements it is just playing with words; the
actual argument may be the same whether concrete or abstract, but a listener or reader will find the abstract version
monotonous and his attention will wander.

If in revising you find successions of abstract sentences,
try to replace most of them with concrete ones.

Too much figurative diction

Figures of speech can add variety to writing, and they
come in amazing variety, from allegory to zeugma. They
can, however, be distracting if misused and monotonous if
overused. The most common figures are the simile, such as
Love is like a blooming flower, in which love is said to be like
a flower; and the metaphor, such as *The boldest flower in
life's garden is love*, in which love is actually taken to be a
flower and life to be a garden.

His campaign has been like a becalmed ship is a fair
enough simile, and the writer might go on to sharpen the
comparison, with campaign workers idly doodling as sailors
whittle scrimshaw. However, continuing this simile could
quickly become tiresome, as voter apathy is likened to failing winds, opponents to cruising sharks, and so on; it is
monotonous to harp on the trivial comparisons that can be
made between one thing and another.

In the last week he has trimmed the sails of his campaign
is a fair enough metaphor, with some useful implications—
the candidate is in control, and his campaign must be picking
up speed. *He has left no stone unturned in trimming the sails
of his campaign*, though not a mixed metaphor of the thigh-
slapping sort gleefully collected by the *New Yorker*, begins
to show the danger of trying to say everything figuratively

rather than directly. Senseless and often ludicrous juxtapositions occur; turning stones has nothing to do with trimming sails. If the writer goes on jumping from one figure to the next, his reader will give up following him, because the monotonous succession of figures will bore him.

Figurative diction can also lead to errors of logic (Rule 4-9). A writer may liken a man's brain to a lightbulb, and then prove that a lightbulb will last forever if it is never turned on, but he has not proved that a man should avoid thinking. A subject that is abstract itself may be enlivened by the use of figures—this is the essential method of many poets—and a complicated subject, such as economics, may be elucidated by discussing it in terms of something simpler, such as a pie, but any figure that befuddles, distracts, or bores should be eliminated.

If you find too much simile and metaphor in your work when you revise, try to cut it down. You may both save yourself embarrassment and clarify your thoughts.

Elegant variation

That man took another individual's hat and *Mother wore a flowered hat, Father proceeded under a homburg, and my pate was graced by a beanie* take care not to repeat a word or a construction—they attempt to be "elegant" by demonstrating the speaker's or writer's ability to find a synonym or alternative construction. This is no way to achieve elegance; it is far better to repeat the straightforward word or construction than to vary it. The variation, though it does not violate rules of grammar, is a misuse of grammar; see Rule 1-5 on parallel constructions. *Mother wore a flowered hat, Father wore a homburg, and I wore a beanie* is fine, and far less boring than a succession of increasingly complicated variations.

This is not to say that words should never be varied. *Mother wore a hat that brought a smile to Father's worn face and somewhat lightened the wearing occasion* is a different sort of error of diction. The various forms of the verb *wear* should be varied, because they have different meanings: *Mother wore a hat that brought a smile to Father's tired face and somewhat lightened the tedious occasion.* Avoiding jarring repetitions of a word used in different senses is not elegant variation; these repetitions should be looked for in the course of revision and should be eliminated. Such repetition occurs very often—perhaps the mind fixates on a word and unconsciously begins to use it in several senses, and unhappy echoes such as *We passed a rubber-tired cart pulled by a tired donkey* result.

Elegant variation pure and simple, as in *The World Series, with the Yankees and Dodgers engaged for the eleventh time in an October duel, promises to be one of the most gripping of fall classics* has won some place in sportswriting and sports announcing, in which a certain humorous resonance is thereby achieved. But the variation is often witless even then.

4-12   Check for clichés and awkward expressions.

Whether a given word or phrase is a cliché or is awkward is, of course, a matter of judgment. Judgment differs from one of us to another, but it is probably fair to say that the more experience we have in public speaking or writing, the harsher our judgment of our own words becomes and yet the less often we have to deal harshly with our own words, because we automatically discard tired and awkward expressions as we write.

The beginning speaker or writer is usually too easily satisfied by the first phrasings that come to mind and may even be delighted that familiar expressions such as *generous to a fault*, *view with alarm*, and *poor as a churchmouse* flow so neatly into place in his composition. They flow too neatly; they will bore the listener or reader.

Some expressions are clichés if addressed to one group but retain their original force if addressed to others. Telling a group of architecture students that a house should be a machine for living would be a mistake—the phrase is far too familiar to them already—but might be a new and interesting thought to a younger and less sophisticated group, such as students in a class in home economics.

The beginning speaker or writer is bound to be awkward. Fluency comes much easier to some than to others, and some of us never achieve it, perhaps because of a limited vocabulary, a lack of self-confidence, or a mind oriented toward the graphic or the mechanical rather than the verbal. Still, every conscientious effort made during the process of revision to find and reword awkward expressions will improve both the speech or written work itself and the speaker's or writer's overall command of language.

4-13   Check grammar, punctuation, and other mechanics.

Even though these matters may have been much on the writer's or speaker's mind from the beginning, and even though the grammar and punctuation of the first draft may have been flawless, they need checking once again. Revisions may have changed the grammar of a sentence or affected the way it should be punctuated, and a final schoolmarmish look at this stage may uncover some surprising lapses.

In a written work of book length, one will almost always find inconsistencies of capitalization and other matters discussed in Chapter 3—even in published books that have been through many drafts and have been read by one or more editors and a proofreader. Periodicals and publishing houses do try to catch these details, along with errors of grammar and punctuation, but they are never perfect at it and are more and more frequently unable to do it, either because they cannot spend the time or because their staff members are not adequately trained. It helps to keep a list of certain decisions that have been made along the way:

> Use comma before *and* in a series
> Spell out numbers to 100, except in the statistical
>   section
> Put titles of the Whitman poems in quotes—not italics
> Capitalize *Farm*, for Brook Farm

Such decisions are for consistency, not for rightness, so it's easy to forget just what decisions have been made unless a list is kept.

4-14   Practice delivering a speech at proper
speed or read a written work at
normal reading speed; seek a test
listener or reader if someone
conscientious is available.

This rule may seem not to need stating; most of us will declaim or reread our work over and over again. But it should be done with the proper attitude; we should be pretending that we are someone else, hearing or seeing the words for the first time. It takes practice to displace ourselves this way and assume objectivity.

A test listener or reader can be invaluable, especially if the listener or reader is representative of the group the speech or written work is for, but it is hard to find a truly conscientious person to play this role. A relative or close friend will rarely be critical enough unless he has been trained in dispassionate evaluation. Many people will snatch idly at some phrase that is quite all right to start with and then harp on it, just to demonstrate acuteness and a willingness to help. A poor listener or reader will not pay attention. A self-absorbed listener or reader will argue that our carefully written history of the dog should concern itself more with the future of the cat.

Choose your test person carefully. For example, suppose you are preparing a paper to be read to a group of executives in your company. Find some executive who is to be in the group, one who is senior to you and whom you would like to flatter, and ask him to read your draft. You will almost certainly have guaranteed yourself one approving eventual auditor, but more than that, you will almost certainly get knowledgeable and helpful advice.

Don't let one test, or even several, overcome your own judgment of your work. You have put in a lot more time and thought than your test people; you may be right and they may be wrong. You will find out when your work reaches its intended audience or readership.

GLOSSARY/INDEX

As well as serving as an index to the preceding four chapters and providing definitions of the terms used in them, the Glossary/Index includes discussions of some individual words, phrases, and constructions that are commonly misused. It is not intended to replace the dictionary, which should be the first reference consulted on most questions involving words rather than sentences.

a, an   *An* should be used only before a word that when spoken begins with a vowel sound. *An ear* and *an heir* are correct. *An hotel* and *an historian* are wrong because the words begin with a sounded *h*, and *an utopia* and *an eulogy* are wrong because the words begin with the sound of a consonantal *y*. Initial-style abbreviations take *a* or *an* according to how they are pronounced: *an FDA report*; *a UNESCO report*.

abbreviations   with periods, Rule 3-10; with commas, Rule 3-11; *Jr., Sr.,* and similar abbreviations in possessive constructions, Rule 2-29 *about*   The word is sometimes redundant, and it has picked up some annoying applications.

They estimated the crowd to be about 25,000 indicates approximation with both *about* and the verb *estimated*. *They estimated the crowd to be about 25,000 to 30,000* is certainly excessive, with the range of numbers giving a third indication of approximation.

Entertainment is what books by celebrities are all about contains a peculiar use of *about* that appeared about two decades ago and may now be going out of fashion; I hope it is. Books by celebrities cannot be said to be about entertainment in any historically traceable sense of the word *about*; they are probably about celebrities. Also, this new usage is offensively glib; the writer adopts a correct but often childish construction (*What's birth control all about, Daddy?*) in hopes its childishness will bully or coax readers into thinking he is ingeniously reducing a complex subject to even-a-babe-can-grasp-it simplicity—really telling them what it's all about. Ugh.

I'm not about to pay him and *He's crazy if he thinks I'm about to pay him* contain another new and peculiar use of *about*; *about to* replaces the straightforward *going to* and intensifies the negative thought. This usage gives an ersatz toughness and cynicism to the expression of those whose language lacks natural flavor. Some dictionaries are doubtless about to include the usage (a correct use of *about to*), which is much in vogue; I advise against it. A vogue usage of this kind can be considered a **cliché**; it may have been effective as a colorful misuse when it was originated, but now it is a crutch.

absolute construction   a phrase that is not an independent clause but is nevertheless not dependent on any particular element in the rest of the sentence. *John having arrived, we began the meeting* contains the absolute construction *John having arrived* (which is not a dangling participle; see Rule 1-21). Interjections and words used in direct address are absolute constructions: *Oh my, I forgot my notes*; *Excuse me, Mr. Chairman*.

Certain adverbs and adjectives that cannot logically be compared, such as *unique* and *infinitely*, are called absolute; see **comparative and superlative**.

abstract diction   speech or writing that makes heavy use of abstract words—those that denote ideas, classifications, qualities, emotions, and other things that exist primarily in the mind rather than in the physical world. Abstract diction can be monotonous (see Rule 4-11), and it is sometimes difficult to follow, especially when chains of abstract nouns are used to form compound adjectives (see Rule 2-36).

active voice   See **voice**.

A.D.   means *anno domini,* "in the year of the Lord," and therefore should precede the year: *Tiberius was born in 42 B.C. and died in A.D. 37.* Also, it should be used only with a year, not with a century: *He died in the first century A.D.* is incorrect. However, this is rather a fussy point; the meaning of a word can change drastically, making its etymology irrelevant, and there is little to be gained by binding *A.D.* forever to its original exact meaning. When being correct with *A.D.* means being clumsy, it is better to follow the herd and use *A.D.* after the year and with centuries.

A.D. and *B.C.* can be replaced by *C.E.* (meaning "current era," "common era," or "Christian era") and *B.C.E.* ("before the current era," and so on). The replacements are significant and desirable in some contexts, but needlessly puzzle readers in others.

address   forms of address, Rules 3-14 to 3-16; punctuation with words used in direct address, Rule 2-10

adjective   one of the parts of speech; a word used to modify the meaning of a **noun**. Often an adjective is misused as an **adverb**; see Rule 1-22. When two or more adjectives are used to modify the same noun, problems may occur with punctuation and with the order of the adjectives; see Rule 1-20.

Adjectival phrases and *adjectival clauses* are so called not because they contain adjectives—often they do not—but because they function as adjectives. *The man wearing the hat is married to the woman who is on his right* contains the adjectival phrase *wearing the hat*, modifying *man*, and the adjectival clause *who is on his right*, modifying *woman*. Since *man* and *woman* are nouns, the modifying phrase and modifying clause are considered adjectival. An adjectival

adverb

clause always includes a relative pronoun—*who* in the example—and is therefore usually called a **relative clause.**

adverb   one of the parts of speech; a word used to modify the meaning of a **verb**, an **adjective**, or another adverb. An adverb can also modify an entire sentence, as in *Regrettably, I lost.* Almost all words that end in *ly* are adverbs (*quickly*; *mostly*), but some are not (*friendly* and *leisurely* are adjectives—though the latter is sometimes awkwardly used as an adverb). Many common adverbs do not end in *ly* (*very*; *quite*); some of these are adjectives as well as adverbs (*better*; *long*) and may require a hyphen to join them to the word they modify to prevent misreading (see Rule 2-33). Often a word that is usually a **preposition** becomes an adverb, as in *Used-car buyers like to trade up*, in which *up* modifies the verb *trade* rather than performing a prepositional function.

Adverbs are often misused as adjectives, as in *I feel badly*; see Rule 1-22. They are also often used when adjectival forms would be better; see *first . . . second* vs. *firstly . . . secondly* and *more important* vs. *more importantly.*

Adverbial phrases and *adverbial clauses* are so called not because they contain adverbs—often they do not—but because they function as adverbs. *He swore when shaving and sang while he showered* contains the adverbial phrase *when shaving*, modifying *swore*, and the adverbial clause *while he showered*, modifying *sang*. Since *swore* and *sang* are verbs, the modifying phrase and clause are considered adverbial.

A *conjunctive adverb* is one used to join clauses or to connect the thought of a sentence to a preceding sentence. In *They won the first two games; however, they lost the series*, the adverb *however* is conjunctive. In *However, they lost the next four games*, the adverb *However* clearly connects the sentence to a preceding sentence and thus is conjunctive. It is also a **sentence modifier**.

aggravate   means *make heavier* or *make worse* but has been misused for so many years to mean *annoy* that the misuse has become a use, accepted as standard in many dictionaries. But those who know enough about the word to use it in its historically correct sense do not use it to mean *annoy*, and those who do use it to mean *annoy* use it only in that sense, presumably because they don't know its historically correct sense. I advise never using it to mean *annoy*.

agreement   in grammar, the change in the form of a word caused by the word's relationship to another word. Some words change their form depending on their **person, number, gender,** and **case.** A subject and its verb should agree in person (Rule 1-10) and in number (Rule 1-11). A pronoun and its antecedent should agree in person, number, and gender (Rule 1-12), and when the pronoun is in apposition it should also agree in case (Rule 1-6). Disagreements such as *Everyone doffed their hats*, in which the singular word *Everyone* is assigned the plural possessive pronoun *their*, are among the commonest errors in English.

all right* vs. *alright   *Alright* is never right.

all together* vs. *altogether   *All together* means *in a group*, as in *We went in to dinner all together. Altogether* means *entirely*, as in *We skipped dinner altogether.*

all* vs. *all of   In a few constructions, *of* is necessary, such as *all of them*, but generally it is optional: *all of the money, all the money.* Usually omitting *of* improves a construction, making it tighter (see Rule 1-4), but the small unstressed word may be desirable in the cadence of a specific sentence. It is wise for a writer to have some consistent personal policy; an optional *of* in one sentence and the omission of an optional *of* a sentence or two later is the kind of inconsistency that, though trivial in itself, makes writing seem characterless.

almost   Often *almost* is illogically used with a comparative adjective or adverb, as in *It is cold today, but it was almost colder last night* and *You drive almost worse than my mother.* The construction is common enough to be considered an idiom rather than an error, but its muddiness is annoying to many; I advise avoiding it.

ambiguity   possession of more than one possible or likely meaning. Ambiguity can be deliberate and useful, as in poetry that is meant to be meaningful on more than one level, but it is usually accidental and confusing. It can have many causes. Frequently **ellipsis** results in ambiguity; see Rules 1-1 and 1-3. Another cause is a pronoun with more than one possible antecedent; see Rule 1-13. Modifiers, particularly adverbs, are sometimes ambiguous because they are positioned carelessly; see Rule 1-20.

ampersand   Except in casual notes, the ampersand, &, should be used only in names of firms—*Smith & Brown, Inc.*—and then only when the firm's known preference is for the ampersand. A comma should not be used before an ampersand: *Smith, Jones & Brown, Inc.*

and/or   a convenient and compact device—it isn't really a word—but an ugly one. It has a place in legal and technical writing, in which precision and compactness are more important than beauty, but even in such writing it is often unnecessarily used when *or* alone would carry the meaning. Elsewhere it should always be avoided, even though avoiding it may require several additional words.

antecedent   the word or phrase that a **pronoun** represents. In *John, who is of royal blood, demeans himself by asking his servants to dine with him*, the pronouns *who*, *himself*, *his*, and *him* all have *John* as their antecedent. Indefinite pronouns such as *anyone* and *whoever* cannot have an antecedent, since they are meant to be indefinite. Interrogative pronouns such as *who?* and *what?* cannot have an antecedent, since the person or thing that such a pronoun represents is unknown. Personal pronouns such as *he* and *they* may not have their antecedents in the same sentence, but there should nevertheless be an unambiguous antecedent somewhere close by or the meaning will be lost. Often pronouns are used excessively and the reader must try to determine for himself which of several possible antecedents a pronoun represents; see Rule 1-13.

antithetical construction   a *not . . . but* construction, in which something is held to be true and something else is held to be untrue: *Her hair was not red but purple.* Sometimes the construction is signaled by *but not* or just by *not*: *Her hair was purple but not garish*; *Her hair was purple, not red.* In more complicated sentences, *not* or *but* is often wrongly positioned; see Rule 1-5. For punctuation of *not . . . but* constructions, see Rule 2-7.

any more vs. *anymore*   The one-word form *anymore* is now accepted as standard in the Merriam-Webster dictionaries and some others when it is an adverb modifying a verb in negative sentences: *Dictionaries just don't care anymore.*

However, *anymore* cannot be used as an adjective, nor as an adverb modifying an adjective or another adverb: *There isn't anymore meat* and *I couldn't come anymore quickly* are wrong; it should be *any more* in both cases.

Those who want to continue using *any more* in every construction despite the partial acceptance of *anymore* should do so. *Anymore* has apparently solidified in imitation of other *any* words such as *anyone, anything, anytime, anyway,* and *anywhere.* But *anymore* is not the same kind of formation as these other words, a fact borne out by the sound of the words; in *anymore,* the *more* gets the stress or there is no stress, but in all the other words, *any* gets the stress.

anytime, sometime   These words are contractions for *at any time* and *at some time.* Whenever the full forms cannot be substituted for the contractions, they should not be contractions but two words: *Come anytime today, but I can't give you any time tomorrow; He said he'd come sometime soon, but the TV may take some time to fix, and we might have to leave it with him for some time.*

apostrophe   use of for the possessive case, Rule 2-29; use of for contractions and dropped letters, Rule 2-30

apposition; appositive   A word is in apposition to another word when it immediately follows the other word to identify or explain it. *Mr. Smith, our chairman, has resigned* contains the appositive *our chairman; Our chairman, Mr. Smith, has resigned* contains the appositive *Mr. Smith.* Words in apposition can be either **parenthetical** or **defining**. Usually if they are parenthetical they are set off with commas and if they are defining they are not set off, though there are exceptions; see Rule 2-1. Words that are in apposition must be in complete **agreement** with the words they are in apposition to; see Rule 1-6. An appositive is not the same as a **complement**, which does not just follow another word but is joined to another word by a verb.

article   a classification including only the two words *the* and *a. The* is called the definite article, *a* is called the indefinite article; *a* changes to *an* when the following word begins with a vowel sound.

as   a tricky word that sometimes is wrongly omitted (see *as well as . . . or better than*) but in the cases below is wrongly included.

He is equally as wrong is redundant; it should be either *He is equally wrong* or *he is as wrong*. However, there are times when *equally as* is correct: *He is famous equally as a playwright and as a novelist*. This avoids *He is as famous as a playwright as as a novelist*, which is correct but unacceptably clumsy. But the statement could be improved; *equally as* is somewhat clumsy too.

They elected John as treasurer needs no *as*; it should be *They elected John treasurer*. See **complement**.

As he said, a mirror should reverse up and down, not just right and left is a careless use of an *as* construction. In an attribution, *as* indicates that the writer agrees with the direct or indirect quotation. If the writer does not agree or does not want to take a stand, it should be *He said that a mirror . . .* or *He said, "A mirror . . ."*; this keeps the writer's opinion out of it.

Consider our connections severed as from this date contains a superfluous *as*; the word has a function in some legal expressions but is usually merely pompous.

as . . . as   joins the elements in a comparison, as in *I play as well as he does* and *I play as much as he does*. The second *as* in the construction introduces a clause in the examples, and it almost always does so, even though the clause may be elliptical. *I love money as much as she* and *I love money as much as her* therefore have different meanings; when the elliptical clauses are filled out, the sentences become *I love money as much as she does* and *I love money as much as I love her*. But in current accepted usage, the second *as* is often taken not as a conjunction introducing an elliptical clause but as a preposition, as in *I am responsible as much as her*, in which the pronoun *her* is in the objective case as the object of a preposition rather than in the subjective case as the subject of an understood verb (*as much as she is*). I advise avoiding such use of *as* as a preposition; see the longer discussion under *than*.

as . . . as vs. so . . . as   There used to be an arbitrary rule that *as . . . as* should be used in positive constructions and *so . . . as* in negative constructions: *You are as hidebound as he*; *You are not so hidebound as he*. The rule is now seldom observed; *as . . . as* is often used in negative constructions, and *so . . . as* can be used in an occasional positive construction, though only in sentences with a negative force: *I doubt if he is so hidebound as you*. I advise using *as* rather than *so* whenever it comes naturally.

as follows vs. as follow   Never use *as follow* to introduce a statement or list. *The people were divided into categories, as follows: men, women, and children* is correct. The word *people* is plural, *categories* is plural, and *men, women, and children* is certainly plural, but none of these is the subject of *follows*. In fact, *follows* has no subject; *as follows* and a very few other expressions (*as concerns, as regards*) are idioms in which the verb has no subject.

as for because or since   *As, because,* and *since* can all be used as subordinating conjunctions—that is, to introduce dependent clauses—but they are not interchangeable. A specific meaning of *as* is *at the same time as*: *As he went down the steps, he slipped*. A specific meaning of *since* is *after the time that*: *Since he slipped on the steps, we have slipped ourselves*. The specific, and only, meaning of *because* is *for the reason that*: *Because he broke his leg, we're being sued*. But both *as* and *since* are often used to mean *for the reason that*: *As he went down the steps, the elevator man didn't see him*; *Since he slipped on the steps, he went away mad*. The result of this usage is that *as* and *since* are often ambiguous; they may carry their special meanings that relate to time, or they may mean *because*. It is too late—by centuries—to pummel *as* and *since* into strict definitions that do not overlap, but nevertheless it is sensible both to reduce ambiguity and to avoid offending those who are careful about usage.

Since for *because* is accepted, as long as there is no ambiguity: *Since it began to rain, I didn't go out* is unambiguous and acceptable; *Since it began to rain, I haven't gone out* may be ambiguous—I may have not gone out for reasons unrelated to the rain—and therefore undesirable. When the dependent clause follows the main clause, a comma or its absence may make *since* unambiguous and therefore acceptable: *I haven't gone out, since it began to rain* uses *since* in the sense of *because*; *I haven't gone out since it began to rain* uses *since* in the sense of *after*. *Since* in the sense of *because* does have a legitimate function; it is less emphatic than *because* and can give a dependent clause a parenthetical effect.

As for *because* is generally not accepted. I advise not using it; if *because* seems too emphatic, *since* should work. Nevertheless, sometimes *as* can be defended. *As he's suing us, I suppose we should postpone the wedding* uses the word not to replace *because* but to replace, and weaken, *since*; the meaning is not *for the reason that* but *in view of the fact that*.

as well as   Often this construction leads to errors of agreement in number between subject and verb, as in *John as well as his parents were at the zoo*. The phrase *as well as his parents* is merely parenthetical; the true subject is *John* and the verb should be *was*. See also **both**, which is sometimes used redundantly with *as well as*.

as well as . . . or better than; as much as . . . or more than   These pairs and similar **correlative** pairs are often incorrectly shortened by omitting the second *as*. *He did as much or more than I did* should have *as* after *much* as well as before it. See Rule 1-2.

attribution   the addition of *he said, John asked, she wrote*, or some similar construction to a direct or indirect quotation to indicate the source. For punctuation with attributions, see Rule 2-11.

Verbs such as *smile* and *frown* have been used for attribution for generations: *"You're a penny short," he frowned.* This practice permits the writer to vary his verbs of attribution and to express very compactly the manner in which something is said, but it is nevertheless absurd, from the strictest point of view, and many readers are annoyed by it. There are many verbs that are not objectionable in attribution but still connote manner, such as *agree, beg, complain, hint, insist, propose,* and *scold*. However, they should not be used just to vary the common *said* and *asked*. A writer may feel that he is overusing *said* and *asked*, but in fact these verbs of attribution are almost invisible to the reader and their repetition is not annoying.

Colorful verbs such as *grunt* and *hiss* are acceptable when they are appropriate—*"Huhn?" he grunted; "Just taste this, my sweet," he hissed*—but *grunt* and *hiss* are ludicrous when the quotation could not actually be grunted or hissed: *"I suppose you consider this an adequate periphrasis," he grunted* (difficult to grunt); *"You will enjoy the cocktail," he hissed* (impossible to hiss).

attributive   An attributive modifier is one that comes just before, or occasionally just after, the modified noun or noun phrase. In *big baby* and *I prefer a baby burping to a baby bawling*, the adjective *big* and the adjectival participles *burping* and *bawling* are attributive. In *The baby is big*, the adjective *big* is not attributive; it is called a predicate adjective, since it is part of the **predicate**. When a string of modifiers precedes the modified word, all the modifiers are attributive: *big bald burping and bawling baby*.

The term is most convenient to describe a noun that is functioning as an adjective. In *Nursery school is a baby heaven*, the words *Nursery* and *baby*, which usually are nouns, function as adjectives, but instead of calling them adjectives we can call them attributive nouns.

auxiliary verb   a "helping" verb, used to form the compound tenses of another verb (see also **compound** and **tense**). *I am going* contains the auxiliary verb *am*; *I have gone* contains the auxiliary verb *have*. The most common auxiliary verbs are forms of *be* and *have*, but *do, can, may, might, must, ought, shall, will, should, could*, and others are also often auxiliary verbs, and some function only as auxiliary verbs. For example, *I shall* has no meaning unless it occurs with another verb or another verb is understood to be occurring with it.

Auxiliary verbs are often contracted: *I have, I've; I would* or *I had, I'd; I would have, I'd've*. The contraction *'ve* is sometimes mistakenly written *of*, because of the similarity in sound: *I'd of baked a cake.*

a while vs. awhile   *Awhile* is an adverb, with the same meaning as the adverbial prepositional phrase *for a while*: *Let's rest awhile; Let's rest for a while.* When *for a while* cannot be substituted for *awhile, awhile* is wrong and should be *a while*: *Spend a while with me.*

behalf of   A lawyer speaks *on behalf of* his client; that is, as his client's agent. A character witness gives testimony *in* *behalf of* a defendant; that is, for the benefit of the defendant. However, the distinction is no longer much observed and is sometimes difficult to draw.

beside vs. **besides**   *Beside* means *alongside*, as in *There was a car beside mine in the lot. Besides* means *in addition to*, as in *There were ten cars besides mine in the lot.*

better   Idiomatic constructions using *better* with *had*, as in *You had better go* and *I'd better go*, are often incorrectly shortened: *You better go*. Either *had* or its contraction, *'d*, must appear in writing and should be heard in speech.

between vs. **among**   *Between* is used with two objects, as in *He stood between his wife and her mother*, and *among* is used when the object is plural or with three or more objects, as in *He stood among his relatives* and *He stood among his wife, her mother, her mother's sister, and her uncle.* However, *between* is also often correct and sometimes is required when there are three or more objects: *It's unlikely that any agreement will be reached between him, his wife, and their therapist* requires *between* because it concerns agreement between each of the three persons and the other two. The choice may make a considerable difference in meaning: *There are few areas of total agreement between grammarians and linguists* means that grammarians generally don't agree with linguists—only two objects are really being discussed, though they both happen to be plural in form—but *There are few areas of total agreement among grammarians and linguists* means that grammarians and linguists, lumped together as a single group, have many conflicting opinions.

black humor   humor directed at matters generally considered to be sad, tragic, or solemn. It can easily be an offensive error of tone; see Rule 4-8.

both   Often *both* is redundant because it is used with words that already include its meaning: *They were both agreed*; *Both are equally at fault*; *Both John as well as his wife wanted to try again.*

brackets   Brackets can be used within parentheses, though this use should generally be avoided; see Rule 2-18 and the introductory discussion preceding it. Brackets are useful primarily within quotations; see Rule 2-19.

bring* vs. *take   These verbs are often confused. They can mean the same thing—*transport* or *escort*—but they have different points of view. *Bring* implies motion toward; *take* implies motion away from. Sometimes the point of view is clear, and one verb is obviously better than the other: *If you take a book from the reference shelf, please bring it back before the end of the day*; *If you must bring uninvited guests to my party I wish you would take them with you when you go*. Sometimes the choice of verb establishes the point of view: *He brought his child to the office* indicates that it is the arrival at the office that is in mind; *He took his child to the office* indicates that it is the departure for the office that is in mind. *Take* is rarely misused, but *bring* is often grossly misused, as in *When you go to the Caribbean, don't bring winter clothes*. *When you come to the Caribbean* would make *bring* appropriate (*come* and *go*, which are rarely misused, have the same relationship as *bring* and *take*).

but   As a **conjunction,** *but* is used to connect things that are opposed in some way but are equal grammatical elements. *He came to the party but didn't stay* has two predicates, *came to the party* and *didn't stay*, which have the same grammatical value, and they are connected by *but*. The word *but* can also be other parts of speech. In constructions such as *Everyone but him was invited*, it is a **preposition** (see Rule 1-9). In *There was no one else there but had been invited* it is a kind of negative **pronoun**, standing for *who . . . not* (*who had not been invited*). In *He is but a gatecrasher* it is an **adverb**, with the meaning of *only* or *merely*.

But is often used unnecessarily: *I do not doubt but that you will succeed*. Since *but* has a negative implication (though it is not a direct negative, such as *not*), this construction has some of the flavor of a double negative. The construction is found in the best writing, because the best writers do make use of it, but ordinarily it should be avoided.

I did not bring but twenty dollars, in which *but* means *only*, is a double negative and is incorrect; *I brought but twenty dollars* is correct.

When a comma occurs after *but*, as in *But, we must do what is best*, it usually is being used in place of a stronger word or phrase, such as *however* or *on the other hand*. The stronger word or phrase should be used to start with.

can vs. *may*   *Can* is used in reference to ability and physical possibility, *may* in reference to permission: *He can swim, so he won't drown*; *He may swim after he has finished his chores*. This distinction is no longer as rigid as it once was; *can* is often used for *may*, especially in negative constructions (perhaps because the contraction *mayn't* has never been popular): *You can't swim until you've finished your chores*. However, the distinction should be observed in formal writing.

Could has almost completely displaced *might* in reference to permission; *He asked if he might go swimming* is quaint, and *She told him he mightn't go swimming* is quainter. When *might* is used, it perversely connotes the possibility of permission rather than permission itself: *I thought he might go if he just mowed the lawn and left the raking till later*.

capitalization   after a colon, Rule 2-15; of directions such as *east*, Rule 3-18; of forms of address, Rule 3-15; of kinship terms, Rule 3-16; of main words in titles, Rule 3-22; of offices and organizations, Rule 3-13; of officials' titles, Rule 3-14; of political and geographical terms, Rule 3-17; of *the* in titles of books and works of art, Rule 3-20; of *the* in titles of newspapers and periodicals, Rule 3-19

case   a form of a noun or a pronoun that indicates its function within a sentence. English has only three cases, the **subjective case**, the **objective case**, and the **possessive case**, and the subjective and objective are the same except for a few pronouns. See Rules 1-6 to 1-9.

clause   a group of words that contains a **subject** and **predicate**, like a **sentence**, but is only part of a sentence. An **independent clause** could stand alone as a complete sentence. *I don't want this hat; it is too small* contains two independent clauses, either of which could stand alone. A **dependent clause** cannot stand alone; it usually includes some word that indicates its dependence on something else in the sentence. *I don't want this hat, which is too small* contains the dependent clause *which is too small*; the relative pronoun *which* indicates that the clause depends on something outside itself, in this example the word *hat*.

cliché   a phrase or figure of speech that has become too familiar and no longer seems clever or forceful, such as *like a* *bat out of hell*. Phrases that are new and effective to one group of listeners or readers may be clichés to other groups; see Rule 4-12.

collective noun   a singular noun that means something plural, such as *group*. Many collective nouns can take either a singular or a plural verb, depending on whether they are being thought of as singular or plural; see Rule 1-11. Various errors of **agreement** occur with collective nouns—for example, a collective noun may be accompanied by a singular verb but then referred to later in the sentence or passage by a plural pronoun; see Rule 1-12.

colon   a mark of punctuation that introduces what follows. It should not be used when the words that follow fit naturally into the grammar of the sentence; see Rule 2-16. The word following a colon usually begins with a capital if it begins a grammatically complete sentence, but there are exceptions to this; see Rule 2-15.

comma   the most common mark of punctuation within sentences, used to separate one word or phrase from another. Its many uses and misuses are dealt with in Rules 2-2 to 2-11 and a few others: after *that, if, when,* and other subordinating conjunctions, Rule 2-8; before *and* or another conjunction in a series, Rule 2-6; before or after direct quotations, Rule 2-11; between an adjective or adverb and the word or phrase it modifies, Rule 2-5; between compound predicates, Rule 2-3; between independent clauses, Rule 2-2; between subject and verb, verb and object, or preposition and object, Rule 2-4; in a series of adjectives, Rule 1-20; in a series of titles that end with punctuation, Rules 3-20 and 3-21; in a series when *and* is omitted, Rule 2-6; position of when used with a closing quotation mark, Rule 2-24; to indicate an understood word, Rule 2-9; to set off a negative element from a positive one, Rule 2-7; to set off names in direct address, Rule 2-10; to set off parenthetical elements but not defining elements, Rule 2-1. See also Rule 2-1 for a general discussion of sentence structure that includes many examples of comma use and Rules 2-12 to 2-14 for examples of commas that should be semicolons.

comparative and superlative   the forms taken by adjectives and adverbs to indicate comparison or degree. Many adjectives and adverbs form the comparative by adding *er* and the superlative by adding *est* (*small, smaller, smallest; soon, sooner, soonest*), but some of the most common have special forms (*good, better, best*), and those of three syllables or more almost always are combined with *more* and *most* instead of changing form (*respectable, more respectable, most respectable*). Using both the *er* or *est* ending and *more* or *most*, as in *more smaller*, is a redundancy and, of course, an error; see also **more, most**.

The superlative form is inappropriate when only two things are being compared: *John and Mary are both good players but Mary is best* is wrong; it should be *Mary is better*. However, in some idioms this rule is disregarded; *It's best to be honest* is technically an error, since there is only one alternative—being dishonest—but is well established in the language.

Comparatives are sometimes used vaguely, as in *older people* and *better stores*. Such vague use should be avoided whenever precision is important, though it too is well established in the language.

Some modifiers cannot logically have comparative or superlative forms. The most often cited is *unique*; it is a so-called absolute adjective, and *more unique, less unique*, and *most unique* are generally considered errors. *More nearly unique* is acceptable, but *more unusual* is a simpler and better way of expressing the meaning. Many other modifiers, such as *complete* and *perfect*, have as much right to be considered absolute as *unique* does but are nevertheless so often used with *more, less*, and *most* that such use cannot be condemned, though it is worth making an effort to avoid it.

comparative elements   elements joined by phrases such as *more than* and *as much as*. Usually elements so joined should be parallel in structure; see Rule 1-5.

complement   a word or phrase that is linked to another word or phrase by a verb to complete the meaning of the verb. *John is the treasurer* contains the subject complement *the treasurer*, completing the meaning of *is*. *They elected John treasurer* contains the object complement *treasurer*, completing the meaning of *elected*. Often a complement is an adjective: *The house is red* and *He painted the house red* both contain *red* as a complement.

Usually a complement must agree in case with the word it is linked to, but common expressions such as *It's me* are acceptable in all but the most formal writing; see Rule 1-6. A complement does not have to agree in number with the word it is linked to (*The main ingredient was onions*; *He made onions the main ingredient*), but this construction often leads to errors of agreement in number between subject and verb; see Rule 1-11. See also **linking verb**.

complex sentence   a sentence that includes at least one **dependent clause**; see Rule 2-1.

composition   the arrangement of words, sentences, and paragraphs in a speech or written work. Chapter 4 discusses several basic aspects of composition.

compound   composed of two or more words or two or more clauses.

A *compound word* can be hyphenated (*city-state*), two or more separate words (*prime minister*), or one solid word (*racehorse*). So-called permanent compounds, such as the three examples in the preceding sentence, must often be looked up in the dictionary, because there is no broad rule governing whether they are hyphenated, separate, or solid. Temporary compound modifiers such as occur in *a bright-seeming child* and *a teacher-shortage problem* do follow rules for hyphenation; see Rules 2-31 to 2-38.

A *compound verb* is one formed of two or more words, such as *window-shop*. The term may also be used for a compound predicate (see below) when the verbs in the compound predicate have no objects or modifiers, and it is sometimes used to mean a verb in a compound tense (see below).

A *compound sentence* is one with two or more independent clauses; see Rule 2-1.

Compound subjects and *compound objects* are merely subjects and objects consisting of two or more elements. *The man and the woman brought pretzels and beer* contains the compound subject *The man and the woman* and the compound object *pretzels and beer*. Compound subjects sometimes cause problems of agreement when they are joined by *or* rather than *and*; see Rule 1-11.

A *compound predicate* is two or more predicates with the same subject. *They eat pretzels and drink beer* has two predicates, *eat pretzels* and *drink beer*.

comprise

A *compound tense* is one that is formed with an **auxiliary verb**; in *I have gone*, *have gone* is a compound tense of the verb *go*. (The phrase *have gone* may be called a compound verb, but is usually called a verb phrase.)

comprise   means *include* or *embrace*, as in *The whole comprises the parts* and *The parts are comprised by* (or *in*) *the whole*. It should not be used to mean *compose* or *constitute*, as in *The parts comprise the whole* and *The whole is comprised of parts*, even though some dictionaries do accept this meaning. It is worth being careful with this word, because misusing it usually indicates ignorance of its correct use, not just loose use. It is used incorrectly much more often than it is used correctly, and the incorrect use will doubtless prevail, but for now the misuse is a giveaway; those who know the meaning of the word are apt to sneer at those who use it loosely.

The meaning of *comprise* is sometimes restricted to statements in which something is said to include everything that something can include. If *comprise* is given this narrow a meaning, *The set of numbers from one to ten comprises four and seven* is a misuse, because the set of numbers from one to ten comprises other numbers as well. This restriction of meaning is not supported by dictionaries but may be understood, and therefore useful, in some contexts.

concrete diction   speech or writing that uses concrete words—that is, words denoting tangible or visible things or actions rather than ideas and emotions. *He wept* is more concrete than *He was sorrowful*. Concrete diction is usually clearer and often more forceful than **abstract diction**, which can be tiresome and monotonous when overdone; see Rule 4-11.

conjunction   one of the parts of speech; a word or phrase used to conjoin, or connect, other words or phrases. The most common conjunction is *and*.

A *coordinating conjunction* is one that connects elements that have the same grammatical value—that is, it is used when neither element is grammatically subordinate to the other. *Read it and weep* uses the coordinating conjunction *and* to connect the two imperative verbs. Other coordinating conjunctions are *or* and *but*. *For*, *yet*, and *so* are sometimes coordinating conjunctions but are frequently difficult to classify. A special type of coordinating conjunction is the *correlative conjunction*, which is found in pairs: *either . . . or*; *not only . . . but also*. Correlative conjunctions are sometimes misplaced in a sentence; see Rule 1-5.

A *subordinating conjunction* is one that joins a subordinate clause—that is, a **dependent clause**—to another clause. There are many subordinating conjunctions, including *after*, *although*, *as*, *because*, *if*, *since*, *than*, *that*, *until*, *when*, and *while*. Usually there should be no comma after a subordinating conjunction; see Rule 2-8.

A *conjunctive adverb* is an adverb such as *however*, *therefore*, *thus*, or *nevertheless* that is used to join a clause to the preceding clause, as in *I was invited; however, I did not go*. It can also "join" a sentence to the preceding sentence—that is, the meanings of the sentences are connected even though they are punctuated as separate sentences: *I was invited. However, I did not go*. Usually a conjunctive adverb is followed by a comma; see the discussion of sentence modifiers in Rule 2-5 and the discussion of introductory constructions in Rule 2-1. It is usually preceded by a semicolon, unless, of course, it begins the sentence; see Rule 2-13.

convince* vs. *persuade   *Convince* is a strong word; it implies winning over, usually against some opposition. *Persuade* is not as strong; it implies talking into, perhaps against little or no opposition and perhaps without producing real conviction (a word based on *convince*). *Convince* is misused whenever it is followed by an infinitive, as in *We convinced him to change his mind*; *persuade* should always be used before the infinitive. *Convince* is correctly used with *that* and *of* constructions: *We convinced him that he was wrong*; *I not only suspect his dishonesty, I am convinced of it*. When neither an infinitive nor a *that* or *of* construction is involved, either *convince* or *persuade* can be used, whichever is more appropriate: *They made a fairly good case for the plan, and we were persuaded*; *They made an excellent case for the plan, and we were convinced*.

coordinate; coordinating   Two or more elements in a sentence are coordinate if they have the same grammatical value in the sentence. *I always wake up when the sun rises and the cock crows* contains the coordinate clauses *the sun rises* and *the cock crows*, both linked to the main clause, *I always wake up*, by *when*. A word such as a **conjunction** is coordinating if it connects coordinate elements; in the example, *and* is a coordinating conjunction.

correlative   Correlative elements are ones connected by certain words that are used in pairs, such as *either* and *or*, *neither* and *nor*, and *not only* and *but also*. See also **conjunction** and Rule 1-5.

could care less   Usually the expression is misused to mean *couldn't care less*. *I could care less* logically means that I do care to some degree. When it appeared in the language it was probably as an ironic elliptical question—*I could care less?*—that when filled out would be something like *Can you imagine that I could care less?* Now it is almost always a statement rather than a question. Both it and the logically correct *I couldn't care less* are tiresome.

couple **vs.** *couple of*   *Couple* is a noun, not an adjective; therefore *We had a couple drinks* should be *We had a couple of drinks*. However, *a couple dozen* and some other phrases are common and can be accepted as informal usages. After all, *a couple of dozen* is worse, since *dozen*, *hundred*, and similar numerical terms are basically adjectives, as in *a couple dozen drinks*, and an adjective can't be the object of the preposition *of*.

dangling construction   a word or phrase, often a participle or participial phrase, that is dependent on something that is either missing or misplaced in the sentence. The word or phrase thus dangles with nothing to relate to or else relates to the wrong thing, as in *Walking down the street, the bridge came in sight*. It should be *Walking down the street, I came in sight of the bridge*, with *I* (or whatever pronoun or other word is appropriate) supplied for the participial phrase to modify. However, certain dangling constructions are accepted; see Rule 1-21.

dash   use and overuse of, Rule 2-17

dates   commas with month, day, and year, Rule 3-8; cardinal rather than ordinal numbers with day of month, Rule 3-9

defining construction   a construction used not just to modify but to identify a word or phrase. *The man in the hat is the* *winner* contains the defining prepositional phrase *in the hat*; *The man who is smiling is the winner* contains the defining relative clause *who is smiling*. Defining constructions are often called restrictive, because they restrict the meaning of the words they modify. Proper punctuation often depends on determining whether an element is a defining construction or a **parenthetical construction**; see Rule 2-1.

dependent clause a clause that cannot stand alone as a sentence but depends on another clause or some word or phrase in another clause; also called a subordinate clause. Dependent clauses can be either parenthetical or defining, and they are punctuated accordingly; see Rule 2-1. They can be either adjectival clauses (also called relative clauses), adverbial clauses, or noun clauses, depending on their function in a sentence; see **adjective, adverb**, and **noun**. A sentence **fragment** is apt to be a dependent clause incorrectly standing alone; see Rule 1-1.

deprecate **vs.** *depreciate*   *Deprecate* means *disapprove*; *depreciate* means *devalue* or *belittle*. However, the words have become hopelessly confused; *deprecatory* and *deprecating* are almost always intended to connote belittling, not disapproval, and *depreciatory* and *depreciating* are taken—that is, mistaken—as errors by almost all readers in contexts such as *He was offended by her depreciatory remarks* and *His manner was humble and self-depreciating*, which are correct. *Deprecate* was once a strong word—the Latin word it is derived from means *avert by prayer*—but over the course of the twentieth century it has all but lost its primary meaning and assumed the meaning of *depreciate* in some contexts. Now *depreciate* no longer seems correct in those contexts. This is a dilemma; we are forced either to be wrong or to seem wrong. I advise using *depreciate* in its standard meaning of *devalue* and in standard contexts, but avoiding *deprecate* altogether; the word is too much misunderstood at present to be useful.

diction   choice of words and grammatical constructions. Chapter 4 discusses some basic aspects of diction; see especially Rules 4-11 and 4-12.

different from **vs.** *different than*   *Different from* is the standard American phrase, except when a clause follows: *The* *present meaning is different from the former one*; *The meaning is different than it was*. The same principle applies to adverbial constructions: *This word is spelled differently from that*; *This word is spelled differently than it was a century ago*. The clause may be highly elliptical, with its verb missing, but *than* is still used: *The word is spelled differently than a century ago*; *She treats him differently than I* (meaning *differently than I treat him*); *She treats him differently than me* (meaning *differently than she treats me*).

The use of *than* with *different* is somewhat peculiar, since *different* is based on the verb *differ*, which always takes *from* or *with* and never *than*. But *from* cannot be directly followed by a clause, except a noun clause—it is a **preposition**, not a **conjunction**—and so if *from* rather than the conjunction *than* is used, something for *from* to have as an object has to be provided, and this something is a more or less cumbersome noun clause: *The meaning is different from what it was*; *This word is spelled differently from the way it was a century ago*. *Different than* saves words and trouble and, peculiar or not, is thoroughly established.

In Great Britain, *different than* is standard whether or not a clause follows: *The present meaning is different than the former one*. The British also often use *different to* when a noun or noun clause follows, which sounds strange to Americans.

digression　a wandering from the point in speech or writing. Digressions are not always bad; see Rules 4-5 and 4-9.

direct object　the word or phrase directly affected by a **transitive verb**. *He gave me all the money* has the direct object *all the money*; the word *me* is an **indirect object**.

disinterested **vs.** *uninterested*　*Disinterested* means *impartial* or *without personal interest*; *uninterested* means *indifferent* or *without any interest*. However, these words have become so confused that it is often better to use *impartial, indifferent*, or some other word that still has a commonly understood precise meaning.

distinguished　The word is much overused in the sense of *eminent* or *respected*. Properly, when something is distinguished it is distinguished from something else. The phrase *distinguished scientist*, it could be argued, implies that the scientist is distinguishable from other scientists, presumably because of his merit rather than his lack of it, but it is still a lazy phrase.

double negative   A double negative is wrong when, on analysis, it reverses the intended meaning, as in *I'm not going nowhere*; with the negatives canceling each other out, the sentence logically means *I'm going somewhere*. In fact, such a double negative is very rarely misunderstood—the double negative is intended and is understood as an intensified negative, not a reversed one. It is nevertheless an immediate indication that the speaker's or writer's diction is substandard.

There are many words formed with the usually negative prefix *in* and a few words formed with the almost always negative prefixes *dis* and *un* that are not negatives: *inflammable*; *disannul*; *unloose*. In these words the prefixes are intensifiers. The existence of such words may account for such condemned double-negative formations as *irregardless*.

The words *hardly* and *but* can carry a negative force and therefore often cause errors: *I haven't hardly any money*; *I haven't but a dollar to my name*.

A double negative is not wrong when the negatives are meant to cancel each other out, as in *I'm not unready* and *Not for nothing was he called Smirking Smith*. Triples can be correct too: *The doctor said that tranquilizers were not only not indispensable but not effective at all when taken routinely*. Multiple negatives often express precise shades of meaning, but are wordy and can force a reader to reread them to untangle them; they should not be used indiscriminately.

double possessive   See **possessive case**.

due to vs. *because of*   Strictly, when *because of* is right, *due to* is wrong, and vice versa. *Due to* is used after a linking verb: *The victory was due to forethought*; *His longevity is due to his diet*. *Because of* is used when there is no linking verb: *Victory was gained because of forethought*; *He has lived a long time because of his diet*. However, *because of* rather than *due to* should be used with a verb in **expletive** constructions: *It was because of forethought that we won*.

Due to is nevertheless very common without a verb, especially to begin a sentence: *Due to his diet, he has lived a long time*. The usage has been accepted in dictionaries and cannot be considered an error. It still is considered an error by many people, though, and is easy to avoid: Never use *due to* without a linking verb.

Because of is common when there is a verb, as in *The defeat was because we had not planned ahead*. Again, this sounds wrong to many people. It does seem to avoid the cumbersome *The defeat was due to the fact that we had not planned ahead*, but there are neater alternatives: *The defeat was due to our failure to plan ahead*; *We were defeated because we had not planned ahead*.

each   should be considered singular in most constructions: *Each of the men doffs his hat*; see Rule 1-12. However, when *each* is not the subject but merely modifies it, a plural subject takes a plural verb: *The men each have a hat*.

each other vs. **one another**   These are now considered interchangeable in most dictionaries, but the distinction formerly made between them is easy enough to maintain: *each other* for two, *one another* for three or more. *John and Mary respect each other*; *John, Mary, and their children respect one another*.

The possessive forms are *each other's* and *one another's*, never *each others'* or *one anothers'*. A following noun is sometimes singular and sometimes plural, and in some cases it can be either: *They respect one another's right to privacy*; *They lied in one another's faces*; *They wore each other's hat* or *hats*.

either . . . or; neither . . . nor   These **conjunction** pairs, which are called **correlative** conjunctions, often cause problems because they are misplaced in a sentence, as in *He was neither poor nor was he rich*; see Rule 1-5. They cause errors of agreement in number between subject and object, as in *Either they or he are wrong* and *Either he or they is wrong*—both are wrong; see Rule 1-11. They also cause errors of agreement in person between subject and object, and sometimes when there is no error the grammar still is jarring: *Either you or I am wrong* is correct but awkward; see Rule 1-10. Mismatched pairs—*neither . . . or* and *either . . . nor*—are, of course, errors.

elegant variation   use of a synonym to avoid repeating a word or use of a different grammatical construction to avoid repeating the same construction. It is called elegant only derisively; it is an amateurish device used in an attempt to seem elegant. Various kinds of variation are desirable in composition, but not elegant variation; see Rule 4-11.

ellipsis   omission of a word, or sometimes several words, that a listener or reader can be expected to supply for himself to complete the meaning of a sentence. Ellipsis is not only permissible but often highly desirable to avoid tiresome repetition; see Rule 1-1. However, certain words should not be omitted even though they are easily supplied by listener or reader; see Rule 1-2. Pronouns are often given the wrong case because they are in elliptical clauses and the error is not immediately evident; see Rule 1-6.
   Points of ellipsis are the three dots that are used to show the omission of words in quoted material and, particularly in written dialogue, to indicate long pauses. For their proper use, see Rules 2-27 and 2-28.

etc.   the abbreviation of the Latin *et cetera* ("and others"), used in English to mean *and so on*. It is a useful abbreviation and is acceptable in many types of writing, but it is usually annoying in narrative, both fiction and nonfiction. It saves space, which is a major virtue in technical writing, but in narrative there is no point in using such a device to save a few words; narrative should be pleasant to read.
   Etc. should be used only when a reader can actually continue the thought or series for himself; it is a more or less transparent evasion when the writer can't himself think of anything to add: *This book should appeal to dozens of special groups: worm farmers, etc.*
   Etc. sometimes causes problems of punctuation. *Stocks, bonds, debentures, options, etc., are the bursar's responsibility* incorrectly has a comma after *etc.*, separating subject and verb (see Rule 2-4).

ex-   causes problems when used with compound nouns, as in *ex-auto mechanic.* It can be replaced by *former*, which requires no hyphen: *former auto mechanic.*

exclamation point   often misplaced when used with other marks of punctuation; see Rule 2-22. Excessive use of exclamation points is amateurish and tiresome; so are doubled and tripled exclamation points.

expletive   a word that temporarily takes the place of the subject or object of a verb. *It is clear that you dislike Bach* and *Make it clear what you dislike about Bach* both use *it* as an expletive. If these sentences are reordered the expletive can be omitted: *That you dislike Bach is clear*; *Make what you dislike about Bach clear*. However, *There are few reasons for disliking Bach* cannot be reordered to avoid the expletive; the sentence would have to be recast. *It is*, *There is*, and *There are* often indicate an expletive construction.

Expletives are essential in some sentences, such as *It is snowing*, and desirable in others, such as *It was John who stole the cookies*, which uses the expletive construction to put an emphasis on *John* that is missing in the straightforward *John stole the cookies*. It is also useful in passive constructions, such as *It is generally believed that John stole the cookies*. However, a succession of sentences that use the expletive construction is monotonous and should be avoided; see Rule 4-11.

false comparison   a comparison between elements in a sentence that cannot logically be compared. The error usually results from omitting more words than the reader can be expected to supply for himself, as in *Profits were not as high as the preceding year*, in which *Profits* and *the preceding year* seem to be directly compared; see Rule 1-2.

farther **vs.** *further*   *Farther* is used only in reference to physical distance: *Don't go farther than the corner*; *He lives on the farther shore*. However, the physical distance may be quite figurative: *Take this reasoning a step farther* has no real involvement with physical distance, but both the verb *take* and the noun *step* have associations of physical motion, and so *farther* can be used. *Further* is used when there is no reference to physical distance: *He didn't discuss it further*; *There was no further discussion*. But *further* is also used in reference to physical distance; it could be used in all the examples for *farther* given above. Thus though *farther* is sometimes wrong, *further* can be used whenever it seems natural.

feel bad **vs.** *feel badly*   *Feel badly* is an error unless *badly* really is an adverb modifying the verb, which it almost never is. In *I feel badly* it is an adjective linked by the verb to the subject, *I*, and thus it should be *bad*, not *badly*. See also **linking verb** and Rule 1-22.

fewer **vs.** *less*   *Fewer* is used in reference to a number of separate items: *There were fewer curtain calls on the second night*; *There were fewer than ten people in the audience*. *Less* is used in reference to an item that either is singular or is being thought of as a unit rather than a collection of separate items: *There was less applause on the second night*; *There was less than a hundred dollars left in the budget*. *Less* has been encroaching on *fewer—There were less curtain calls*—and some dictionaries have accepted its use for *fewer*, but the distinction is still worth making; failure to make it is considered a sign of ignorance by many people.

figurative diction   diction that employs figures of speech, such as the **metaphor** and the **simile**. Figurative diction is vital in many kinds of poetry and is also important in many kinds of prose. It is not the opposite of **concrete diction**, since many figures of speech are highly concrete: *He turned his face to the wall* is more concrete than the straightforward *He gave up hope*. In fact, figures are often used to express concretely something that otherwise would have to be expressed in **abstract diction**, and thus they make expression more vivid. However, they can be poorly chosen or overused; see Rule 4-11.

first . . . second **vs.** *firstly . . . secondly*   Either may be used to introduce successive items in an argument, but they should not be mixed; if the argument starts out with *firstly* it should go on with *secondly*, *thirdly*, and so on. I prefer the forms without *ly*; they are brisker, and when one has a choice of using an adjectival or an adverbial form and the meaning is essentially adjectival, one might as well use the adjectival form.

flourishes   words or phrases added to dress up a sentence. *I venture to say*, *Far be it from me to suggest that*, and *If I may be so bold* are familiar flourishes. They are usually

for

clichés; see Rule 4-12. Nevertheless, they cannot always be condemned, since they can add humor or nuance; see Rule 1-4.

for   can begin a clause or a sentence, either as a conjunction or as a preposition. The danger is that when it is a preposition it will be momentarily misunderstood as a conjunction, and vice versa. The following uses the conjunction: *He went bankrupt. For his creditors, who had been hounding him for months, would wait no longer.* The following uses the preposition: *He went bankrupt. For his creditors, who had been hounding him for months, he had only pennies in assets.* Both uses are correct, but they are unfair to the reader; he has to wait to the end of the sentence to find out if he has guessed right on the meaning of *for.* If a sentence or clause begins with *for,* the next few words should make its meaning apparent.

foreign words   Excessive use of foreign words is offensive; it seems to call attention to the speaker's or writer's sophistication. When a foreign phrase is used as an adjective, it should not be hyphenated as would be a corresponding expression in English; see Rule 2-38. Relatively unfamiliar foreign words are usually italicized; see Rule 3-23.

formal   I have used the term in this book to characterize speech or writing in which informality is inappropriate, and it is probably clear enough to most. But these days the word *formal* suggests pompous adherence to convention, and informality is considered always a virtue. It is true that almost any category of speech or writing can have an informal character, from a eulogy to a Supreme Court decision; even the aggressively formal language of contracts has been deformalized, by law in some states. Nevertheless, some categories of speech and writing remain formal, requiring the writer or speaker to demonstrate self-respect as well as respect for his subject, for those he addresses, and for the occasion. The standards of the day permit some informalities in formal contexts but not others. When I advise that a certain construction or usage should be avoided in formal writing, I do not mean it should be avoided by the pompous—I mean it should be avoided by all of us in contexts we consider formal or suspect our readers will consider formal.

forms of address   See Rules 3-15 and 3-16.

fragment   a group of words that has been punctuated as a complete sentence but cannot be a complete sentence; see Rule 1-1.

ful **vs.** *fuls*   Words such as *cupful* and *handful* are sometimes given odd plural forms: *cupsful*; *handsful*. The correct forms are *cupfuls* and *handfuls*. If it is really the container rather than the quantity that is plural, the word *full* is used, not the suffix *ful* or *fuls*: *There were several bucketfuls of water on the floor* means that there was enough water to fill a bucket several times; *There were several buckets full of water on the floor* means that there were several buckets and they were full of water.

gender   the classification of nouns and pronouns as masculine, feminine, or neuter. English has very few changes in **inflection** to indicate the different genders, but nevertheless errors do occur with pronouns; see Rule 1-12. The masculine singular personal pronoun—*he*, *him*, *his*—has been used for centuries to refer to an antecedent that may be either masculine or feminine, as in *Everyone has his own tale to tell*, but sometimes it is obviously inappropriate, as in *Every divorced person has his own tale to tell*. In such cases it is better to use both genders: *his or her own tale*. See also **sexism**.

generic   relating to a whole group or class of things; not specific. A generic term is one such as the word *company*, which can refer to any company, or the phrase *chairman of the board*, which can refer to any chairman of the board. In *the Ajax Company*, the word *company* becomes part of a **proper noun** and is no longer a generic term; see Rule 3-12. In *The meeting was held in the absence of the Chairman of the Board*, the phrase *Chairman of the Board* refers to a specific person and a specific office, and thus is no longer just a generic term, but the capitals should nevertheless usually be avoided; see Rule 3-14. Trademarks such as *Kleenex* and *Fiberglas* are not generic terms and should be capitalized, though many trademarks have become generic terms; see Rule 3-12.

geographical regions and features   capitalization of names for, Rule 3-17; capitalization of directions such as *east* used to refer to regions, Rule 3-18. See also Rule 3-12 on generic terms.

gerund   a verb form that looks like a **participle**, usually ending in *ing* or, with an auxiliary verb, in *ed*, but that is used as a noun rather than as an adjective. *Drinking is a vice* has the gerund *Drinking*, used as the subject of the sentence. *A drinking man is an honest man* uses *drinking* as an adjective, modifying *man*; here *drinking* is a participle rather than a gerund. However, even when an *ing* or *ed* form of a verb is used as an adjective it may be a gerund, since a gerund, like any other noun, can modify another word. *A drinking bout* uses *drinking* as a gerund, not as a participle; the bout is not drinking, it is a bout of drinking.

A gerund can be in either the present tense or the present perfect tense—*Swilling is a pleasure, having swilled is not*—but its tense has no effect on the tense of any other verb in a sentence; see Rule 1-15.

A gerund can have a subject and an object: *She doesn't like his ignoring her*. The object is in the **objective case**, like the object of any verb, but the subject should be in the **possessive case**, since the subject of a gerund "owns" the action expressed by the gerund. *She doesn't like him ignoring her*, with the subject of the gerund the objective *him* rather than the possessive *his*, is accepted by many authorities but ignores a distinction that can often be important; see Rule 1-7.

got* vs. *gotten   Both are correct past participles of the verb *get*. Either can be used as an auxiliary verb in combination with *has* or *have*, with the meaning of *become* or *been*: *He has got tired of it*; *I have gotten fired*. In this construction *gotten* is more common in the United States, *got* more common in Great Britain.

Got and *gotten* are not always interchangeable. When the idea of possession is intended, *got* is used, merely intensifying the sense of *has* or *have*, and *gotten* cannot be used: *He has got a brother*. When the idea of obtaining is intended, *gotten* is used, although *got* too can be used and in Great Britain usually is used: *He has gotten a postponement*. Thus the choice of *got* or *gotten* can be significant: *He has gotten the money* can mean only that he has obtained the money; *He has got the money* probably means simply that he has the money, except in Great Britain. When *had* rather than *has* or *have* is part of the construction—that is, when the tense is not perfect but past perfect—there is no such distinction; both *got* and *gotten* indicate obtaining, not possession: *He had gotten the money from his father*; *He had got the money from his father*. Again, *gotten* is usual in the United States.

grammar   the system of inflections (changes in the form of a word, such as to show whether a noun is singular or plural) and syntax (order of words in a sentence) that makes it possible to form sentences out of words. Strictly defined, grammar cannot be good or bad, right or wrong; it is the collection of conventions that exist in a language as it is actually spoken and written, not as it should be spoken and written and not as it may be spoken and written by special classes of people, such as the well-educated, the educators, and the writers of books on grammar. The grammar of an individual speaker or writer is nevertheless an indicator of his social and educational background, his intelligence, and his interest in and awareness of the sensibilities of those he addresses. I have used the terms *grammar* and *grammatical* rather loosely throughout this book, as explained in the introduction to Chapter 1, to discuss what should be rather than what is.

he or she vs. **he/she, s/he**   The formations *he/she* and its inflections and *s/he* should almost never be used; they are not words or valid compounds. If *he* is not permitted to mean either sex, it is better to use *he or she* no matter how often this straightforward compound must be repeated, or else to obviate the problem by using plurals whenever possible. See **sexism**.

hopefully   an adverb meaning *in a manner full of hope* or *in a hopeful manner. Hopefully, he approached the two-dollar window* uses the word correctly. *Hopefully, his loss will teach him a lesson* misuses it; it is a **dangling construction**, because *Hopefully* has nothing to modify except the verb *teach* or the whole sentence, and the word's meaning doesn't permit it to modify either.

hyperbole

Many other adverbs can modify whole sentences; *Unfortunately, he lost his bet*; that is, his loss of the bet was unfortunate. If the adverb *hopeably* existed, it too could modify a whole sentence: *Hopeably, his loss will teach him a lesson*; that is, that his loss will teach him a lesson can be hoped. But *hopefully* cannot modify a whole sentence; it must modify a verb, and the verb it modifies must have something animate as its subject—something capable of feeling hope. (Note that the adjective *hopeful* does not always require something animate to modify, because it can mean *hope-inspiring*, as in *The outlook is hopeful*.)

The misuse of *hopefully* does fill a need. The correct constructions it is misused for, such as *Let us hope that* and *It is to be hoped that*, are wordy. They often make what was intended merely as a modifier into the main clause, forcing the more important part of the thought to be just a noun clause: *It is to be hoped that his loss will teach him a lesson.* They are intrusive as parenthetical constructions—*His loss, let us hope, will teach him a lesson*—and not genuinely parenthetical; the speaker or writer of the example does not mean *His loss will teach him a lesson*, because he doesn't know for certain that the loss will teach him a lesson, and so *let us hope* is necessary to the meaning, not parenthetical.

Because the misuse is useful, it may eventually be entirely acceptable; most dictionaries already accept it. However, at this time it is perhaps the most controversial usage in the language. Those who condemn it are apt to consider it not only questionable or sloppy but despicable. Therefore I advise never misusing *hopefully*.

hyperbole a figure of speech that employs exaggeration to strengthen the meaning. *He raised a million objections* is a hyperbolic way of saying *He raised several objections* or *He was very critical. I almost keeled over* is hyperbolic for *I was surprised*; it is also a use of **metaphor**, since it is boats, not people, that keel over. Hyperbole is a standard method of emphasizing meaning; it may be imprecise but it is not intended to deceive, as other forms of exaggeration may be. Like any figurative diction, it can be overused; see Rule 4-11. It is often easy to puncture: "There are thousands of reasons why I can't make a donation." "Name ten." "Well . . ."

hyperurbanism   an error in grammar that results from a misunderstanding and misapplication of a grammatical rule. A child may be corrected repeatedly about the misuse of the objective case in sentences such as *Johnny and me were kicked out of class*, which is a simple error in grammar, and conclude that *Johnny and I* is always better, leading to hyperurbanisms such as *The dean kicked John and I out of college*, which is an unnatural error in grammar. Often a hyperurbanism is painfully unnatural, as in *The dispute is only between he and I*; the speaker or writer falls for it because he suspects his own ear and thinks the unnatural is more dignified and more apt to be correct than the natural.

He eats as an animal can be considered a hyperurbanism; too much fear of *like*, which should not ordinarily be used as a conjunction, leads to strained diction.

hyphen   a mark used to connect the elements of **compound** words and to indicate that a word has been divided at the end of a line. Some compound words, especially compound nouns, do not have the hyphen but are written as two or more separate words, and others are written as a single solid word. Although there are general principles that affect the formation of compound nouns, so many exceptions to them exist that one must rely largely on the dictionary, as explained in the discussion preceding Rule 2-31. The hyphen to indicate division of a word at the end of a line should be positioned between syllables; dictionaries generally use centered dots or other symbols to show where words can be divided.

Hyphens are not used with many prefixes, such as *un* and *pre*, that are not independent words. Instead these prefixes combine solidly with another word; see Rule 2-31. Hyphens are used with some other prefixes, such as *all* and *self*, that do exist as independent words; see Rule 2-32.

Hyphens should be used between the elements of many compound adjectives. They are often omitted or misused. The principles governing them are quite complicated; adjectival combinations of some parts of speech require the hyphen but combinations of others do not, and some combinations are hyphenated if they occur before the word they modify but not if they occur after it. See Rules 2-33 to 2-37.

ic vs. ical

Several miscellaneous situations in which the hyphen causes problems are discussed in Rule 2-38.

ic vs. ical   *Geologic* and *geological* mean the same thing in most contexts, but *historic* and *historical* are different; a *historic event* is an important one, a *historical event* is merely one that happened in the past. In general, an adjective ending in *ical* merely has a somewhat broader meaning than the same adjective ending in *ic*, but it may have the same meaning or it may have a very different meaning. When in doubt, check the dictionary definition carefully; avoid errors such as *In classic times slavery was common.*

When there is no apparent difference between the *ic* and the *ical* form of an adjective, there is a tendency in the sciences and social sciences to use the *ic* form, which is shorter and seems more precise whether it is or not, and this can be annoying. In *The report includes parenthetic observations on biologic distinctions that may have influenced the data,* the rare forms *parenthetic* and *biologic* seem to be used only to put the reader in his place; the common *parenthetical* and *biological* have exactly the same meaning in this context, but they might allow the reader the illusion that the writer considers him an equal.

imperative mood   the mood of verbs used to express commands and instructions. *Pay me immediately* and *Go straight till the next light* are imperative constructions. The second-person pronoun *you* is understood as the subject of the imperative verb. The verb form is almost always the same as the form that goes with *you* in the **indicative mood**, but in fact the imperative form is based on the infinitive—it just happens that for every verb except *to be*, the infinitive form is the same as the form for the second person. *Be good* demonstrates that actually the infinitive form is used. The infinitive form can also be seen in the occasional constructions that occur with the imperative in the third person, as in *Somebody hold the ladder or I'll fall*; the indicative form with the third-person pronoun *somebody* would be *holds*.

Although the imperative is not necessarily impolite— *Please accept this reward* and *Forgive me* are imperative— sometimes an imperative expression is softened by being put in the indicative mood or **subjunctive mood** and phrased, but not punctuated, as a question: *Will you attend to this immediately*; *Would you let me know as soon as possible.*

imply **vs.** *infer*   *Imply* means *hint or suggest*; *infer* means *draw a conclusion*: *He implied in his remarks that I was a crook*; *I inferred from his remarks that he considered me a crook. Infer* is often misused for *imply*, and some dictionaries now accept the misuse as standard. However, there is no reason at all to misuse it, since the precise and equally short *imply* is available. Those who are careful about *infer* consider its misuse a giveaway of ignorance.

independent clause   a clause that could stand alone as a **sentence**. *I came in the door, and the burglar went out the window* contains two independent clauses. *As I came in the door the burglar went out the window* contains only one independent clause, *the burglar went out the window*; the addition of *As* has made *I came in the door* a **dependent clause**, modifying the independent clause.

Sentences containing two or more independent clauses are called compound sentences; see Rule 2-1. For proper punctuation of compound sentences, see Rules 2-2, 2-12, and 2-13.

indicative mood   the most common mood of verbs, used to make straightforward statements or ask questions about facts. *I went to the party* and *Will you go to the party?* are both in the indicative mood. *Go to the party!* is in the **imperative mood**. *Would you go to the party if I were going?* has both its verbs in the **subjunctive mood**; it concerns not facts but possibilities and conditions.

indirect object   the word or phrase indirectly affected by a verb. *He gave me all the money* has the indirect object *me*; the phrase *all the money* is the **direct object**. The preposition *to* is understood to precede the indirect object. When the preposition is supplied, which has to be done when the indirect object does not directly follow the verb, the indirect object becomes a prepositional phrase: *He gave all the money to me.*

An **intransitive verb** cannot have a direct object, but may occur with a prepositional phrase that functions somewhat like an indirect object: *He seems honest to me.* (The intransitive verb *seems* in this example is of a special type; see **linking verb**.)

infinitive   the familiar base form of a verb that usually is preceded by *to*. *I want to go* contains the infinitive *to go*. *I want to help solve the problem* contains the infinitive *to help* and also the infinitive *to solve*, with the *to* omitted for the second infinitive. Some grammarians have devised complicated rules to govern when *to* can be omitted, when it cannot be, and when it is optional, but one can almost always rely on the ear alone; errors are extremely rare. However, leaving out an optional *to* is sometimes undesirable. *I want to help, encourage, and to sustain the intellectually needy*, with *to* supplied for the third infinitive but not the middle one in the series, is faulty parallelism; see Rule 1-5.

Split infinitives, such as *to genuinely help*, with a modifier between *to* and the verb, are not errors but nevertheless annoy many people and should therefore be avoided; see Rule 1-20.

Infinitives do not function as active verbs but instead as nouns (*I want to go* uses *to go* as the direct object of *want*), adjectives (*He is the man to see* uses *to see* to modify the noun *man*), or adverbs (*I was happy to leave* uses *to leave* to modify the adjective *happy*). Nevertheless, they can have subjects and objects—both of which are in the objective case: *I told him to call me*. The reason that the subject of an infinitive is in the objective case is that it is always also the object of a verb or preposition; thus in *For him to call was rare*, the subject of the infinitive, *him*, is also the object of the preposition *for*.

Infinitives also have tense: *To err is human; to have erred is also human*. The proper tense for the infinitive depends on the relationship of the time expressed by the infinitive to the time expressed by the main verb; see Rule 1-15. The present infinitive frequently expresses expectation, purpose, or compulsion, and thus its time is actually future rather than present: *I expect to go*; *I am to go in the morning*; *I was to go in the morning*.

Infinitives can be misused. The infinitive of purpose should not be used unless there really is some idea of purpose to express; *I worked all day to end up exhausted* would be better as *I worked all day, ending up exhausted*, and *I worked all day to discover I hadn't accomplished anything* would be better as *I worked all day but discovered I hadn't accomplished anything.*

Infinitives can easily be misplaced so that their function is not clear: *He advised those who had not been trained to solve the problem* is ambiguous, because *to solve the problem* can go either with *advised* or with *trained.* Especially when they are adverbial, infinitives must be positioned carefully or sometimes eliminated in favor of another construction; see Rule 1-20.

inflection　　a change in the form of a word to indicate its function and meaning. Some pronouns are inflected to indicate their **case** (*he, him, his*), **number** (*he, they*), **person** (*I, you, he*), and **gender** (*he, she, it*). Nouns are inflected to indicate case, although the subjective and objective cases are the same, and number. Verbs are inflected to indicate person, though only in the present tense, and even in that all but the third person singular are the same (*I cook, you cook, he cooks*). A few verbs, like *can*, aren't inflected at all to show person. The verb *to be* has more inflections for person than other verbs, with three forms in the present (*am, are, is*) and two forms in the past (*was, were*). Verbs are also inflected to show **tense** (*I cook, I cooked*), with auxiliary verbs helping to form many of the tenses (*I am cooking, I have cooked*), and to show **mood** (*He cooks; I insist that he cook*). Adjectives are not inflected, except for the demonstrative adjectives *this* and *that*, which have the plurals *these* and *those*. The comparative and superlative adjective endings *er* and *est* are usually considered not inflections but suffixes, since they alter the basic meaning of an adjective rather than merely indicating its function.

initials　　whether to use periods with, Rule 3-10

interjection　　one of the parts of speech; a word or phrase used to express feeling rather than meaning, usually as an exclamation. *Oh dear, it's raining* contains the interjection *Oh dear; I'd like to help, but, darn, I'm broke* contains the interjection *darn.* Interjections have no grammatical connection with a sentence they are part of; they are quite independent and can stand alone as complete sentences: *Oh dear! Damn! Hurray!* If they are connected to a sentence, they are almost always set off by commas or other marks of punctuation, like parenthetical constructions, which they basically are; see Rule 2-1. However, an interjection does not have to be set off if a writer wants to indicate a spoken delivery with no pauses around the interjection: *Oh I don't know about that*; *We could surrender, but oh the shame we would face.* Similarly, *I'd like to help, but darn, I'm broke* may suggest spoken delivery better than the original example above with the comma after *but*.

into vs. in to   *Into* is a preposition, as in *He went into his office*, in which it is part of the adverbial prepositional phrase *into his office. In to* is an adverb plus a preposition, as in *He went in to lunch*, in which *in* directly modifies the verb *went* and *to* is a preposition with the object *lunch*. When *into* is misused for *in to* the result is sometimes ludicrous: *He turned his uniform into the supply sergeant* states that the uniform was transformed into the sergeant, not handed over to him.

intransitive verb   a verb that does not have an **object**. A **transitive verb** transmits its action from a subject to an object: *The bat hits the ball.* An intransitive verb does not pass its action along: *The ball disappears.* Intransitive verbs do not require an object to complete their meaning.

Many verbs can be either transitive or intransitive. *The child plays* uses the verb *play* intransitively; *The child plays poker* uses it transitively. Other verbs, such as *lie* (tell a falsehood), *sleep*, and *smile*, are always intransitive, except in a special construction in which they are given an object that repeats the meaning of the verb: *He lied a terrible lie*; *He slept the sleep of the just*; *He smiled an ambiguous smile.* A few, such as *lie* (lie down), cannot be transitive even in this special construction.

An intransitive verb can never be in the passive voice. If an active verb is made passive, its object becomes its subject; *The bat hits the ball* becomes *The ball is hit by the bat.* But an intransitive verb has no object to be made its subject, and so the verb can't be made passive, since with very few exceptions (see *as follows* vs. *as follow*) a verb must have a subject. Even an imperative verb, as in *Go away*, has the understood subject *you*. See also **linking verb**.

introductory construction   a word, phrase, or clause that precedes the main clause of a sentence; see Rule 2-1. A comma after an introductory construction is usually helpful to indicate that the main clause is about to start, but this principle is sometimes misapplied: *In view of the circumstances, we chose to build a house* properly has a comma after the introductory construction, but *In view of the road, is a poor place to build a house*, which uses the prepositional phrase *In view of the road* not as an introductory construction but as the subject of the sentence, incorrectly has a comma between the subject and its verb; see Rule 2-4. *In view of the road, we saw a good site* uses the phrase *In view of the road* not as an introductory construction but as a modifier, and the main problem is not the comma but the ambiguous position of the modifier, which makes it difficult to tell whether it modifies the verb *found* or the noun *site*; see the discussion of inverted sentences in Rule 2-5. *We decided that, in view of the circumstances, we should build a house* uses the comma correctly after *circumstances* but incorrectly after *that*; see Rule 2-8.

inversion   in a sentence, a word order that is not the standard one. *"Not guilty" was the verdict* inverts **subject** and **complement** to put extra emphasis on *"Not guilty." Hurt in the accident were two bystanders* puts the subject at the end of the sentence and inverts the usual order of auxiliary verb and base verb; *Two bystanders were hurt in the accident* is the standard order. Inversion can create ambiguity (see Rule 2-5) and, since inverted sentences tend to sound unnatural anyway, can conceal various grammatical errors, especially errors of **agreement**, that would be automatically avoided in a straightforward sentence. Inversion is often used for no purpose other than to provide variety of sentence structure; such variety is desirable (see Rule 4-11) but inversion is a poor way to achieve it.

italics   slanted, scriptlike type, as distinguished from roman type. On the typewriter and in handwriting, italics are indicated by underlining. Italics have the effect of providing emphasis in writing in the same way rises in volume, pitch, or intensity provide emphasis in speech. They are often overused for this purpose; even two or three italicized words in a paragraph can create a gushy, gesturing effect that is annoying to the reader.

Italics are used for the titles of certain written works, musical compositions, and works of art; see Rules 3-19 and 3-20. They are also used for unfamiliar foreign terms; see Rule 3-23. They may be used instead of quotation marks in some circumstances, as I have used them in this book for examples and for words under discussion; see Rule 2-26. They are almost always used for the names of specific ships, as in S.S. *United States*; note that initials preceding the name, such as S.S. and H.M.S., are not italicized. They are often used for the names of specific airplanes or spacecraft—*Air Force One*; *Mariner IV*—but roman may be used for these as well; different publications and publishing houses have different policies, and a writer may decide his own policy as long as he thinks it out carefully and follows it consistently. Thus one might decide to use roman for Air Force One, which is actually the Air Force numerical designation for the plane the President happens to be using rather than a true name, but to use italic for *The Spirit of St. Louis*.

it is, there is, there are   In these constructions, *it* or *there* temporarily takes the place of the true subject. In *It is true that there is no school today*, there are two such constructions. The subject is *that there is no school today*. The use of *It is* makes it possible to avoid the awkward *That there is no school today is true*. The use of *there is* is essential; *No school is today* isn't English. Sometimes the true subject never appears in the sentence, especially in familiar idioms such as *It is cold*, in which the true subject—*the weather*, or perhaps *the temperature*—is understood. See also **expletive**.

It is can be followed by a true subject that is plural: *It is friends we need*. In this respect it is like any construction with a **complement**; the verb *is* agrees in number with the subject, *It*, not the complement, *friends* (see Rule 1-11). But when a relative clause follows the true subject, the verb in the relative clause usually agrees with the true subject, not with *It*, in number and person, even though logically the antecedent of the relative pronoun is *It*: *It is friends that are needed*; *It is I that am friendless*. However, although *It is friends that is needed* and *It is we that is friendless* are wrong to everyone's ear, *It is I that is friendless*, in which *I* and *is* agree in number but not in person, has its defenders. Particularly in negative constructions, *is* may sound better even when it disagrees with the true subject in both number and person: *It is not I that is friendless, it is you that are friendless*; *It is not you that is friendless, it is I that am friendless*. Since there is disagreement on the point, each of us can follow his own ear. See also *what is* vs. *what are*.

There is and *there are* don't create this problem: *There is no school*; *There are no classes*. If the true subject is singular, *is* is correct; if the true subject is plural, *are* is correct. However, careless errors are common, especially when the true subject is separated by other words from *There is*: *There's eventually going to be objections* is incorrect.

There is is often used when the true subject is a compound subject, and therefore plural, but its first element is singular: *There is a car and two chickens in his garage*. Although this disagreement in number of verb and subject cannot be defended logically, it sometimes seems preferable to careful agreement: *There are a right way and a wrong way of doing everything*, while correct, is unnatural. Perhaps there isn't a right way; *there is*, like *it is*, is a highly idiomatic construction in English, and idiom often ignores right and wrong. Generally, *there are* will work when the true subject is plural; if it seems unnatural, we have the choice of recasting to avoid it or accepting *there is* as an idiomatic exception to the standard rules of agreement.

it is I vs. *it is me*   The first is correct but sounds stilted; the second is grammatically incorrect, since *me* is being used as a subject **complement** and should be in the **subjective case**, but sounds more natural. Usually *it is me*, and especially the contraction *it's me*, should prevail; see Rule 1-6.

its vs. *it's*   *Its* is the possessive form of the pronoun *it*: *The pen was missing its cap*. *It's* is the contraction of *it is* or *it has*: *It's snowing, though it's never happened here in September before*. *It's* is often carelessly and sometimes ignorantly used for *its*.

Jr., Sr.   These abbreviations should normally be preceded by a comma, and followed by a comma if the clause or sentence continues: *John Smith, Jr., was there*. They can cause problems; see Rule 3-11.

kind   When it is singular, *kind* should not be used with the plural demonstrative adjectives *these* and *those*. Therefore *these kind of stories* is an error; the plural *stories* has been allowed to change *this kind* to *these kind*.

However, *this kind of stories*, though grammatically correct, does not sound quite natural. When everything is plural—*these kinds of stories*—there is no problem, but if the topic is one specific kind, not several kinds with something in common, the plural is illogical: *I used to like stories about baseball, but these kinds of stories bore me now*. It is usually possible to make everything singular instead: *this kind of story bores me now*. When the plural has to be used with *kind of*, it usually sounds natural enough: *I don't like this kind of beans*.

Note that *these kinds of* followed by a singular, as in *these kinds of story*, is grammatically correct, and it usually sounds natural.

The *kind of* construction is somewhat overused. Often it is better to use an *of this kind* construction: *Stories of this kind bore me now*, when only one kind has been mentioned, and *Stories of these kinds bore me now*, when two or more kinds have been mentioned, are both correct, and both sound natural.

Kind of is much too common as a vague qualifier, as in *I was kind of busy* and *I kind of had to cut her short*. All it generally signifies is that the speaker or writer has no confidence in his own expression and feels apologetic. It is a colloquial construction and has been around kind of a long time but is kind of annoying in speech or writing that is kind of formal.

kinship terms   when to capitalize, Rule 3-16; set off with commas in direct address, Rule 2-10

lay vs. lie   These verbs are often confused; in the past tense even many well-educated people make errors.

Lay is a **transitive verb** meaning *place* or *put*. Its past tense is *laid*, and its past participle is also *laid*. *I am going to lay the money on the table. He would not take the money, so I laid it on the table. "I have laid the money on the table," I said.*

Lie is an **intransitive verb** meaning *recline*; it is often used with the adverb *down* or with a prepositional phrase such as *on the bed.* Its past tense is *lay*—just like the present tense of the other verb, which is the source of much of the confusion—and its past participle is *lain. I decided to lie down. I lay on the bed for a while, then muttered to myself, "I have lain here long enough."*

Among educated people the most common error is using *lay* for *laid,* as in *He lay the book on the table.*

leave vs. let   In most contexts, *leave* is obviously nonstandard for *let: Leave us go now* and *We should leave him sink or swim* are incorrect. *Leave* is idiomatic in some common constructions: *Leave me be; Leave him alone.* However, since *Let me be* and *Let him alone* are equally idiomatic, *leave* might as well be saved for contexts in which its basic meaning, *go away from,* is relevant.

less   See *fewer* vs. *less.*

let's you and me vs. let's you and I   *Let's you and me* is a contraction of *Let us, you and me,* in which the pronouns *you* and *me* are in **apposition** to the pronoun *us.* Since *us* is in the objective case, as the object of *Let, you* and *me* must be in the objective case (see Rule 1-6). Therefore *let's you and I* is wrong.

Let's you and him is clearly illogical if the contraction is expanded to *let us you and him. Let's us* is clearly redundant, since the expansion is *let us us.* The constructions are well established as colloquial idioms, but neither they nor the correct *let's you and me* are appropriate in anything but the most informal or deliberately folksy context.

like for as, as if, or as though   The word *like* can be several parts of speech, but it should not be used as a **conjunction**—that is, it should not be used to replace *as, as if,* or *as though,* all of which are subordinating conjunctions. Essentially, this means that *like* should not be used to introduce a clause. *She looks just like I used to look at her age* is wrong, because *like* introduces a clause; *like* should be *as. She acts like she wants to be admired* is the same error; *like* should be *as if* or *as though.*

Like is properly used as a **preposition:** *She looks just like me at her age* is correct; note that the pronoun *me* is in the objective case, as the object of *like;* and that there is no verb in *like me at her age*—it is not a clause.

like for *as, as if,* or *as though*

The difficulty is that the phrase following *like* may be elliptical and may include an understood verb, as in *She takes to
it like a duck to water,* which is technically incorrect, since
when the ellipsis is filled out the phrase becomes *like a duck
takes to water,* and *like* should be *as. Like* is thoroughly
established in many similar elliptical idioms—*He played it
like a pro; He eats like an animal.* We can keep filling in the
ellipsis until something like correctness results—*She takes
to it in a way like the way a duck takes to water,* and so on—
but it is tiresome to make a sentence increasingly unnatural
just to justify what our ears tell us is acceptable. Although it
is impossible to give invariable rules for what is acceptable
and what is not, it is worth noting that certain verbs, such as
act, work and others with similar basic meanings, seem to
combine naturally with *like* followed by an elliptical clause:
It acts like a plow and works like a dream.

Often we must rely on our ears rather than on any hard-
and-fast rule. A bad ear coupled with a fear of *like* causes
real problems; *He eats as an animal* and *He played it as a
pro* just do not sound like English. Adding a verb, either the
appropriate one or a form of *do,* makes such sentences English again—*He eats as an animal does*—and perhaps this is
the best solution for the uncertain.

Like as a conjunction does have many defenders among
the well-educated and even among grammarians. *It looks like
we won't be able to go* certainly wouldn't offend most people. Even *She looks like I used to* offends few people, and
She looks like Mary used to, with the subjective case following *like* not so apparent, offends even fewer. Many other
prepositions, such as *after,* can be conjunctions; why not let
like be one, when so many educated people use it as one?
There is no good reason, except a reason that for the purposes of this book must be considered not only good but
unassailable: The use of *like* as a conjunction has become a
shibboleth; those who condemn it do so very strongly.
Therefore I advise avoiding use of *like* whenever a clause
with a verb follows and being suspicious of it even when the
verb is elliptical—remembering, however, that using *as*
when *like* is actually correct or idiomatically correct is worse
than misusing *like;* see **hyperurbanism.**

Like seems capable of ever new misuses. Its use as a
vague qualifier or modifier in speech, as in *She was like not*

interested in me at all and *I was trying to get a laugh out of her for like twenty minutes*, is particularly objectionable; *like* becomes a verbal tic and infests every sentence. The indecisive, apologetic overtones it gives sentences may have a kind of charm, as may the adolescents who use it, but it amounts to an admission by the speaker himself that his expression is poor.

linking verb a special kind of **intransitive verb** that links its subject to a **complement**. In *The cat seems nervous*, the verb *seems* links *The cat* to the adjective *nervous*. In *He became president*, the verb *became* links *He* to the noun *president*. The most common linking verb is *be*, as in *The cat is gray*, but there are many others, such as *appear*, *remain*, and *grow*. Almost all can be used in other senses in which they are not linking verbs, but when they express some kind of being, seeming, or becoming, they are linking verbs.

Linking verbs are not complete in themselves (as are other intransitive verbs: *He slept*) but require another word or a phrase to complete their meaning, somewhat as a **transitive verb** requires an object to complete its meaning. But the complement of a linking verb is not an object; it should be in the subjective rather than objective case: *The culprit was he*, not *The culprit was him*. There are idiomatic exceptions to this rule, especially in **expletive** constructions such as *It's me*; see Rule 1-6.

I feel badly is an error because *feel* is functioning as a linking verb in the sentence, and the pronoun *I* cannot be linked with the adverb *badly*; see Rule 1-22. It should be *I feel bad*, linking the pronoun to an adjective—unless, of course, *badly* is actually meant to be an adverb, as in *I feel badly since my stroke and can no longer pick locks*, in which *feel* is not a linking verb.

literally means *actually* or *without exaggeration*. In careless writing and speech it often has the opposite meaning—*figuratively*—or has no meaning at all beyond a vague and unnecessary intensification. *He was literally floored* and *He was literally caught red-handed* are misuses unless he actually collapsed on the floor or his hands were actually red. *He was literally flabbergasted* is a misuse because *flabbergast* doesn't have a truly literal meaning; all *literally* does in the sentence is intensify *flabbergasted*, which is intense enough as it stands. Often *literally* actually weakens an expression instead of strengthening it.

Literally should be saved for contexts in which it indicates that an expression is intended in its literal rather than its figurative sense: *He was literally insane with grief and had to be confined in a psychiatric hospital*; *When the bride threw the groom rather than her bouquet down the stairs, the bridesmaids below were literally crushed.*

loan vs. lend   *Loan* is primarily a noun, *lend* is only a verb. *Loan* has long been accepted as a verb, and the past-tense form *loaned* is much more common than *lent*. As a minor nicety, I advise using *loan* only as a noun.

may   See *can* vs. *may*.

mechanics   The mechanics of a language are the various rules and principles that govern its use and make it more than a succession of meaningless syllables. In this book, Chapter 1, on grammar, Chapter 2, on punctuation, and Chapter 3, on miscellaneous matters such as capitalization and conventional uses for italics and quotation marks, are concerned with mechanics. Some of the mechanics of English, such as spelling, are not covered in the book. Chapter 4, on diction and composition, is largely concerned with matters that go beyond mechanics.

metaphor   a figure of speech in which something is spoken of in terms of something else, as in *Love is a shy flower*. *He sails close to the wind* is a straightforward statement if the context is sailing, but is a metaphorical statement if the context is business ethics. Metaphors are useful and often effective, but can be overused; see the discussion of figurative diction in Rule 4-11.

The metaphor should not be confused with the **simile**, which is similar but makes an explicit comparison: *Love is like a shy flower*. The term *metaphorical* is often misused to characterize any figurative diction: *When I say I almost fainted I am not being metaphorical* is an error; *I almost fainted* may be **hyperbole** but is not metaphor. It should be *I am not exaggerating*.

modifier   a word, phrase, or clause that modifies another word, phrase, or clause. Adverbs and adjectives are obvious modifiers, but the term is broad and includes phrases and clauses that have adverbial or adjectical functions; see **adjective** and **adverb**. Modifiers should not dangle without something to modify; see Rule 1-21.

mood   The mood of a **verb** indicates whether the verb's sentence or clause concerns matters of fact (the **indicative mood**), expresses a possibility (the **subjunctive mood**), or is a command (the **imperative mood**). Sometimes the word *mode* is used instead of *mood*. See the discussion preceding Rule 1-17.

more, most   *More* is a comparative form and *most* is a superlative form; if they are used with adjectives or adverbs that are already comparative or superlative, they are redundant. They are rarely misused when the words they modify are clearly comparative or superlative, as in *Truth is more stranger than fiction*, but even the well-educated sometimes misuse them with words such as *preferable*, which is comparative in meaning even though not in form: *Both usages are acceptable, but the first is more preferable* is therefore an error also.

Most should not be used to make a superlative out of a modifier that includes the word *well*, as in *the most well-known painter* and the *most well-respected lawyer*. Either *most* should be dropped and the modifier itself made superlative or the modifier should be altered so that *well* is not included: *the best-known painter*; *the most respected lawyer*. Similarly, *more* should not be used to make a comparative out of a modifier that includes *well*; *more well-known painter* and *more well-respected lawyer* should be *better-known painter* and *more respected lawyer*.

more important vs. *more importantly*   I advise using *more important*, if only because those who condemn *more importantly* do so very strongly. But the issue is not simple.

An adverb can modify an entire sentence, as in *Fortunately, it did not rain*, and there is no reason why such an adverb cannot itself have an adverbial modifier, as in *Less fortunately, there was an attack by killer bees*. However, the function of a sentence-modifying adverb is often more adjectival than adverbial—it does not modify an action or a quality, as adverbs usually do, but a statement or the meaning of a statement, which can be thought of as a thing. Therefore, when there is a choice between using an adjectival form and using an adverbial form to modify an entire sentence, the adjectival form may be preferable.

More importantly is probably the most common adverb-plus-adverb combination used to modify entire sentences: *More importantly, we forgot to bring the beer*. But there is a choice with *more importantly*; the adverb-plus-adjective form is just as common: *More important, we forgot to bring the beer*. This can be considered elliptical for *What is more important, we forgot to bring the beer*. I recommend the adverb-plus-adjective form for *more important* and for any similar sentence modifier whenever it does not seem unnatural.

Note that we do not have an option when the adverb-plus-adverb sentence modifier can be considered to modify the verb in the sentence, as in *Less frequently, we hold our celebrations indoors*, in which *Less frequently* can be taken either as modifying *hold* or as modifying the entire sentence.

Ms., Mrs., Miss   The title *Ms.*, which is not a true abbreviation but nevertheless has a period, has been in use for several decades in business correspondence to address a woman whose marital status is unknown. It is currently associated with feminism, because, like *Mr.*, it does not indicate marital status. Many women do not like it. It is often used archly, making it a sneer rather than a courtesy. I advise not using it for a woman whose marital status is known unless it is the woman's own preference.

Mrs. should not ordinarily be used with a woman's given name: *Mrs. John Smith* is correct; *Mrs. Mary Smith* is not. However, a divorced woman may prefer *Mrs. Mary Smith* if she has retained her married surname.

Mrs. should not be used with a maiden name or another name that a woman uses professionally and is not her husband's name. If Mary Smith is an actress married to John Brown, she is Mrs. Brown but Miss Smith.

No title at all should be used if *Mr.* is not used for men in the same context. *The committee included John Brown, George Smith, and Miss Jane Jones* (or *Mrs. James Jones*) is discriminatory; if Brown and Smith don't need a tip of the hat, neither does Jones. Referring to a woman by her last name alone was formerly considered rude in most contexts and still bothers some people, but it is preferable to false or unwanted courtesy.

myself, yourself   These are reflexive or intensive pronouns (see **pronoun**). They should not be used when ordinary pronouns will do. *She invited myself and my wife to dinner* has a hoity-toity flavor that is quite objectionable.

neither . . . nor   See *either . . . or*.

nicknames   Quotation marks are sometimes used to enclose nicknames but are rarely necessary; see Rule 2-26.

nominal   a word or group of words that functions as a noun in a sentence. Nouns themselves are nominals. In *His smiling suggested what he thought*, the gerund phrase *His smiling* is a nominal, acting as the subject of the sentence, and the clause *what he thought* is a nominal, acting as the object of the sentence. The term *substantive* means the same thing.

none   a pronoun that often means *not one* and is treated as singular, as in *None of the men has retired*. However, it can also mean *not any* and be treated as plural, as in *None of the trees in the forest are deciduous*. Often it can take either a singular or a plural verb with no significant change in meaning.

nonrestrictive   See **parenthetical construction**.

nor   See *or* vs. *nor*.

no sooner . . . than vs. *no sooner . . . when*   Since *no sooner* is a comparative construction, *than* must be used; *when* is incorrect. *No sooner had I hung up the phone than it rang again* is correct, not *when it rang again*.

not . . . but   an **antithetical** construction, used to distinguish a negative element from a positive one. Often the negative element is set off with commas, as in *He went to college, not to play football, but to get a degree*. However, I advise omitting these commas in most cases; see Rule 2-7.

   I did not bring but twenty dollars, in which *but* means *only*, is incorrect because it is a double negative; *I brought but twenty dollars* is correct.

noun   one of the parts of speech; a word that names a person, place, or thing. A primary function of nouns is to serve as subjects or objects in sentences. In *John ate fish in Japan*, the noun *John* is the subject of the verb *ate*, the noun *fish* is the object of the verb, and the noun *Japan* is the object of the preposition *in*. Most nouns can also serve as adjectives, simply by being placed before another noun: *Reagan proposal*; *California wine*; *fish dinner*. However, excessive use of nouns as adjectives should be avoided; see the discussions of clumped compound modifiers in Rule 2-36 and the discussion of abstract diction in rule 4-11.

Noun phrases and *noun clauses* are so called not because they contain nouns—often they do not—but because they function as nouns. *His speaking so fast suggested he was nervous* contains the noun phrase *His speaking so fast*, acting as the subject of the verb *suggested*, and the noun clause *he was nervous*, acting as the object of the verb.

Proper nouns are those that name a specific person or place, such as *John* and *Japan*; they are capitalized.

Common nouns are all other nouns—those naming things, such as *fish*, *district*, and *peace*. When a common noun is used in the name of a specific person or place, it becomes part of a proper noun phrase and is capitalized, as in *District of Columbia*. A proper noun phrase can name a specific thing rather than a person or place: *Nobel Peace Prize*. See also **generic** and Rule 3-12.

number   in grammar, an **inflection** that indicates whether a word is singular or plural. The number of a verb and its subject should agree; see Rule 1-11. The number of a pronoun and its antecedent should also agree—a rule frequently broken, as in *Everyone clapped their hands*; see Rule 1-12.

numbers   The treatment of numbers in written material is often inconsistent or otherwise faulty. A basic problem is when to spell out a number and when to use figures for it; see Rules 3-1 to 3-5. The plural of a number in figures usually requires no apostrophe; see Rule 3-6. Inclusive numbers joined by a hyphen are often misused, as in *from 1890-93*; see Rule 3-7. For other problems with numbers and hyphens, see Rule 2-38.

object   a word or group of words in a sentence that is affected by the action of the sentence's verb or by a preposition. In *The man with her is my husband*, the pronoun *her* is the object of the preposition *with*. Many verbs can have both a direct object and an indirect object; in *I gave him money*, the noun *money* is the direct object of *gave* and the pronoun *him* is the indirect object. The indirect object has a prepositional relationship to the verb, even though the actual preposition, which is usually *to*, does not appear. If the indirect object is separated from the verb, there is a preposition and the indirect object becomes part of a prepositional phrase: *I gave money to him*.

objective case   the case of a noun or pronoun that is being used as the object of a verb or of a preposition. Only a few pronouns have a distinctive **inflection** for the objective case: *I, me; he, him; she, her; we, us; they, them; who, whom; whoever, whomever*. Other pronouns and all nouns have the same form in the objective case that they have in the **subjective case.** Nevertheless, since the inflected pronouns are very common, mistakes are frequent; see Rules 1-6 to 1-9.

obligated **vs.** *obliged*   *Obligated* suggests duty, as in *I was obligated to finish writing the book. Obliged* suggests either constraint, as in *I was obliged by my tax situation to sell my stamp collection*, or gratitude, as in *I was obliged to the IRS for its mercy*. These past participles are often confused, though confusion is rare with their base verbs, *oblige* and *obligate*; *to oblige someone* means to do him a favor or force him to do something, whereas *to obligate someone* means to make him aware of a debt or duty by somehow doing him a favor.

of **for** *have* **or** *'ve*   *If you'd given me the figures earlier, I'd of been better prepared* is an example of an increasingly common error. The word *of* is pronounced very much like the contraction *'ve* but cannot be substituted for it. A novelist may sometimes use *of* instead of *'ve* in dialogue to indicate a contraction that is drawled or pronounced in a nonstandard way, but many readers doubtless suspect the novelist does not know better.

off vs. off of   *Off* is sufficient by itself: *He jumped off the roof*; *Please get this tick off me.* An added *of* is superfluous, though it is not wrong and may seem desirable in the cadence of a specific expression: *How much money did you make off of that deal?*

only   The word is frequently placed carelessly so that it is not clear what it modifies; see the discussion of adverbs in Rule 1-20.

onto vs. on to   *Onto* is a preposition, as in *The key fell onto the sidewalk* and *He added the tax onto the bill.* It can usually be replaced by either *on* or *to*: *The key fell on the sidewalk*; *He added the tax to the bill. On to* is an adverb plus a preposition, as in *We drove on to the gas station*, in which *on* modifies the verb *drove* and *to* is a preposition with the object *gas station.* Misuses can cause misreading. *We drove onto the bridge* means that we began to cross the bridge; *We drove on to the bridge* means that we continued driving till we reached the bridge.

or vs. nor   In some constructions, both *or* and *nor* are correct: *He cannot read or write*; *He cannot read nor write.* The second example, which is actually elliptical for *He cannot read, nor can he write*, no longer sounds natural unless special emphasis is intended for the word after *nor*: *He will not withdraw nor reduce his demands.* In a **correlative** construction, *or* must be used after *either* and *nor* must be used after *neither*: *He can neither read nor write*; *He refuses either to withdraw or to reduce his demands.*

organization   in composition, the relationship and order of ideas. Some basic principles of organization are discussed in Rules 4-4 and 4-5.

out vs. out of   *Out* is sometimes sufficient by itself: *He threw it out the window.* Here an added *of* is superfluous, though it may be desirable in the cadence of a specific sentence. However, *of* is often required, as in *He drew it out of his pocket* and *He made money out of that deal. Out* cannot replace *out of* in the same way that *off* can replace *off of.*

parallel structure   For parallel structure within a sentence, see Rule 1-5; see also the discussion of elegant variation in Rule 4-11.

immediately apparent whether the subject is singular or plural; see Rule 1-11. Problems of agreement also occur between pronoun and antecedent; see Rule 1-12. Plural and possessive forms are often confused, especially when a plural is also possessive; see Rule 2-29.

Plurals of lowercase letters usually require an apostrophe for clarity (*p's and q's*), but plurals of figures do not (*1980s*); see Rule 3-6.

An English noun typically forms its plural by adding *s* or *es*, but there are many exceptions, and sometimes more than one form is correct; when in doubt, use the dictionary to determine the correct or preferred plural. One item not covered in dictionaries: A proper noun ending in *y*, such as *Mary*, does not form its plural in the regular way—that is, by changing the *y* to *i* and adding *es*—but simply by adding *s*, as in *Last night there were three Marys at the party*. There are some exceptions, such as *the Rockies* and *the Ptolemies*.

When a possessive form used as a noun, such as McDonald's (the fast-food chain), is made plural, we usually pronounce the form with an *es* added—McDonald'ses—but this looks peculiar in writing. *There were two McDonald's on the same block* is acceptable; I advise against *McDonald'ses* unless there is some point in indicating pronunciation (as in dialogue). In most writing the problem can be avoided: *There were two McDonald's restaurants*.

plus The voguish use of *plus* to replace *and in addition* or a similar phrase is objectionable: *They gave him a raise, plus he got a corner office*. English has many conjunctions and conjunctive constructions; why borrow *plus* from the chaste language of mathematics and corrupt it? Phrases such as *principal plus interest* are, however, acceptable in financial contexts, since they make use of the mathematical sense of the word. I have used phrases such as *apostrophe plus s* and *adverb + adjective* in this book; this borrowing of *plus* is conventional in writing on language.

points of ellipsis the three dots—or four dots, if a period is included—used to indicate omissions in quoted material and pauses in speech. See Rules 2-27 and 2-28.

political divisions and subdivisions capitalization of, Rule 3-17

parentheses position of with other marks of punctuation, Rule 2-18. See also the discussion preceding Rule 2-18.

parenthetical construction a construction used not to identify a word or phrase but merely to provide further information about it. A construction within parentheses is, of course, parenthetical: *John (who won the tournament) is smiling*. Instead of a pair of parentheses, a pair of commas or a pair of dashes can be used to set off a parenthetical construction: *John, who won the tournament, is smiling*; *John—who won the tournament—is smiling*. Parenthetical constructions are often called nonrestrictive, because they do not restrict the meaning of the words they modify. In *The man who won the tournament is smiling*, the clause *who won the tournament* is no longer parenthetical; it is a **defining construction**, restricting the meaning of the word *man*. Proper punctuation often depends on determining whether a construction is parenthetical or defining; see Rule 2-1.

participle a form of a **verb** that is used as an adjective and in compound tenses. The present participle ends in *ing*: *The drinking man is laughing* contains the participle *drinking*, used as an adjective to modify *man*, and the participle *laughing*, used with the auxiliary verb *is* to form the present progressive tense of the verb *laugh*. The past participle usually ends in *ed*, but many verbs form the past participle irregularly: *The elated man has drunk too much* contains the past participle *elated*, used as an adjective to modify *man*, and the irregular past participle *drunk*, used with the auxiliary verb *has* to form the present perfect tense of the verb *drink*.

Participles sometimes seem to act as adverbs, as in *The man didn't want to go staggering home*, in which *staggering* seems to modify *go*, describing the manner of the man's going rather than the man himself. If we try to consider *staggering* a participle used as an adjective, we have to imagine some word for it to modify, since none appears in the sentence. Instead, we can consider *go staggering* to be a special compound tense of the verb *stagger*, with *go* an auxiliary verb.

Not all forms that look like participles are participles. In *The man drinking from the bottle should pay for more than the drunk portion*, *drinking* and *drunk* are participles. However, in *The drunk man has been having a drinking bout*, *drunk* is not a participle but an ordinary adjective, and *drinking* is not a participle but a **gerund**. The man has not been drunk in the sense that a bottle is drunk, he is drunk; the bout is not drinking in the sense that a man can be drinking, it is a bout of drinking.

When the present participle is used as an adjective, it is active in relation to the word it modifies: *an annoying man*. When the past participle is used as an adjective, it is passive in relation to the word it modifies, unless it is combined with a participial form of an auxiliary verb: *An annoyed customer complained*; *Having annoyed everyone, the man left*. Thus the tense of a participle is primarily an indicator of active and passive rather than an indicator of time.

However, a participle used as an adjective should be in the tense that is logical in relation to the tense of the main verb in the sentence—the present participle indicates time that is the same as the time of the main verb, and the past participle with an auxiliary verb indicates time that is previous to the time of the main verb; see Rule 1-15. Loose use of the present participle to indicate action just before that of the main verb, as in *Crossing the room, he sat down*, should be avoided; see Rule 1-16.

A *participial phrase* is an adjectival phrase (see **adjective**) that is based on a participle. *Diminishing in the distance, the road leading to the foothills seemed endless* contains the participial phrases *Diminishing in the distance* and *leading to the foothills*, both modifying *road*. Participial phrases are sometimes misused or misplaced in a sentence so that it is not clear what they modify; see Rule 1-20. Note that in *The guide advised following the road*, the phrase *following the road* is not a participial phrase; *following* is not a participle but a gerund, and the phrase is used not as an adjective but as a noun, the object of the verb *advised*. Also note that an *ing* form of a verb in a prepositional phrase, as in *we were committed to following the road*, has to be a gerund rather than a participle; see **preposition**.

If a participle used as an adjective does not have anything to modify, it is a **dangling construction**: *Trudging toward the foothills, the road seemed endless* has a dangling participial phrase; see Rule 1-21.

parts of speech   Words are traditionally divided into eight parts of speech: **adjective**, **adverb**, **conjunction**, **interjection**,

noun, **preposition**, **pronoun**, and **verb**. However, these classifications are accurate only when they are used to categorize a specific word in a specific context, because many words can be more than one part of speech. They actually characterize the relationship a word has to other words rather than the word itself. Thus the word *dog*, ordinarily thought of as a simple noun, can easily escape that classification; the phrase *dog food* uses it as an adjective.

passive voice   See **voice**.

period   the full-stop mark that ends a declarative sentence. In an interrogatory sentence the question mark replaces the period; in an exclamation the exclamation point replaces the period. A true period—that is, one that indicates the end of a sentence—cannot be used with the comma, semicolon, colon, dash, question mark, or exclamation point, but can be used with a closing parenthesis or bracket (see Rule 2-18) or with a closing quotation mark (see Rules 2-23 to 2-26).

The period that indicates an abbreviation, as in *Mr. Smith* and *Smith & Co.*, is not a true period; it can occur with all the marks of punctuation except the period itself. When an abbreviation with a period ends a declarative sentence, the single period serves both purposes; it is not doubled.

The three dots that indicate omissions and pauses are not true periods either but points of ellipsis; see Rules 2-27 and 2-28.

person   in grammar, the form of a pronoun or a verb that indicates who is making a statement and whom it is being made about. *I am* has subject and verb in the first person; *you are* has subject and verb in the second person; *he is* has subject and verb in the third person. *We are* and *they are* are plural forms for the first and third person; *you are* is the same in the singular and the plural. A subject and its verb should agree in person (Rule 1-10), and a pronoun and its antecedent should agree in person (Rule 1-12). This agreement is so basic a part of the language that errors are rare, but they do occur.

place names   capitalization of, Rules 3-17 and 3-18

plural   The **number** of a noun, pronoun, or verb can be either singular or plural. Problems of **agreement** in number can occur between subject and verb, often because it is not

possessive case   the case of a noun or pronoun that indicates ownership. The ownership can be quite vague; *John's block* would not usually indicate that John owns the block but merely that he lives on it. The possessive case normally turns a noun or pronoun into an adjective, since the possessive noun or pronoun modifies the thing possessed. However, a certain kind of possessive, called an independent possessive, functions like a noun, as in *My hamburger fell in the fire, so I ate John's*, in which *my* is an ordinary possessive pronoun but *John's* is an independent possessive; see Rule 1-19 and the discussion of disagreement in case in Rule 1-12.

Nouns typically form the possessive by adding an apostrophe plus *s* in the singular and just an apostrophe in the plural, but there are many complications and exceptions; see Rule 2-29.

Some of the personal pronouns have special forms for the independent possessive—*mine, yours, hers, ours, theirs*. These forms do not have apostrophes. One frequently sees the forms *your's, her's, our's*, and *their's*; they are wrong and indicate a very shaky knowledge of English, though they were standard in previous centuries.

The word *of* can often replace the possessive case: *the government's role; the role of the government*. However, very often when *of* is used, the possessive case can be or must be used too: *John's friend; a friend of John's*. This so-called double possessive is difficult to explain. The basic reason for it is that while the possessive case usually does indicate actual—if often loose—ownership, the word *of* can indicate not only ownership but also a so-called partitive relationship; it can indicate that something is a part of something else or made of something else. Thus we can say *a slice of cake*, using the partitive *of*, but not *a cake's slice*. In certain situations this partitive implication of *of* intrudes when simple ownership is intended—sometimes disturbingly, as in *a cake of Mary*, which carries the possible but unintended meaning that the cake is part of Mary or made from Mary. To avoid ambiguity and to stress that ownership, not a partitive relationship, is intended, the possessive case is therefore used along with *of* or else the possessive case is used alone: *a cake of Mary's; Mary's cake*. Yet in many other situations the partitive implication of *of* does not intrude and the double possessive is not used: *the arrival of Mary* cannot be *the arrival of Mary's*. Sometimes the double possessive makes a distinction in meaning: *a picture of John* means a picture with John as its subject; *a picture of John's* means a picture owned by John.

precipitate vs. precipitous   *Precipitate* means *sudden* or *hasty*, as in *a precipitate decision*. *Precipitous* means *steep*, as in *a precipitous path*.

predicate   the part of a sentence that expresses what is predicated—that is, set forth—about the subject of the sentence. The predicate includes the verb and also any object, modifier, or complement of the verb. In many simple sentences that have their words in standard order, such as *The boy came slowly into the room*, everything that follows the subject, in this case *The boy*, is the predicate. However, in *Slowly into the room came the boy*, the predicate precedes the subject; and in *The boy came slowly into the room, carrying his books*, the participial phrase *carrying his books* is not part of the predicate but part of the subject, modifying *boy*.

A *compound predicate* contains two or more verbs that have the same subject, as in *He sleeps too much and works too little*. Usually the elements of a two-verb compound predicate should not be separated by a comma; see Rule 2-3.

predominant vs. predominate   *Predominant* is the adjective; *predominate* is the verb. Therefore *predominantly*, not *predominately*, is the adverb. *The hardwoods predominate in eastern woodlands*; *Hardwoods are predominant*; *The trees are predominantly hardwoods*.

prefixes and suffixes   Prefixes are added at the beginning of a root word; *unkind* has the prefix *un*, added to *kind* to reverse its meaning. Suffixes are added at the end of a root word; *kindness* has the suffix *ness*, added to the adjective *kind* to make it a noun. Most common prefixes combine solidly with the root word, but some require a hyphen; see Rules 2-31 and 2-32.

preposition   one of the parts of speech; a word used to indicate direction, motion, or position or some logical or conceptual relationship. A preposition always has an object—which is a noun or pronoun or some construction acting as a noun, such as a gerund—and it relates that object to some other word in the sentence, usually a noun or a verb. In *He went to France*, the preposition *to* relates its object, the noun *France*, to the verb *went*. In *The man in tweeds is English*, the preposition *in* relates its object, *tweeds*, to the noun *man*. There are many prepositions in English; common ones include *with, without, for, against, on, under, between, of, during, among, through, by, above, below, after,* and *before*. There are also many compound prepositions, such as *far from, close to,* and *because of*.

Some words that can be prepositions can also be conjunctions: *He appeared before me* uses *before* as a preposition, with the object *me*; *He appeared before I did* uses *before* as a subordinate conjunction, joining the clause *I did* to the rest of the sentence. Note that when *before* is a preposition, its object is in the objective case; see Rule 1-9. If *before*, or any similar word that can be either a preposition or a conjunction, is followed by a clause, such as *I did* in the second example, it is a conjunction.

Some words that can be prepositions can also be adverbs: *The ship beat up the coast* uses *up* as a preposition, with the object *the coast*; *The bosun beat up the mate* uses *up* as an adverb, modifying the verb *beat*—at a glance, *the mate* may look like the object of *up*, but actually it is the object of the verb-plus-adverb combination *beat up*. When such a word does not have any apparent object, it is an adverb: *Let's see what turns up*; *Darkness closes in*; *The food ran out*. In *He got through by cheating*, *through* is an adverb and *by* is a preposition; *through* has no object, but *by* has the object *cheating*. In *He got by through cheating*, *by* is an adverb and *through* is a preposition.

A *prepositional phrase* is a phrase including a preposition, its object, and any modifiers of the object. A preposition can't ordinarily stand alone but has to be part of a prepositional phrase, since a preposition requires an object. However, the prepositional phrase can be quite scrambled, as in *That's the drawer I put it in*; unscrambled, the sentence is *I put it in that drawer*, and the prepositional phrase is *in that drawer*.

Note that it is permissible to end a sentence with a preposition, despite a durable superstition that it's an error. Errors such as *He showed me where to stand at* are wrong not because the preposition *at* is at the end but because it shouldn't be in the sentence at all.

Prepositional phrases usually have adverbial or adjectival functions and sometimes can act as nouns. *Before breakfast is the time for prayers in the monastery* uses *Before breakfast* as the subject of the sentence (the usual function of a noun), *for prayers* to modify the noun *time* (the usual function of an adjective), and *in the monastery* to modify the entire sentence (the usual function of an adverb). They often modify entire sentences as introductory constructions: *In view of the foregoing, please disregard our previous letter.* Adverbial and adjectival prepositional phrases are often carelessly positioned, making it unclear what they modify; see Rule 1-20.

pronoun   one of the parts of speech; a word that represents a noun. There are several types of pronouns.

Personal pronouns are *I*, *you*, *he*, *she*, *it*, *we*, and *they*, along with their forms for the possessive case and objective case—*my* and *mine* for the possessive, *me* for the objective, and so on.

Intensive pronouns are special forms of personal pronouns used to add emphasis. In *John himself is going*, the pronoun *himself* is intensive.

Reflexive pronouns are the same as intensive pronouns in form but are used differently. In *John selected himself* and *She loved John for himself*, the pronoun *himself* is reflexive.

Reciprocal pronouns include *each other* and *one another*; they express a reciprocal, or mutual, relationship, as in *They loved each other*.

Relative pronouns include *who*, *whom*, *whose*, *which*, and *that* when these words are used to introduce relative clauses. Most of them also have indefinite forms (see below).

Interrogative pronouns include *who*, *whom*, *whose*, *which*, and *what* when these words are used to introduce questions, including indirect questions. In *I wonder what is happening*, the pronoun *what* is interrogative.

Indefinite pronouns include *someone*, *anyone*, and *one*; *either* and *each* unless they are adjectives; and the relative pronouns *whoever*, *whomever*, and *whichever*. They are called indefinite because it cannot be definite what they represent.

Demonstrative pronouns include *this*, *that*, *these*, and *those*. When these words are used as modifiers, as in *this book*, they are no longer pronouns but demonstrative adjectives.

Many pronouns, unlike nouns, have different forms in the **subjective case** and **objective case**, and mistakes are frequent; see Rules 1-6 to 1-9. A pronoun that is the subject of a verb should agree with the verb in person and number; see Rules 1-10 and 1-11.

If a pronoun has an **antecedent**, it should agree with the antecedent in number, person, and gender; see Rule 1-12. Often the meaning of a pronoun is unclear because there is more than one grammatically possible antecedent in the sentence; see Rule 1-13.

A pronoun can itself be the antecedent for another pronoun, as in *She blames herself*. However, a possessive pronoun, unless ı is an independent possessive, functions as an adjective and thus cannot be used as the antecedent of another pronoun; see Rule 1-19.

proper noun   a noun that names a specific person, place, or thing and that is capitalized. *John*, *Boston*, and *Texaco* are proper nouns; *man*, *city*, and *corporation* are common or **generic** nouns. Exact definitions of the term differ; some dictionaries limit proper nouns to nouns that cannot logically take a limiting modifier such as *this* or the articles *a* or *the*, which rules out such nouns as *Christian* (derived from the proper noun *Christ*) and allows *France* to be a proper noun but not, apparently, *the United States*. A broader definition is more serviceable: Any noun that is customarily capitalized—that is, capitalized in a dictionary—can be considered a proper noun, including common items identified by trademarks, such as *a Ford*. In addition, within a given piece of writing, any noun or noun phrase that the writer chooses to capitalize to indicate that it has a specific rather than a general meaning can be considered a temporary proper noun; for example, *the Chairman of the Board* and similar titles are apt to be capitalized in a company's reports.

The question of whether a given noun is proper or generic can therefore be restated; in practice the question is merely whether or not to capitalize a given noun, which is covered in Rules 3-12 to 3-18.

provided vs. *providing*   As conjunctions meaning *if* or *on the condition that*, both are now accepted by most dictionaries. *Providing* was formerly considered incorrect, and since there are many who object to it still, I advise using *provided*.

punctuation   the subject of Chapter 2; see the introduction to the chapter and Glossary/Index entries for the individual marks of punctuation.

question mark   often incorrectly used after indirect questions; see Rule 2-20. When it occurs with other marks of punctuation its position is always logical; see Rule 2-21.

quotation marks   used for direct quotations but not indirect quotations; see Rule 2-23. When a closing quotation mark is used with another mark of punctuation, its correct position may violate logic; see Rule 2-24. With certain exceptions, single quotation marks should be used only within double quotation marks; see Rule 2-25. Quotation marks can be used to set off unfamiliar terms, nicknames, and words used in a peculiar way, but this use can be overdone; see Rule 2-26. They are conventionally used to set off the titles of short stories, songs, and some other works; see Rule 3-21.

reason is because   a common redundancy; it should always be replaced by *reason is that*. The error is most common when the phrase is interrupted. *The reason for the error, when we analyze it, is because the redundancy seems to add emphasis* is wrong; *is because* should be *is that*.

redundancy   unnecessary repetition of meaning, as in *consensus of opinion*, which means simply *consensus*. The term is often loosely used to mean phrases that are not actually redundant but merely excessively wordy, such as *at the present time* for *now* and *a sufficient number of* for *enough*. Both redundancy and wordiness are discussed in Rule 1-4.

relative clause   a clause that begins with a relative pronoun, though the relative pronoun may not actually appear in the clause but be understood. *He is the man who robbed the bank* contains the relative clause *who robbed the bank*. *He is the man whom they arrested* contains the relative clause *whom they arrested*; as is frequently the case when the relative pronoun is objective rather than subjective and the relative clause is a **defining construction** rather than a

286

parenthetical construction, the relative pronoun can be omitted: *He is the man they arrested.* However, such grammatically permissible omissions are not always advisable; see Rule 1-3.

Since a relative clause begins with a relative pronoun (whether actually present or understood), and since a relative pronoun cannot have as its antecedent anything but a noun or pronoun or some construction being used as a noun, a relative clause has the function of an adjective—it modifies the antecedent of the relative pronoun. Therefore relative clauses are often called adjectival clauses (see **adjective**).

Certain indefinite pronouns such as *whoever* are usually considered relative pronouns but cannot have an antecedent. It is moot whether clauses formed with such pronouns can be considered relative clauses; in *Whoever robbed the bank, they arrested the wrong man*, the *Whoever* clause doesn't relate to anything and certainly isn't adjectival. Such a clause can be considered an **absolute construction**.

restrictive   See **defining construction**.

reverend   The word is merely an adjective, like *honorable*. When it is used as a title of courtesy for the clergy it is almost always misused. The proper forms are *the Reverend John Smith, the Reverend Mr. Smith*, and *the Reverend Mr. and Mrs. Smith*. The abbreviation *Rev.* can be used in any of these forms. The article *the* is required. Improper forms include *Reverend John Smith* (with no article), *the Reverend Smith, the Reverend,* and *the Reverend and Mrs. Smith*.

However, the misuse is not a new one. In previous centuries, *reverend* was used as a title just like *doctor*; current correct forms are based on the relatively recent codification of forms of address in Great Britain. Furthermore, many members of the clergy do not object to *Reverend Smith* or other improper forms, and some of them use these forms themselves. I advise using the current correct forms to avoid seeming ignorant.

revision   an important stage in composition, covered in Rules 4-9 to 4-13. Revision can be harmful or overdone; see the discussion preceding Rule 4-9.

semicolon   a mark of punctuation that has functions similar to those of the comma but that is stronger. It often either can be or should be used to separate independent clauses; see Rules 2-12 and 2-13. It is also often needed to separate items in a series when some of the items already contain commas; see Rule 2-14.

Unlike the comma, the semicolon is positioned logically when it is used with a closing quotation mark; see Rule 2-24.

sentence a group of words that begins with a capital letter and ends with a period, a question mark, or an exclamation point. Less evasive definitions are hard to defend; see the discussion preceding Rule 1-1. Some basic principles of good sentences are covered in Rules 1-1 to 1-5. For a discussion of types of sentences and sentence structure, including definitions of simple, compound, and complex sentences and parenthetical, defining, and introductory constructions within sentences, see Rule 2-1.

Sentences can be classified as declarative, interrogative, exclamatory, and imperative; these classifications should need no definition.

sentence modifier a modifier that modifies everything else in its sentence, not just a specific word or phrase. *Unhappily, the Yankees lost* is a very pure example of a sentence modifier; if *Unhappily* is considered to modify only the verb *lost*, the meaning is quite different. Unless *Unhappily* is meant to describe the manner in which the Yankees lost rather than the fact that they lost, it can't be considered to modify just the verb. However, usually a word or phrase can be taken as a sentence modifier or an ordinary adverbial construction modifying a verb without any significant difference in meaning. In *After the sixth inning, the Yankees folded*, the prepositional phrase *After the sixth inning* can be considered either an adverbial modifier of *folded* or a sentence modifier; the meaning is the same. The term is convenient to classify adverbs and adverbial phrases that do not have specific words to modify.

Sentence modifiers can be well buried in their sentences. *The season was nevertheless terrific* buries the adverb *nevertheless*, but the adverb modifies the whole sentence, not just the verb *was* or the adjective *terrific*. The sentence-modifying adverb also acts as a conjunction, joining the thought of its sentence to a preceding sentence; see **adverb**.

A sentence modifier is by nature a **parenthetical construc-**

tion, since it does not define anything in its sentence, and is therefore usually set off by commas or other marks of punctuation (see Rules 2-1 and 2-5). However, in *The season was nevertheless terrific* and similar sentences in which the role of the sentence modifier is clear without parenthetical commas, the commas can be omitted; if they are put in they may give more emphasis to the sentence modifier than is desired.

serial comma   the comma as used in a series, as in *men, women, and children.* A comma before *and* and other conjunctions in a series of three or more items—the so-called final serial comma—avoids several problems; see Rule 2-6. A series of adjectives may or may not need to be separated by commas; see the discussion of adjective chains in Rule 1-20.

sexism   The English language is conspicuously sexist in two principal ways: The word *man* occurs as a suffix in many nouns denoting functions, titles, or occupations, such as *chairman*; and the masculine pronoun is used in the third person singular when the antecedent could be either masculine or feminine, as in *Everyone has to live his own life*.

Some words can have the word *woman* as a suffix, such as *policewoman* and *committeewoman*, and nothing prevents replacing *man* with *woman* in any word, though *postwoman* and *radiowoman* may not please every ear. But many people who object to sexism in language want gender removed from most nouns, not just changed from masculine to feminine; they feel the gender indication is often patronizing or disparaging. They have a point. *Usherette* uses the diminutive suffix *ette* to indicate gender; *poetess* adds the *ess* feminine suffix to a word that can indicate either sex as it stands (the word *poet* actually comes from a Latin feminine, *poeta*); and *woman photographer*, *lady photographer*, and *girl photographer* add a modifier as if the noun would inevitably be taken as masculine unless so modified. Some people object even to *masseuse*, *heiress*, and *actress*, which are long-established words and are usually used in contexts in which gender is important. And some object to *male prostitute* and *male nurse*, as just backhand versions of the forehand slam *female doctor*.

Often a noun ending in the suffix *man* can be replaced by another noun or compound that has no apparent gender;

letter carrier can replace *postman* and *radio operator* can replace *radioman*. A less happy solution is using the word *person* as a suffix, as in *chairperson*. Some such new coinages have begun to lose their abrasive unfamiliarity, and perhaps some will become genuine English words rather than self-conscious scrapes and bows in the direction of sexual equality, but it seems questionable whether they really avoid sexism anyway—they are not usually used for men, just for women.

The pronoun problem is just as troublesome. The careful use of *he or she*, *him or her*, and *his or her* is one solution, but not a graceful one when the construction must be repeated again and again; and for genuine equality *he or she* has to be alternated with *she or he*, and the alternation adds to the gracelessness and self-consciousness. Formations with slashes—*he/she* and *s/he*—are ugly. The least annoying solution is to evade the problem by making any noun that will become the antecedent of a pronoun plural, so that *they*, *them*, *their* can be used. But though this solution may not annoy readers, it certainly annoys writers, who must forego the privileges the masculine pronoun has for millennia enjoyed in English and its root languages and keep the issue of sexual equality always in their consciousness, no matter how remote the issue may be from what they are writing about.

But consciousness and unconsciousness are at the root of the problem of sexual inequality. It is undeniable that the language, like the cultures in which it has developed, is sexist, and that its speakers, both men and women, are sexist. It is also undeniable that until recently we—both men and women—were largely unconscious of this sexism; when we were conscious of it, we were complacent about it if male, resigned if female, and monkeying with the language was all but unthinkable. Now we are forced to think about sexism. Like a great many other men and also a great many women, I am annoyed at being forced to think about it and by the effect the issue is having on the language, but I cannot say that I have never been sexist in my own behavior or that I am not now—all I can say is that the commotion about gendered nouns and personal pronouns has made me much more conscious of the pervasiveness of discrimination against women and at least somewhat less sexist in my behavior. Quibbles about specific gendered words may be trivial, but the spirit behind the quibbles is not; the spirit should be respected, and during this period when both language and culture are changing in the direction of sexual equality, the quibbles must be taken seriously. Tired japes such as "So let's change *manhole* to *personhole* and *craftsmanship* to *craftspersonship*" advertise the danger that the antisexists are putting the language in, but they also advertise the hidebound and language-reinforced discrimination that the antisexists are attempting to eliminate.

How careful should we be to avoid sexism in language? I think we should be very careful—but also careful not to let avoidance of sexism distort our expression or distract a reader or listener. Each writer or speaker must consider his readers or listeners and devise his own policy, and these days he must do it consciously. In this book I have allowed myself to use masculine personal pronouns when the antecedent could be either masculine or feminine. In many sentences I have been forced into *or* constructions, especially *writer or speaker*, and I did not want to have to stir *his or her* into many such sentences; I also think that *or she, or her*, and *or hers* often read like gallant little bows in the direction of feminism and are therefore sexist anyway. I have not wanted to use plurals, because this book is concerned with a matter essentially singular—each reader's, each person's, use of language; *Writers and speakers must devise their own policies* seems diffuse and weak to me. So I have made my own judgment about pronouns, and it has been to follow the sexist convention—but I have made it consciously and for reasons I consider adequate. Ten years from now, perhaps, I might judge differently; and a century from now, both language and culture may have changed.

shall vs. will   An elaborate distinction was once made between these two forms. To express merely the future, *shall* was used in the first person (that is, with *I* and *we*) and *will* was used in the second and third persons (with *you, he* and *she*, and *they*). To express necessity or determination, *will* was used in the first person and *shall* in the second and third persons. The negative contraction of *shall* was *shan't*, which is exceedingly rare today. *I shall probably stay up late; I'm* *tired but I will keep going till I finish. You will probably turn in early, but you shall give me a hand here first, or I shan't be able to finish.*

Will has almost completely displaced *shall*, however. Very few Americans sense the distinction, and very few ever use *shall*, except in questions, such as *Shall we go?* It is still used in contracts and other legal documents, in which it does quite properly express compulsion or obligation but is perceived by most of us as just another lawyerly stiffness: *In such circumstance the property shall revert to Mortgagee.*

Those who do use *shall*, perhaps admiring its archaic flavor, often misuse it: *You shall probably turn in early.* This merely seems a little stilted to most of us. But to well-educated British people and to Americans who do understand the distinction between *shall* and *will* and whose ears are attuned to it, such a misuse is gross; it gives the speaker or writer away as ill-educated and laughably pretentious. Even in England, *will* is now acceptable where *shall* was once prescribed, but *shall* where *will* is prescribed is wrong both there and here.

simile   a figure of speech in which something is said to be like something else, as in *Love is like a shy flower.* See **metaphor**.

simplistic   means *excessively simple* or *overly simplified*, as in *His theory was simplistic, because it ignored various inconvenient facts.* It should not be used to mean merely *simple.*

singular   The **number** of a noun, pronoun, or verb can be either singular or **plural**. Problems of **agreement** in number can occur between subject and verb, often because it is not immediately apparent whether the subject is singular or plural; see Rule 1-11. Problems of agreement also occur between pronoun and antecedent; see Rule 1-12.

so . . . as   See *as . . . as* vs. *so . . . as.*

sometime vs. *some time*   See *anytime, sometime.*

spelling variants   This book does not deal with incorrect spelling; anyone in doubt about the spelling of a particular word should consult a dictionary. However, sometimes more than one spelling of a word is correct, and a choice has to be made.

American dictionaries of desk size and larger often give two spellings of the same word: *honor, honour; civilize, civilise; connection, connexion; judgment, judgement; leaped, leapt; offense, offence; theater, theatre; program, programme; traveler, traveller; gray, grey.* Each dictionary has some way of indicating which spelling it considers primary, as explained in the dictionary's introduction. Usually the secondary spelling is one common in Great Britain but uncommon in the United States. There is little point in using any spelling but the primary one. A surprising number of people seem to consider British spellings chic, like British haberdashery, but such spellings are apt to be perceived as amateurish or pretentious if the writer is American.

Toward, backward, and a few other words are often heard and seen with an *s: towards, backwards.* The *s* is not wrong, and probably almost all Americans use it in both speech and writing some of the time. Nevertheless, American book, magazine, and newspaper editors routinely take the *s* out— which is justifiable, except in carefully reported or composed dialogue, because very few Americans always use the *s*; their inconsistent use of it is unnoticed in speech but is apt to be noticed in writing, and so it might as well be made consistent.

Simplified spellings such as *thru* and *tho* are acceptable only in casual notes. Some others, such as *cigaret* and *employe*, have been pushed by major newspapers and magazines but have failed to displace older spellings; they are correct, in the sense that dictionaries include them, but they annoy many readers. A few, such as *omelet* and *catalog*, have achieved parity or better with older spellings.

split infinitive   an infinitive with some interruption between *to* and the verb itself, as in *to humbly ask.* It is not an error, though it was formerly regarded as one and is still offensive to some; see Rule 1-20.

Sr.   See *Jr., Sr.*

style   Generally, the word *style* means *manner*, and style in language is the choice of diction and tone that makes one person's expression different in manner from another's.

However, among those involved professionally in writing, *style* can also mean a collection of rules and conventions for capitalization, use of italics, and other details of written English; style in this restricted sense is the subject of Chapter 3.

subject   a word or group of words in a sentence or clause that is responsible for the action of the verb. In *I gave him money*, the pronoun *I* is the subject of the verb *gave*. A verb must have a subject, though in the **imperative mood** the subject is usually not expressed but understood—*Give him the money* has the understood subject *you*—and there are a few idioms with subjectless verbs (see *as follows* vs. *as follow*).

A verbal—that is, a verb that is an **infinitive**, **participle**, or **gerund**—can be said to have a subject, though the relationship between subject and verbal is not exactly like the relationship between subject and verb. In *My giving him money enabled him to satisfy his clamoring creditors*, the gerund *giving* has the possessive pronoun *My* as its subject, the infinitive *to satisfy* has the objective pronoun *him* as its subject, and the participle *clamoring* has the noun *creditors* as its subject. A participle almost always requires a subject, since it is either an adjective that requires something to modify or else part of a compound tense of a verb; see Rule 1-21 for a few exceptions.

Gerunds and infinitives often do not require a subject, since a gerund functions as a noun itself and an infinitive can function as a noun or as an adverb.

subjective case   the case of a noun or pronoun that is being used as the subject of a verb. Nouns and many pronouns have the same form in the subjective case and **objective case**, but the pronouns *I*, *he*, *she*, *we*, *they*, *who*, and *whoever* have different forms for the objective, and frequently the wrong case is used for these pronouns. See Rules 1-6 to 1-9.

subjunctive mood   the mood of verbs used to express possibility rather than actuality—that is, to express what something might be or do, should be or do, or must be or do rather than what something actually is or does. See the discussion preceding Rule 1-17.

Subjunctive forms usually look like past-tense forms of the indicative mood. In *Last summer I would cut the grass every Saturday*, the verb phrase *would cut* is indicative, a special past tense of *cut* that expresses repeated or habitual action. In *I would cut the grass if we had a lawnmower*, the verb phrase *would cut* is subjunctive; it does not indicate past action but possible present or future action. When the intended meaning is both subjunctive and past, the subjunctive form goes an extra step into the past: *I would have cut the grass if we had a lawnmower*. The wrong tense is sometimes used; see Rule 1-14.

There are certain distinctive subjunctive forms. *He holds his temper* and *He is polite* contain the indicative forms *holds* and *is*; *I insist that he hold his temper* and *I insist that he be polite* contain the subjunctive forms *hold* and *be*, which are the same as the form of the present infinitive. They keep this form regardless of the tense of the main verb: *I had insisted that he be polite, but he lost his temper*. In certain uses of the subjunctive in conditional constructions, *were* is used with the first person and third person singular instead of *is*, *am*, or *was*: *I am glad I am rich and he is not* is indicative; *I would be glad if I were rich and he were not* is subjunctive. See Rule 1-17.

Rule 1-17 provides a general discussion of the distinctive *were* subjunctive form. A common error is to use this form when the context is not subjunctive at all. Here are some examples of such errors.

She knew that if she were to graduate she would have to study harder is an example of an error common among educated people; the *if* clause is not quite an ordinary conditional clause but expresses both uncertainty and purpose, and *would* seems to be a subjunctive form that matches well with *were*. But actually *would* is not subjunctive but merely the past tense of *will,* and the *if* clause should not be subjunctive. This is apparent if the whole sentence is put in the present tense: *She knows that if she is to graduate she will have to study harder*. Therefore *she knew that if she was to graduate* is correct.

He asked me if I were rich is an error whether or not I am in fact rich. The *if* clause is a special construction used in indirect quotation; the equivalent using direct quotation is *He asked me, "Are you rich?"* Again, putting the sentence in the present helps expose the error; in modern English it is *He asks me if I am rich,* not *He asks me if I be rich,* though that would have been correct a century ago.

If he were disappointed he did not show it is an error whether or not he actually was disappointed. *If he were disappointed he would not have shown it* is also an error; the *if* clause should indeed be subjunctive, because it is intended to be contrary-to-fact, but the wrong tense is used. It should be *If he had been disappointed he would not have shown it,* with the subjunctive verb form taking an extra step into the past (see also Rule 1-14). In the present tense the contrary-to-fact statement is *If he were disappointed he would not show it,* and when it is put in the past tense both verbs have to change. This is not the case, however, when an *if* clause is not involved. When *I wish I were rich* is put in the past tense it becomes *I wished I were rich;* the form *I wished I had been rich*, though more logical and perhaps not incorrect, is unnatural.

The errors discussed above all yield readily to a single logical test—putting them in the present tense to see what becomes of *were*; if it becomes *am* or *is*, it is logical to insist that *were* is wrong in the past tense; and if it remains *were*, it may be necessary to change *were* to *had been* in the past tense. However, it must be admitted that for this and many other points of usage, logic cannot be the only determinant. Many educated people overuse *were*; they may be trying too hard to be elegant, like those who use *between you and I*, but it is just as likely that they have heard and used *were* all their lives in constructions in which it is now considered incorrect, and for them it is natural. One could say that as distinctive subjunctive forms die out of the language they have vacated almost all present-tense constructions but are showing a ghostly vivacity in past-tense constructions. I advise putting down the ghosts, though, simply to avoid seeming pretentious or unsure of modern usage.

subordinate clause   a clause that is dependent on another clause or some word or phrase in another clause; see **dependent clause**.

substantive   a word or group of words that functions as a noun in a sentence; a **nominal**.

superlative   See **comparative and superlative**.

syntax   the arrangement of words to form sentences. The alphabetical word list *all are in made meaningful of order* *sentences some up words* does not make a sentence, but when these words are rearranged according to syntactical conventions they do make a sentence: *All sentences are made up of words in some meaningful order.* Syntax can thus be considered word order. Syntax is one of the two basic parts of grammar; the other is **inflection**. English could get by as a language without any inflections—it very nearly does in some dialects of English—but it could not be a language without syntax.

Errors of syntax include failures to make elements in a sentence parallel in structure when they are parallel in meaning (see Rule 1-5) and failures to position modifiers unambiguously (see Rule 1-20).

telephone conversations   One side of a telephone conversation can be difficult to punctuate; see a suggestion in Rule 2-28.

tense   the form of a verb that expresses the time of action of the verb. The basic tenses of a verb are present, past, and future—*I cook, I cooked, I will cook*—but there are many others; see the discussion preceding Rule 1-14. When there are two or more verbs in a sentence, often their tenses must be in an exact relationship to one another; *I arrived just as he will leave and she greets me* clearly misuses tenses. However, just as often there is a choice of tenses, and sometimes the choice affects the meaning and sometimes it doesn't; see Rule 1-14.

Participles, infinitives, and gerunds have tenses, which are sometimes misused; see Rules 1-15 and 1-16.

The past tense in English is typically formed by adding *ed*, or just *d* if the present tense of the verb already ends in *e*: *I cook, I cooked*; *I serve, I served*. However, a great many verbs, including most of the commonest ones, have irregular forms for the past tense, and some have still other forms for the past participle, which is used to form other tenses: *I drink, I drank, I had drunk*. Some verbs have both a regular and an irregular form for the past; the past tense of *I leap* can be either *I leaped* or *I leapt*. The verb *spit* can be either *spit* or *spat* in the past. If in doubt, use a dictionary; when there is more than one form a dictionary usually indicates a preference.

than   A word used to introduce the second element of an unequal comparison, as in *John is older than Mary*. It is always associated with a comparative modifier, such as the adjective *older* in the example, or with one of a few other words that contain the idea of comparison, such as *different* and *differently*, *other*, *rather*, and *else*. When *than* is not associated with a comparative modifier, it is being misused, as in *Scarcely had we sat down to eat than the phone rang*, which should be either *Scarcely had we sat down to eat when the phone rang*, replacing *than* with *when*, or *No sooner had we sat down to eat than the phone rang*, replacing the adverb *scarcely*, which is not comparative, with the comparative *no sooner*.

Than is almost always a conjunction introducing a clause, even though the clause is very often elliptical; the expanded form of *John is taller than Mary* is *John is taller than Mary is tall*. Because of ellipsis, sentences with *than* are frequently ambiguous: *John praises Mary more than Jane* can mean either that John praises Mary more than he praises Jane or that John praises Mary more than Jane praises Mary. The ellipsis is not usually a problem, because the context generally makes it clear which meaning is intended, but it can be a problem, and a difficult one for the writer to catch, because he already knows what his meaning is; see Rule 1-3.

When *than* is followed by a personal pronoun, the case of the pronoun is determined by its function in the *than* clause—that is, by whether it is subject or object. Thus *John loves money more than she* and *John loves money more than her* are different statements; when the elliptical *than* clauses are expanded they become *John loves money more than she loves money* (or *than she does*) and *John loves money more than he loves her* (or *than he does her*).

Unfortunately, however, the explanation above is too simple. In fact, *than* is often used as a preposition, followed by the objective case, as in *John is older than her*. If *than* is considered a conjunction, *her* is obviously wrong; the expanded form would be *John is older than her is old*. Older dictionaries considered this prepositional use incorrect, but many modern ones do not. The objective case is particularly likely to be used after *than* when the first element of the comparison—that is, the one before *than*—is functioning as object rather than subject: *John has dated taller girls than her.* Logically this is incorrect; it does not mean *John has dated taller girls than he has dated her*, it means *John has dated taller girls than she is tall*. But there is no denying that objective pronouns are commonly found after *than* when the subjective would be required if *than* were being considered a conjunction. And as in *It's I*, careful use of the subjective case may sound quite stilted.

One solution is to avoid highly elliptical clauses after *than*, providing just enough—usually simply a form of verb such as *do*, *be*, or *have*—to make it clear that *than* is indeed functioning as a conjunction. As a happy by-product, this prevents ambiguity. *John has had older partners than her* thus becomes either *John has had older partners than she is* or *John has had older partners than she has*. (The word order in the first sentence can be improved: *John has had partners older than she is*.) The subjective-case pronoun might sound stilted standing alone, but it sounds quite natural when a verb is provided for it.

Than whom, as in *He has dated Mary, than whom no one is taller*, is a special case. Clearly it should be *than who*, once the grammatical relationships are unscrambled—*no one is taller than Mary is*, with *whom* replaced by its antecedent, *Mary*. But it is *than whom*—not just in modern dictionaries and books on grammar, but in older ones. I advise avoiding the construction altogether; aside from its annoying violation of logic, it is cumbersome.

than any vs. than any other   In a comparison with *than any*, the first element is often part of the second element, as in *John has lost more at the track than any gambler in town*. Since John is one of the gamblers in town, this sentence is illogical; John can't have lost more than he himself has lost. The addition of *other*, or some other qualifying word, makes the sentence logical: *John has lost more at the track than any other gambler in town*.

However, *other* should not appear if the second element in the comparison already has an adequate qualifier—that is, a qualifier that excludes the first element—or if the second element does not include the first element anyway. *The new chairman is ruder than any other previous chairman* has an unnecessary and illogical *other*. So does *Poor John has lost more in his retirement plan than any other gambler in town*;

thankfully

poor John is apparently not one of the gamblers in town in the first place but a man trying to save for the future.

thankfully   The word means *in a thankful manner*, as in *He wrote thankfully to his benefactor*. It should not be used as a **sentence modifier**, as in *Thankfully, it did not rain*. See **hopefully**, which is much more commonly misused in the same way and is discussed at length. There is little excuse for misusing *thankfully*, since common words such as *fortunately* are available to replace misuses.

that   When used as a conjunction to introduce a clause, as in *We hope that you will win*, *that* usually can be omitted and often is better omitted, but it should not be omitted if ambiguity results; see Rule 1-3. It can also often be omitted when it is a relative pronoun; see *that* vs. *which*.

That should not be used before a direct quotation. *He said that "War is unlikely"* should be either *He said, "War is unlikely"* or *He said that war is unlikely*. See also Rule 2-23.

That as a relative pronoun can refer to a person, as in *the child that I saw*.

But that, as in *I don't doubt but that she is rich*, is questionable but nevertheless common in good writing; see **but**.

that vs. which   As relative pronouns, *that* and *which* can be kept strictly apart; *that* can be used only for defining relative clauses and *which* only for parenthetical relative clauses (see the discussion of defining and parenthetical constructions in Rule 2-1). However, although *that* is indeed used only for defining clauses, *which* is used for both types: *I'm returning this book, which you lent me* uses *which* in a parenthetical clause, and *I'm returning the book which you lent me* uses it in a defining clause. Note that *I'm returning this book, that you lent me*, using *that* in a parenthetical clause, does not seem natural and is not considered correct. The error is most likely to occur when there are two parallel relative clauses, perhaps because the speaker or writer thinks it is desirable not to use the same pronoun twice: *I'm returning this book, which you lent me and that I liked very much*. The second relative clause could omit the pronoun entirely, but it should not have *that* as its pronoun, since it is not a defining clause.

There is some value in making a strict distinction between *that* and *which*—that is, using *which* only for parenthetical clauses. The consistent use of the pronouns can add precision and clarity to expression, reinforcing the punctuation of sentences (parenthetical constructions are almost always set off by commas or other marks of punctuation, and defining constructions are not) and emphasizing grammatical relationships. But occasionally *which* may seem better in a defining clause. It may even be necessary, as in the combination *that which*, in which *that* is a demonstrative pronoun and *which* a defining relative pronoun; imposing the strict distinction results in the unpleasant doubling *that that*.

That can often be omitted in a relative clause, because the relative clause—always a defining one, as explained above—is so closely bound to its antecedent. *I'm returning the book that you lent me* and *This is the day that we've been waiting for* might even be criticized as unnecessarily wordy; *I'm returning the book you lent me* and *This is the day we've been waiting for* are better. If the *that* clause is separated from its antecedent, *that* is usually needed—*I'm returning the book, the one on economics, that you lent me*—but it is almost always better not to separate the *that* clause and its antecedent in the first place.

the   whether to consider part of the title of a published work, Rules 3-19 and 3-20; whether to capitalize within a title, Rule 3-22

there is, there are   See *it is* and **expletive**.

this, these   *This* is a demonstrative pronoun, as in *It rained yesterday, and this kept us from going*. Its particular usefulness is that its antecedent can be an entire preceding clause or preceding sentence. It should not be used when it has a specific word as its antecedent—that is, when it is merely displacing the pronoun *it* or sometimes even *he*: *I offered him a dollar, and this was rudely rejected*; *The head-waiter approached me, and this was a lordly man. These* is similarly misused, as in *I knew some of the board members, and these introduced me to others*, in which *these* should be *they*. Note, however, that *this* and *these* are correct, and unavoidable, in a construction such as *I've had good pie before but this is delicious*, in which *this* is not actually a demonstrative pronoun referring to the *pie* earlier in the sentence and earlier eaten, but a demonstrative adjective with another *pie* being understood for it to modify and being eaten now.

time of day

It must be admitted that this (a defensible use of *this*, its antecedent being the entire paragraph above) is rather a small point. But *this* and *these* do sound strained and somewhat prissy when they have specific antecedents and can be replaced by other pronouns.

time of day   See Rule 3-5.

titles   of books, independently published poems, plays, movies, musical compositions, paintings, sculptures, and other works of art, Rule 3-20; of newspapers and periodicals, Rule 3-19; of officials, Rule 3-14; of parts of books, short stories, essays, articles, features in periodicals, and short musical compositions and parts of longer ones, Rule 3-21

tone   the manner in which a writer or speaker addresses a reader or listener. In a spoken address, both tone of voice and choice of words affect overall tone; in writing, choice of words—that is, diction—determines tone. See Rules 4-6 to 4-8.

too   means *excessively* or *also* and has a function in various idioms. In its *excessively* meaning it is sometimes used unnecessarily, and sometimes an idiom forces it to be used illogically. *John is too pigheaded* has an unnecessary *too*; how pigheaded is too pigheaded? *He was too dishonest to be president* cannot do without the *too* because the idiom requires it, but the sentence certainly implies that some degree of dishonesty is acceptable; if this implication is not intended, the sentence should be recast to avoid the idiom.

In its *also* meaning, *too* is frequently set off with commas: *You, too, are an Aries*. It is indeed essentially parenthetical in this sentence, and parenthetical constructions are generally set off with punctuation (see Rule 2-1). However, an overriding principle of modern punctuation is to use none when it performs no helpful function and cannot be heard when a sentence is spoken. I advise not setting off *too* unless setting it off is helpful in some way. *You too are an Aries* is smoother.

trademarks   should be capitalized; see Rule 3-12. The most convenient reference work for checking trademarks is the *Trade Names Directory* (Gale Research Company), which most public libraries have.

Owners of trademarks are obliged to use special symbols

with them—an R or TM within a circle—in their advertisements; if they don't, they may lose the legal right to exclusive use of a trademark. The general public is under no such obligation.

transitive verb   a verb that has an **object**. A transitive verb transmits its action from a subject to an object: *The bat hits the ball.* Some verbs do not pass their action along and cannot have an object: *The ball disappears.* See **intransitive verb**.

transpire   means *become known* or *come to light*, as in *It transpired that he had been the culprit all along*, but it is often very loosely used to mean *happen*, as in *Something funny transpired on my way to the office.* The loose usage is now accepted in many dictionaries, and it must be admitted that the *become known* meaning is none too pure either; the word has quite different older meanings and modern technical meanings. However, I advise not using it to mean *happen*; in this meaning it seems pretentious or pointlessly whimsical, and is apt to be considered a sign of ignorance by those who are aware of the *become known* meaning.

try and vs. *try to*   *Try and* is solidly established in the language in constructions such as *Try and stop me* and *I'm going to try and reach her at home.* It nevertheless means nothing but *try to. Try and* cannot be considered an error—it's an idiom—but it has a decidedly informal flavor. I advise using *try to* in any kind of writing or speech; even in the most casual speech it doesn't sound stilted.

uninterested   See *disinterested* vs. *uninterested.*

unique   should not be given a comparative or superlative form (*more unique, most unique*); see **comparative and superlative**.

upon vs. *on*   When *upon* can be replaced by *on*, which is almost always, *on* is usually better: *I put the book on the table* and *On reflection I picked it up again* are better than *I put the book upon the table* and *Upon reflection I picked it up again.* The words mean the same thing, though *upon* may sometimes seem stronger and better, as in *His schemes, built upon one another for so long, tumbled in disarray. Upon* may sometimes be clearer when direction is meant, not just position; *The child jumped on the upper bunk* may mean the child was using the bunk as a trampoline, but *The child jumped upon the upper bunk* suggests a single movement from one place to another. In general, *upon* seems slightly pompous when *on* is equally natural and is stilted when *on* is more natural.

usage   manner of use. The word is not synonymous with *use*: *I object to his use of my typewriter* means I object to his using it at all; *I object to his usage of my typewriter* means I think he misuses or abuses it. In discussing language, *usage* relates to generally accepted standards of manner of use, as in *Words change their meanings over the years, and usages that were derided by Samuel Johnson are correct usages today.* Using *infer* when *imply* is meant is faulty usage. *It's me* is acceptable usage in all but the most formal writing even though it violates a grammatical principle (see Rule 1-6).

Whether a usage is acceptable often depends on the context, for there are levels of usage—informal, colloquial, slangy, vulgar—between the clearly correct and the clearly incorrect. The best way to determine usages of a specific word and the degree of acceptance of a specific usage used to be to read the word's dictionary definition carefully. But some modern dictionaries, including the latest editions of the Merriam-Webster dictionaries, make few attempts to distinguish correct and incorrect usage and levels of usage; they describe how the language is used rather than prescribing how it should be used. Thus when we want a prescription rather than a description we often have to consult an older dictionary, a modern dictionary such as *The American Heritage Dictionary* that does make usage distinctions, or one of the many specialized dictionaries and handbooks of usage. This Glossary/Index includes entries on some of the most common problems of usage.

used to, use to   a construction used to indicate continual or habitual action in the past, as in *We used to play tennis. Use to* is used for negative statements, as in *We didn't use to play it as much*; it is correct but seems clumsy to many. It is better to eliminate *use to* or avoid it by recasting.

verb   one of the parts of speech; a word that expresses an action or a state of being. Every sentence, except some exclamations and elliptical sentences (see **ellipsis**), must have a verb. *He saw that it was good* contains the verbs *saw* and *was*.

A verb that has an object is a **transitive verb**; one that does not is an **intransitive verb**. A transitive verb can be either active or passive; see **voice**. An intransitive verb may be of a special type called a **linking verb**.

A verb can change its form to indicate its **tense**, its **mood**, and its **number**.

A *verbal* is one of three special forms of a verb: a **gerund**, an **infinitive**, or a **participle**.

A *verb phrase* is a verb form that includes both a basic verb and an **auxiliary verb**.

voice   the form taken by a **transitive verb** to indicate whether the subject of the verb is the verb's agent—that is, is acting—or is the verb's recipient—that is, is being acted upon. In the active voice, the subject is the verb's agent: *I hit the ball* has *I* as both subject and agent. In the passive voice, the subject is the verb's recipient, and the agent is indicated by a participial phrase with *by*: *I was hit by the ball* has *I* as the subject but *the ball* as the agent.

A sentence in the active voice means the same as a sentence in the passive voice if the object of the active sentence is made the subject of the passive sentence and the subject of the active sentence is replaced by a participial phrase with *by*: *I hit the ball* means the same as *The ball was hit by me*, and *The ball hit me* means the same as *I was hit by the ball*. Note that the subject of the active verb does not become the object of the passive verb; it remains the agent of the verb.

A passive verb must be a transitive verb—that is, one that has an object when it is in the active voice—because if it had no object in the active voice there would be nothing to become its subject in the passive voice, and a verb must have a subject (though the subject of an imperative verb usually does not appear in the sentence but is understood).

Sometimes an active verb has both a direct and an indirect object: *I sent him the letter* has the direct object *the letter* and the indirect object *him*. When such a sentence is made passive, either the direct object or the indirect object becomes the subject, but they can't both become the subject: *The letter was sent him by me*; *He was sent the letter by me*.

The object that remains an object is called the retained object.

The passive voice is wordier than the active voice, and it is often comparatively clumsy. When it is used excessively, it makes expression seem vague and evasive. However, it has many legitimate uses; see Rule 1-18.

were* vs. *was   *Were* is used instead of *was* with *I* and *he* in certain subjunctive constructions; see Rule 1-17.

what is* vs. *what are   In some constructions, *what* functions as both a demonstrative pronoun and a relative pronoun, like the combinations *that which* and *those which*: *The money is what is important*; *Rules we can understand are what are needed*. As may be apparent in the second example, *what are* often is troubling; regardless of what its antecedent is, *what* seems much happier in singular constructions. But if it can be replaced by *those which* and not by *that which*, it is functioning as a plural and can have a plural verb.

What is needed are rules we can understand demonstrates the problem caused by the tendency of *what* to be considered singular regardless of its meaning: First *what* is the subject of the singular verb *is*, then it is the subject of the plural verb *are*. The plural noun *rules* is responsible for the plural *are*, but it should not be; *rules* is merely the **complement** of *are*, not its subject, and should not be allowed to determine the number of the verb (see Rule 1-11). The sentence should be either *What are needed are rules we can understand* or *What is needed is rules we can understand*. The second is not only grammatically correct but logical too; even though the topic, *rules we can understand*, is plural in form, it can be thought of as representing a singular idea— the understandability of the rules to us—rather than an explicitly plural idea such as *six rules*. In fact, when *what* is replaced by *that which* or *those which*, *that which* may be better even when the topic is plural in form: *That which is needed is rules we can understand* is better than *Those which are needed are rules we can understand*, which focuses too strongly on the rules and not strongly enough on the understandability.

When there is only one verb, no such problem of agreement occurs, and it is grammatically correct and almost always idiomatic to let the persistent singularity of *what* determine the number of the verb: *What we need is rules we can understand* and even *What we get is six incomprehensible ones. What . . . are* is also correct in these sentences but not as natural.

It is possible to approach this issue differently and devise a system in which *what* always means *that which* and is never allowed to mean *those which*—that is, to be plural. *Rules we can understand are what is needed* can be defended; *what is needed* is merely the complement of *are* and doesn't have to agree with it in number. *What are needed are rules we can understand* would be considered wrong. However, I believe it is better to allow *what* to mean *those which* and be a plural. Thus my advice is merely never to use both a singular and a plural verb with *what* as the subject; either both verbs should be singular or both should be plural.

when and **where** in definitions   *Overacting is when the actor tries too hard* and *A solecism is where you make some mistake in grammar* are childish constructions. Adults sometimes switch them around and complicate them, but they remain childish and incorrect: *When you make some mistake in grammar it's called a solecism.* Actually, when you make some mistake in grammar you probably get away with it and the mistake isn't called anything. Sometimes the *when* or *where* construction is an unnecessary complication and can just be eliminated: *A solecism is a mistake in grammar.* Sometimes a *what* construction can replace or correct the *when* or *where* construction: *Overacting is what an actor does when he tries too hard.*

When and *where* are, of course, quite correct in constructions that are not definitions but ordinary statements: *Teatime is when we bring out the Scotch; Jerez is where sherry originated.*

whether vs. **whether or not**   When *or not* can be omitted, it might as well be. In *I don't know whether or not to go*, it can be omitted; in *I am going whether or not he goes* (or *whether he goes or not*), it cannot be.

Errors occur in long sentences with *whether or not*: *I am going whether or not John, who said he had the minutes of the last meeting prepared and could let me take them, goes or not.* This reduces to *I am going whether or not John goes or not*, which is redundant. It should be either *I am going whether or not John goes* or *I am going whether John goes or not*; the statement does require an *or not* but it can't have two.

who, whom; whoever, whomever   There is no question that *who* and *whoever* are the correct forms for the **subjective case** and *whom* and *whomever* are the correct forms for the **objective case**. Nevertheless, *who* and *whoever* are often used when the principles of grammar call for the objective case, and such usage is acceptable in speech and in most writing when the pronoun is not directly preceded by a verb or preposition; see Rule 1-8. However, the opposite flouting of grammatical principles—using *whom* or *whomever* when the subjective case is called for—is never acceptable; see the discussion of pronouns as part of their own phrases or clauses in Rule 1-6.

Than whom is the correct form even when the subjective form *who* seems clearly called for: *John, than whom there is no more skillful sailor, nevertheless capsized.* I advise avoiding the construction entirely; see **than**.

whose vs. of which   *Whose* seems to be based on the pronoun *who*, which can be used only with persons, and therefore the rule used to be that *whose* should not be used except when its antecedent is a person. Such usages as *These are the organizations whose members generally vote twice* and *Show me a street whose inhabitants don't love it* were condemned. The correct forms were *These are the organizations of which the members generally vote twice* and *Show me a street the inhabitants of which don't love it*, which to modern ears seem in far worse trouble than could be caused by using *whose* to represent a thing rather than a person. Therefore *whose* is now accepted as able to have a thing as well as a person as its antecedent.

Nevertheless, *whose* still seems inelegant to some people when it can be avoided easily, and sometimes it is still incorrect. It should not be used as an interrogative pronoun with an inanimate object as its referent, as in *Whose climate is better, Florida's or California's? I met that author whose book I read* is a conventional use of *whose* with a person as its antecedent, but *I read that book whose author I met* is clumsy; it should be *I read that book by the author I met* or some similar rewording.

whose* vs. *who's These are so often confused that something worse than mere carelessness must often be the problem. *Who's* is the contraction of *who is* or *who has*, as in *I wonder who's here* and *I wonder who's been invited. Whose* is the possessive form of *who*, as in *I think I know whose woods these are* and *Whose woods are these? Whose* is sometimes also a possessive form of *which*; see ***whose* vs. *of which***.

worth In constructions such as *ten dollars' worth*, the apostrophe is often omitted. It is required, as is evident from other phrases such as *his money's worth.*

your* vs. *you're Like *who's* and *whose*, these are confused surprisingly often. *Your* is a possessive pronoun, as in *This is your life. You're* is the contraction of *you are*, as in *You're going to have to live your own life.*

The error *your's* is sometimes seen. It should be *yours*. It is a special form that the pronoun *you* has when it is an independent possessive; see **possessive case**.